THE PETER MYTH

THE PETER MYTH

Karl L. Oakes

RESOURCE *Publications* • Eugene, Oregon

THE PETER MYTH

Copyright © 2020 Karl L. Oakes. All rights reserved. Except for brief quotations in critical publications or reviews, no part of this book may be reproduced in any manner without prior written permission from the publisher. Write: Permissions, Wipf and Stock Publishers, 199 W. 8th Ave., Suite 3, Eugene, OR 97401.

Most of the Scripture quotations in this work are taken from the Holy Bible, King James Version.

Scripture quotations marked (NIV) are taken from the Holy Bible, New International Version®, NIV®. Copyright © 1973, 1978, 1984, 2011 by Biblica, Inc.™ Used by permission of Zondervan. All rights reserved worldwide. www.zondervan.com The "NIV" and "New International Version" are trademarks registered in the United States Patent and Trademark Office by Biblica, Inc.™

Resource Publications
An Imprint of Wipf and Stock Publishers
199 W. 8th Ave., Suite 3
Eugene, OR 97401

www.wipfandstock.com

PAPERBACK ISBN: 978-1-7252-7420-4
HARDCOVER ISBN: 978-1-7252-7421-1
EBOOK ISBN: 978-1-7252-7422-8

Manufactured in the U.S.A.   10/07/20

TO DENITA,
my long-suffering wife,
the love of my life,
and the most generous human being I have ever known;
for her patience with this twenty-five year project,
for her cheerful, unflagging help and support,
and for feigning interest in what must have seemed
a dry and desolate wasteland.

History is written by the winners.
—George Orwell

History is written by the victors,
but eventually the truth comes out.
—Bui Diem,
South Vietnamese ambassador to the US

Contents

Preface ix

Abbreviations xi

Introduction xiii

1	The Background of the Galatian Heresy	1
2	Founded on Fables	21
3	Peter, the Bishop of Rome	36
4	The Teaching Develops and Spreads	47
5	The Church Organizes and Worships	60
6	The Fathers of Uncleanness	75
7	The Primitive Eucharistic Meal	83
8	The Introduction and Acceptance of Paul	97
9	The Evolution of the Catholic Canon	108
10	The Meaning of the Eucharist	121
11	The Roman Reformation	127
12	Easter: The Catholic Passover	140
13	Heresy and Dissent in the Great Church	150
14	Chronology: Setting the Record Straight	156

Supplemental Material	171
The Earliest Witnesses to the New Testament Books	173
The New Testament in Historical Context	175
Epistle of Peter to James	189
Epistle of Clement to James	193
The Didache	201
Bibliography	207
Index	211

Preface

Where did the Catholic Church come from? Ask any Roman Catholic this question and, without a moment's hesitation, he will tell you they are the heirs of St. Peter. He was the first pope, leading and guiding the young Christian movement from Rome.

However, there is not a single, solitary scrap of Scripture that unequivocally places Peter at Rome. Not one. In the Acts of the Apostles, we read of Simon Peter at Joppa, at Caesarea, he made a trip up to Syrian Antioch, and he played a major role in the Jerusalem Council in AD 49. When Paul wrote to the saints at Rome in AD 57, he greeted about twenty of the faithful by name—but not Peter, the bishop who was supposedly sitting on the *cathedra*. Paul was imprisoned in Rome from AD 60 to AD 62, and wrote at least five epistles during this period. Again, Peter is strangely missing.

Paul is likewise missing from all of the genuine Catholic writings from the close of the New Testament AD 70 until the middle of the second century. The Christian missionary who carried the gospel to the Gentile world, the theological genius who authored over one-half of our New Testament, is never mentioned by name nor are his epistles cited. This is even more astounding when you realize how extensive this body of literature is.

- *The Epistle of Peter to James*
- *The Epistle of Clement to James*
- *The Recognitions of Clement*
- *The Homilies of Clement*
- *The Didache*
- *Second Clement*

- *The Epistle of Barnabas*
- *The Apology of Aristides*
- *Peri Pascha* (On the Passover)
- *The fragments of Papias*
- *The writings of Hegisippus*
- *The Shepherd of Hermas*
- Justin Martyr's *First Apology*
- Justin Martyr's *Second Apology*
- *Dialogue with Trypho the Jew*

These books, the literary output of the *Ekklesia Katholika* for almost 80 years, present a picture of the apostolic period that is completely at odds with the New Testament. Instead of ministering to Jewish believers, as in the Bible, Peter travels up the coastline of Lebanon and Syria, preaching to great crowds and debating Simon the Magician. In this alternate universe, he spends the last twenty-five years of his life as the bishop of Rome and is succeeded by Clement.

The Peter Myth advances a provocative new understanding of church history. Far from being the heirs of St. Peter, the *Ekklesia Katholika* is shown to be the offspring of the false apostles, the oldest heresy of Christendom. The evidence produced in this book proves beyond a shadow of a doubt that the conventional wisdom on Catholic origins, accepted by billions of believers, was in fact the grand deception of the ages.

Abbreviations

1 Apology	*First Apology*, Justin Martyr
Addaeus	*Teaching of Addaeus the Apostle*
Against Heresies	*Against Heresies*, Irenaeus
Against Marcion	*Five Books against Marcion*, Tertullian
Antiquities	*Antiquities of the Jews*, Flavius Josephus
Ep Apostles	*Epistle of the Apostles*
Ap Const	*Apostolic Constitutions*
Ap Trad	*Apostolic Traditions*
b.	Babylonian Talmud
Barsamya	*Martyrdom of Barsamya*
Ep Barnabas	*Epistle of Barnabas*
G Barnabas	*Gospel of Barnabas*
Clement to James	*Epistle of Clement to James*
Dialogue	*Dialogue with Trypho the Jew*, Justin Martyr
Didache	*The Lord's Teaching Through the Twelve Apostles to the Nations*
Did Apost	*Didascalia Apostolorum*
Eccl Hist	*History of the Church*, Eusebius
Homilies	*Homilies of Clement*
Ig to Eph	*Epistle of Ignatius to the Ephesians*

ABBREVIATIONS

Ig to Romans	*Epistle of Ignatius to the Romans*
j.	Jerusalem Talmud
Life	*Life of Constantine*, Eusebius
Marcion	*Marcion: The Gospel of the Alien God*. Harnack, Adolf. Eugene, Oregon: Wipf & Stock, 2007.
m.	Mishnah
Muratorian	*Muratorian Canon*
Panarion	*Panarion*, Epiphanius
Peter to James	*Epistle of Peter to James*
Polycarp to Phil	*Epistle of Polycarp to the Philippians*
Mar Polycarp	*Martyrdom of Polycarp*
Prescrip	*Prescription Against Heretics*, Tertullian
Recognitions	*Recognitions of Clement*
Refutation	*Refutation of all Heresies*, Hippolytus
Shape	*Shape of the Liturgy*. Dix, Gregory. New York: Seabury, 1983.
Shepherd	*Shepherd of Hermas*
Simon Cephas	*Teaching of Simon Cephas in Rome*
Stromata	*Stromata*, Clement of Alexandria
Syriac Teaching	Syriac *Teaching of the Apostles*
t.	Tosephta
Thomas	*The Acts of the Holy Apostle Thomas*
Wars	*Wars of the Jews*, Flavius Josephus

Introduction

Where did Catholicism come from? How did it originate? What is its connection with the church we read about in the New Testament?

Many theories have been floated over the years to explain their origin, but in truth no one knows. The Catholics themselves have supplied us with a ready-made answer in their founding documents. They are the heirs and successors of Jesus Christ. The Lord gave the keys of the Kingdom to Peter, he founded the church at Rome, and his successors have governed the church ever since. This is what was believed by the Fathers of the Church, and it is what is believed today. Those men—earnest, zealous, and quite convinced of the surety of their faith—had been led astray by their own misleading propaganda.

The problem historically is that their founding mythology does not line up with the New Testament. Actually, it is worse than that. The traditions of the Church contradict the Word of God at almost every turn. We are told that Peter was the bishop of Rome for twenty-five years, but the Acts of the Apostles tells us otherwise. Simon Cephas was at Jerusalem, Joppa, Caesarea, and Antioch on the Orontes, but he was never at Rome. The apostle Paul explicitly said that Peter ministered to the circumcision, not the Greeks and Romans.[1]

Catholic tradition also insists that Simon Peter brought the resurrection message to Antioch and served as its first bishop. However, as the story is related in Acts 11, Peter didn't have a thing to do with the first Gentile church. The Bible gives the credit to unnamed men from Cyprus and Cyrene, and Paul and Barnabas were the first apostles to teach the Antiochene Christians.

1. Galatians 2:7–8.

There is also the view—common among Protestants—that the *Ekklesia Katholika* succeeded the apostles, but it was corrupted by worldliness. The usual culprits for this corruption are the Roman Emperor Constantine and Pope Sylvester, the pope at the time. Despite being an unbaptized catechumen, Constantine meddled in the affairs of the Great Church and even presided over the opening of the Council of Nicaea. It cannot be denied that many elements of paganism were introduced in the fourth century: candles, the veneration of icons, Marian devotion, and a new feast celebrated at the time of the winter solstice we know as Christmas.

The Catholic Church undoubtedly goes back into the first century. The staple dogmas of Catholicism—the keys of binding and loosing, the Roman bishopric of Peter, the succession of bishops, and the reliance on tradition—can all be traced back to the very ancient *Epistle of Clement to James* and *Epistle of Peter to James*. The *Didache* was written so close to the apostolic age that the community still had itinerant "apostles." Addressed to the Nations—meaning Gentiles—it laid the foundation for a Jewish form of Christianity completely apart from the Pauline missions. The *Didache* is cited almost verbatim by the early second century *Epistle of Barnabas* and the third century *Didascalia Apostolorum*.

We shall, in this work, connect the events and controversies of the New Testament with the earliest writings of the historic Church. The false apostles who refused to accept the ruling of the apostles in Acts 15 are identified as the "apostles and prophets" of the Catholic *Didache*. A seamless history of Catholic Christianity will be constructed from the time of the apostles until we reach solid ground at the end of the second century. We will show that the church which declares itself to be "Holy, Catholic, and Apostolic" was indeed apostolic, but not in the way it is claimed.

1

The Background of the Galatian Heresy

AD 30 to AD 60

> For in Jesus Christ neither circumcision availeth anything,
> nor uncircumcision; but faith which worketh by love.
>
> —GALATIANS 5:6

The full story of the first century Christian church has never been told. There is an abundance of clues scattered through the New Testament and the patristic literature, but they have been overshadowed by counterfeit documents designed to mislead and deceive. And mislead they have. The actual history of the period is dominated by a messy doctrinal dispute, false teachers who rejected the authority of the apostles, and a colossal deception, all culminating in an unrecorded schism. This is not what usually comes to mind when people think of the followers of Christ.

The Christian tradition that captured the western world grew out of a dispute over the Law of Moses. God had revealed the Torah, the glory of Israel, on Mount Sinai amidst thunder and lightning and billowing smoke. The Mosaic covenant promised a wonderful life to those who would live within its borders, but it was subject to limitations. The blessings of Torah were given to a specific people (the house of Jacob), who inhabited a certain land (Israel), and they were restricted to natural life. Eternal life was never part of the bargain and, in fact, one influential sect, the Sadducees, did not even believe in life after death.[1]

> If ye walk in my statutes, and keep my commandments, and do them; then I will give you rain in due season, and the land shall yield her increase, and the trees of the field shall yield their fruit. And your threshing shall reach unto the vintage, and the vintage shall reach unto the sowing time: and ye shall eat your bread to the full, and dwell in your land safely. And I will give peace in the land, and ye shall lie down, and none shall make you afraid: and I will rid evil beasts out of the land, neither shall the sword go through your land.
> —Leviticus 26:3–6

When Christ came, he delivered the good news of the Kingdom of Heaven to the house of Israel.[2] Later, he expanded the mission to include every nation and tongue,[3] but his first followers were the sons and daughters of Abraham. They continued to offer sacrifices, attend synagogue, and keep the holy days.[4] After the resurrection—and probably during the 50-day countdown to Pentecost—they withdrew from the synagogues, and the apostles laid the foundation for a Christ-centered fellowship. They established separate gatherings for worship, instituted the breaking of bread to commemorate the risen Christ, and designated Sunday as the Christian day of fellowship.[5] "And they continued stedfastly in the apostle's doctrine and fellowship, and in breaking of bread, and in prayers."[6]

The young church grew by leaps and bounds the first few years. Three thousand souls were added on the day of Pentecost; in a short time, the total number of believers reached five thousand men;[7] and, after Ananias was struck dead, it increased again by "multitudes."[8] The first Christians broke bread in private homes, and if each gathering held twenty or thirty people, there would have been hundreds of them in Jerusalem alone. To put this into perspective, the city of approximately 90,000[9] inhabitants had

---

1. Matthew 22:23, Acts 23:8
2. Matthew 10:6.
3. Matthew 28:19.
4. John 9:22; 12:42; 16:2; Matthew 5:23–24; 23:2–3; Luke 23:56.
5. "And upon the first day of the week, when the disciples came together to break bread, Paul preached unto them" (Acts 20:7).
6. Acts 2:42.
7. Acts 4:4.
8. Acts 5:14.
9. Josephus quotes the 4th century BC philosopher Hecatus of Abdera: "But there

480 synagogues.[10] The light of the glorious gospel even penetrated into the Temple. "The number of disciples multiplied in Jerusalem greatly, and a great company of the priests were obedient to the faith."[11]

All of this was happening within the walls of Jerusalem—in full sight of all Israel. The Sadducean establishment initially reacted to the mass apostasy with threats and intimidation, but after several public confrontations in the Temple, they stepped it up to beatings and imprisonment. A flashpoint was reached with trial and stoning of Stephen. Leaving the leadership behind in Jerusalem, many of the disciples fled north to Samaria and Syria.

That was when the door of salvation begins to open to the Gentiles. Although they had been given a mandate to "go and teach all nations," the Christian leaders never mapped out a strategy to reach the countless millions outside the covenant. The apostles seemed almost reticent to tackle the complexities of the Gentile issue. This was, after all, uncharted territory, and they did not want to get it wrong. We get the distinct impression from the early chapters of Acts that God reserved the matter to himself, taking an active role in shaping events and enlightening minds. The Holy Spirit had been promised to guide them into all truth and so gradually, step by step, the young apostles were led to an understanding of his will.

The Hebrew church inherited an attitude that did more to hinder the furtherance of the gospel than the height of the mountains or the vastness of the sea. The purity laws, as practiced in the first century, made it impossible for devout Jews to develop personal relationships with non-Jews and they placed severe restrictions on business relationships. Gentiles (*Goyim* in Hebrew) were deemed to be like men with running sores, meaning they were ritually unclean in the highest degree.[12] Uncleanness was believed to be transmittable, like a contagious disease. A conscientious Jew would therefore never set foot in the house of a Gentile for fear of being contaminated, and sitting down to sup at the same table would be unthinkable. The Pharisees, the "separated ones," would not even eat with common folk, the *Am Ha'aretz*, much less with the uncircumcised. How would they ever be able to break bread together and drink from the same cup as brothers in Christ?

Peter was the instrument God used to move them beyond such a narrow view of the divine plan. One day, while up on the rooftop praying, Peter

---

is one strong city (in Israel), about 50 stades in circumference, which is inhabited by 120,000 or thereabouts. They call it Jerusalem" (*Against Apion* 1). Jonah provides us with another yardstick when he describes Nineveh, a much larger city: "120,000 souls who do not know their right hand from their left" (Jonah 4:11).

10. *J. Megillah* 73d.
11. Acts 6:7; John 12:42.
12. t. *Zabim* 2.1; *Sifra on Leviticus* 15.2.74d.

fell into a trance and saw a large sheet filled with wild beasts let down to the ground. "And there came a voice to him, Rise, Peter; kill and eat. But Peter said, Not so, Lord; for I have never eaten anything that is common or unclean. And the voice spoke unto him the second time, What God hath cleansed, that call not thou common."[13] This was done three times, after which three men immediately knocked on the door. Peter and several others were then led to a Roman military officer in Caesarea named Cornelius. As he entered the centurion's house, the meaning of the vision suddenly dawned on Peter. "Ye know how that it is an unlawful thing for a man that is a Jew to keep company, or come unto one of another nation; but God hath shewed me I should not call any man common or unclean."[14] As Peter preached, the Holy Spirit fell upon the assembled men, just as He had on the Jews the day of Pentecost, and it was accompanied with the same miracle of tongues. The implication was not lost on Peter—"What was I, that I could withstand God"—and Cornelius was baptized.

When Peter got back to Jerusalem, he was chastened for eating and mixing with uncircumcised men. He carefully rehearsed the whole incident for them, from beginning to end. The other apostles recognized the hand of God, and rejoiced that "God hath also to the Gentiles granted repentance unto life."[15] Thus was the young church delivered from the rigid traditions that had grown up around the purity code.

The next phase for Gentiles involved the conditions of discipleship. Would they also need to keep Torah—like the Jewish believers—or did God have something different in mind for them? Because this question is so inextricably bound up with the whole conversion process, we will make a short digression at this point.

Converts to Judaism—known as "strangers" or *Ger* in Hebrew—came in two degrees of commitment. The God-fearers were Gentiles who were loosely attached to the Jewish way of life by marriage or personal conviction. This ill-defined term is not even used in the Talmud, but in general they worshipped the God of Abraham as the one true God, observed the moral aspects of the Law, and contributed the annual half-shekel tax toward the maintenance of the temple. They were the "devout" Greeks mentioned so often in the Acts of the Apostles. Cornelius, the centurion of Caesarea, "a devout man who feared God with all his household," was one.[16] Because of their respect for the *Tanakh* (Hebrew scriptures) and acceptance of its lofty ethics, the God-fearers proved

---

13. Acts 10:13–15.
14. Acts 10:28.
15. Acts 11:18.
16. Acts 10:2.

to be fertile soil for the gospel. In city after city, Paul formed the nucleus of the Christian church from the Gentile fringe of the synagogues.

The second category, the *Ger Tzedek* or proselytes of righteousness, were full proselytes who entered the covenant through a tripartite ritual involving circumcision, immersion, and an offering. The prospective convert was first questioned about his motivation for joining a persecuted people. If he answered, "I know this, and I am not worthy to give my neck to the yoke of him who spake the word and the world came into existence," he was accepted.[17] He was then instructed in the "lighter and weightier commandments" of the Law. If he still was not dissuaded, he was circumcised. After the wound healed, he was immersed in water or, as we would say, baptized. Finally, the convert would bring his first sacrifice—usually a bird offering—to the temple. He was now considered a son of Abraham, and expected to observe the 613 commandments of Torah.

The saints who had been persecuted during Stephen's time found safe harbor in what is now Lebanon, Syria, and Cyprus. Although the gospel was only being propagated within the Jewish communities, some Greeks at Antioch heard the Word and a "great number" turned to the Lord.[18] Antioch was a sophisticated cosmopolitan city—the third largest in the Roman Empire—and it contained a sizable Jewish community.[19] Josephus tells us that a large number of Antiochene Greeks had become Jewish proselytes.[20] Barnabas was sent from Jerusalem to shepherd the situation, and he saw the unmistakable evidence of God's favor in their lives. These *Christianoi*, or "followers of Christ" as they were now called, knew nothing of the Law; only faith in Christ Jesus. Antioch thus had the distinction of possessing the first Gentile church. Paul and Barnabas taught there a full year, witnessing the same spiritual miracle in the lives of these Gentiles as they had among the believers in Israel.

From this point on, the evangelization of the Gentile world centers on Paul. He and Barnabas left Syria to bring the resurrection message to central Anatolia. Most of the towns in this region had Jewish settlers, and they used the local synagogues as their base of operations. Using messianic passages from the Law and Prophets, they declared Jesus of Nazareth to be the long-awaited hope of Israel. In town after town, the leaders of the synagogues rejected their message and stirred up opposition. At Antioch of Pisidia, Paul announced that, from thenceforth, they would direct their ministry to the

17. b. Yev 47a.
18. Acts 11:19.
19. *Wars* 7.43.
20. *Wars* 7.45.

Goyim.[21] On the return trip, Paul and Barnabas separated out those who had believed, formed churches, and ordained elders. They returned to Syria, where they abode "a long time."[22]

During their extended stay in Antioch, sometime around AD 48, Peter came up to see the Greek church for himself. He initially embraced the new converts as full brothers in Christ.[23] However, after some zealous believers from Judaea arrived, he stopped sitting at table with them and the younger apostles—even Barnabas—followed his example. Paul had a face-to-face confrontation with Peter, arguing forcefully for their freedom in Christ. These men told the Antiochene church it was absolutely necessary for them to be circumcised. They were, in effect, saying that *Goyim* had to become full Jewish proselytes and live within the bounds of Torah to be saved. Paul had a heated exchange with these men, and the matter was finally brought before the apostles and elders at Jerusalem.

The Gentile issue had been simmering on the back burner for almost two decades, and it had finally reached the boiling point. Acts 15 preserves a complete transcript of the meeting convened by the apostles circa AD 49. After some initial discussion, Peter came out strongly against the yoke of Torah, reminding them that God had given the Holy Spirit to the *Goyim* as well as to them. Paul followed up by rehearsing the manifold blessings that had been showered on the Gentile believers at every turn.

When James rendered his decision, he reached back into their storied past for a precedent. In Leviticus 17 and 18, Moses named four abominations that were prohibited even to the strangers who sojourned among them. They were not to eat meat offered at the altars of demons, consume blood, eat animals which had died or been torn, or engage in the sexual liaisons common among pagans. James co-opts this list, even using the same sequence as the Lawgiver. "For it seemed good to the Holy Ghost, and to us, to lay upon you no greater burden than these necessary things; That ye abstain from meats offered to idols, and from blood, and from things strangled, and from fornication: from which if ye keep yourselves, ye shall do well."[24] These four practices were deeply offensive to Jewish sensibilities, and James was asking the Gentiles to accept the same minimal courtesies so the two peoples could be united into one.

This decision only applied to Gentiles. The Palestinian Christians continued to circumcise their children and live as Jews. As the Jerusalem elders

---

21. Acts 13:46.
22. Acts 14:28.
23. Galatians 2:11–14.
24. Acts 15:28–29.

said to Paul on his last home visit in AD 58. "Thou seest, brother, how many thousands of Jews there are which believe; and they are all zealous of the law: and they are informed of thee, that thou teachest all the Jews which are among the Gentiles to forsake Moses, saying that they ought not to circumcise their children, neither to walk after the customs."[25] Paul was told to go out and publicly demonstrate that he walked according to the Law.

What do we know about the opposition or, as Paul called them, the Circumcision Party?[26] His first encounter with these men seems to have been at Antioch.[27] They were Pharisees[28] and almost certainly teachers of the Law.[29] Paul, who had sat "at the feet of Gamaliel and been taught according to the perfect manner of the law," was not impressed.[30] To him they were simply "false brethren brought in unawares"—nothing more—and he did not even bother to learn their names.[31]

> **The Oral Law**—As teachers of the Law, the Pharisees were often asked to provide guidance on what was permissible. They tried to keep the people a safe distance from forbidden ground or, as they put it, to "build a fence around the Torah." The body of legal opinions which resulted is known as the Oral Law, and to the Pharisees, it was just as binding as the Written Law.
>
> Moses forbade work on the Sabbath, but what exactly constitutes work? We are given a definitive answer in the Mishnaic tractate *Shabbat* 7:2. "A. The generative categories of acts of labor [prohibited on the Sabbath] are forty less one: B. (1) he who sews, (2) ploughs, (3) reaps, (4) binds sheaves, (5) threshes, (6) winnows, (7) selects [fit produce}, (8) grinds, (9) sifts, (10) kneads, (11) bakes; C. (12) he who shears wool, (13) washes it, (14) beats it (15) dyes it; D. (16) spins, (17) weaves, E. (18) makes two loops, (19) weaves two threads, (20) separates two threads. . ."

The Pharisees (or "separated ones") were the largest branch of Judaism. Because they taught and officiated in the local synagogues, they had the support of the common people. The Pharisees taught that the divine revelation given at Mt. Sinai was not only the written law, the five books of Moses, but it also included the oral law. Known as the "traditions of the

---

25. Acts 21:20–21.
26. Galatians 2:11–12.
27. Acts 15:1.
28. "But there rose up certain of the sect of the Pharisees which believed, saying, that it was needful to circumcise them, and to command them to keep the law of Moses" (Acts 15:5).
29. 1 Timothy 1:7.
30. Acts 22:3.
31. Galatians 2:4.

elders" in the New Testament, this body of rabbinical rulings had built up over the centuries as a kind of case law to interpret the words of Moses.

The second defining characteristic of the Pharisees was a belief in the priestly sanctity of all Israel.[32] The purity expected of priests and Levites in the Temple was extended into the homes of ordinary Israelites, particularly at mealtime. The cleanliness required of priests was made mandatory in the kitchen, and food on the table was considered to be like offerings on the altar. The rituals taken from the temple service include the washing of hands, the boiling of pots and pans, and the various blessings recited over the food. All of these have become staples of Jewish domestic piety.

The Circumcision Party

The Circumcision Party argued that the Law was eternal, that God's written covenant with man did not expire just because the Messiah had arrived. They had some Scripture on their side. Jesus himself kept the commandments, and he instructed his disciples to observe the temple rites and respect the authority of the rabbis.[33] In the Sermon on the Mount, at the very beginning of his ministry, the Lord sought to show a continuity between the Torah and his teachings.

> Think not that I am come to destroy the law, or the prophets: I am not come to destroy, but to fulfill. For verily I say unto you, Till heaven and earth pass, one jot or one tittle shall in no wise pass from the law, till all be fulfilled. Whosoever therefore shall break one of these least commandments, and shall teach men so, he shall be called the least in the kingdom of heaven: but whosoever shall do and teach them, the same shall be called great in the kingdom of heaven.
> —Matthew 5:17–19

The meaning of fulfill is admittedly open to interpretation. The Greek word itself means "to become" or "come to pass," or—as we might say—"to complete." Paul's understanding of the term can be found in two epistles he wrote to combat the Judaizers. "For all the law is fulfilled in one word, even in this; Thou shalt love thy neighbor as thyself."[34] "Love worketh no ill to his

---

32. Exodus 19:5–6.
33. Matthew 8:4; 23:2–3; 23:23.
34. Galatians 5:14.

neighbor: therefore love is the fulfilling of the law."[35] If we love our neighbor as ourselves, we are completely and perfectly satisfying the demands of the law.

> The Epistle of Peter to James was one of the founding documents of the Catholic Church. This fraudulent letter was composed very close to AD 70. It was designed to connect the false apostles with the Jerusalem church and thus give their converts confidence in their ministry.

The arguments advanced by the legalists have been preserved in the earliest literature of the historic Church. *The Epistle of Peter to James* has "Peter" warning the flock against a Christian evangelist who is disparaging the law and teaching others it was obsolete. It is an obvious reference to Paul. Directly contradicting the decision reached by the apostles in Acts 15, these men openly proclaim the "eternal continuance" of the Torah.

> For some from among the Gentiles have rejected my legal preaching, attaching themselves to certain lawless and trifling preaching of the man who is my enemy. And these things some have attempted while I am still alive, to transform my words by various interpretations, in order to the dissolution of the law; as though I also myself were of such a mind, but did not freely proclaim it, which God forbid! For such a thing would act in opposition to the law of God which was spoken by Moses, and was borne witness to by our Lord in respect of its eternal continuance; for thus he spoke: 'The heavens and the earth may pass away, but one jot or one tittle shall in no wise pass from the law.'
> —*Epistle of Peter to James* 1

The *Apostolic Constitutions* offers three justifications for Christians to observe the law, including the previous passage from the Sermon on the Mount. This fourth century Syrian document was the great literary storehouse of the ancient Church, preserving many old liturgies, church orders, ecclesiastical canons, and archaic material no one knew what to do with. The following passage takes us back to the days of their founding.

> Remember ye the law of Moses, the man of God, who gave you commandments and ordinances. Which law is so very holy and righteous, that even our Savior, when on a certain time He healed one leper, and afterwards nine, said to the first, 'Go show thyself to the high priest, and offer the gift which Moses commanded for a testimony unto them;' and afterwards to the nine, 'Go show yourself to the priests.' For nowhere has He dissolved

---

35. Romans 13:10

> the law, as Simon [i.e. Paul] pretends, but fulfilled it; for He says, 'One iota, or one tittle, shall not pass from the law until all be fulfilled.' For he says, 'I am not come to dissolve the law, but to fulfill it.' For Moses himself, who was at once the lawgiver, and the high priest, and the prophet, and the king, and Elijah, the zealous follower of the prophets, were present at our Lord's transfiguration in the mountain, and witnesses of His incarnation and of His sufferings, as the intimate friends of Christ, but not as enemies and strangers. Whence it is demonstrated that the law is good and holy, as are the prophets.
> —*Apostolic Constitutions* 6.1.19

For reasons that will become clear in the next chapter, Simon the Magician was their code name for Paul.

Paul dismissed these strident, misguided men as "false brethren" when he confronted them at Antioch. They did not appear to be much of a threat. However, once they began meddling in the churches he had founded, Paul began to view them in a harsher light. They were now "false apostles." "For such are false apostles, deceitful workers, transforming themselves into the apostles of Christ. And no marvel; for Satan himself is transformed into an angel of light. Therefore it is no great thing if his ministers also be transformed as the ministers of righteousness; whose end shall be according to their works."[36]

We may possess the actual identities of these men. The same roster of names appears—with only minor deviations—three times in the Clementine literature: twice with twelve names and once with sixteen.[37] They play up the similarity with the twelve apostles of the Lord, so we presume four were added later to their staff. The list is a blend of truth and fiction—Clement was certainly fictitious—but by embedding the names in their sacred text, they were able to establish a plausible link between the apostles and the men teaching the alternate gospel.

> Therefore the next day, I Clement, awaking from sleep before dawn, and learning that Peter was astir, and was conversing with his attendants concerning the worship of God. There were sixteen of them, and I have thought good to set forth their names,

---

36. 2 Corinthians 11:13–15. The false apostles had an equally unflattering view of Paul. "They do not know who is my precursor Simon. For if he were known, he would not be believed; but now, not being known, he is improperly believed; and though his deeds are those of a hater, he is loved; and though an enemy, he is received as a friend; and though he be death, he is desired as a savior; and though fire, he is esteemed as light; and though a deceiver, he is believed as a speaker of truth" (*Homilies* 2).

37. *Homilies* 2.1; *Recognitions* 2.1, 3.68.

as I subsequently learned them, that you may also know who they were. The first of them was Zacchaeus, who was once a publican, and Sophonias his brother; Joseph and his foster-brother Michaias; also Thomas and Eliezer the twins; also Aeneas and Lazarus the priests; besides also Elisaeus, and Benjamin the son of Saphrus; as also Rubilus and Zacharias the builders; and Ananias and Haggaeus the Jamminians; and Nicetas and Aquila the friends . . . ..
—*Homilies of Clement* 2.1

> One of the founding books of the sectarians was the *Preaching of Peter*. It has been lost to history, but two recensions have survived: the *Recognitions of Clement* and the *Homilies of Clement*. Often called the Clementine literature or the pseudo-Clementines, they are a fictitious account of Peter's ministry and teachings.

The ringleader of the movement may have been Zacchaeus, who always comes first in these lists. He is singled out for more attention and honor in the pseudo-Clementines than anyone other than Clement. At Caesarea, the hometown of Zacchaeus, Peter endows him with all the authority and pretensions of a medieval pope.

> I have ordained Zacchaeus as a bishop for you, knowing that he has the fear of God and is expert in the Scriptures. You therefore ought to honor him as holding the place of Christ, obeying him for your salvation, and knowing that whatever honor and whatever injury is done to him, redounds to Christ, and from Christ to God. Hear him therefore with all attention, and receive from him the doctrine of the faith.
>
> Whosoever will, then, let him come to Zacchaeus and give his name to him, and let him hear from him the mysteries of the kingdom of heaven.
> —*Recognitions of Clement* 3.66, 3.67

Zacchaeus may have had a second, baser motivation for his activism. *Homilies* 3.71 sounds like a man laying guilt on others in order to feather his own nest.[38]

> Zacchaeus alone having given himself up wholly to labor for you, and needing sustenance, and not being able to attend to

---

38. Paul accused the false apostles on Crete of preaching for financial gain. "Whose mouths must be stopped, who subvert whole houses, teaching things they ought not, for filthy lucre's sake" (Titus 1:11).

his own affairs, how can he procure the necessary support? Is it not reasonable that you are to take thought for his living? Not waiting for him to ask you, for this is the part of a beggar. But he will rather die of hunger than submit to do this. And shall you not incur punishment, not considering that the workman is worthy of his hire?

What do we know about this man? Luke tells us he and his colleagues were Pharisees.[39] Zacchaeus lived in the Roman capital of Palestine—Caesarea—and had been a publican or tax collector.[40] He had a brother named Sophonias, who was also involved in the movement.[41] Zacchaeus fancied himself to be a "good and eloquent man,"[42] and "expert in the Scriptures."[43] The picture which emerges is that of a proud Pharisee, learned in the law and unwilling to submit to the authority of the apostles. This shadowy figure, who is remembered in Catholic tradition as the first bishop of Caesarea, may have been the man Paul debated at Antioch.[44]

The Crisis Deepens

The false apostles tried every tactic they could to discredit Paul, and drive a wedge between him and the churches he had founded. They challenged his doctrine, disputed his apostleship, cast doubt on his claims of direct revelation, and questioned his standing with the mother church. They made him out to be a renegade and a rogue, preaching on his own without authorization from James. This was their initial approach, and we can read about it in the pages of the New Testament.

One of their strategies was to follow Paul and win over his converts. As incredible as it sounds, this plan has been preserved in the oldest stratum of Church literature. They have Peter speaking in this fictional account.

> He addressed us to the following effect: 'Let us, my brethren, consider what is right; for it is our duty to bring some help to the nations, which are called to salvation. You have heard that Simon [i.e. Paul] has set out, wishing to anticipate our journey. Him we should have followed step by step, that whosoever he

---

39. Acts 15:5.

40. *Homilies* 2.1 It is possible that a later interpolation confused this Zacchaeus with the Zacchaeus in Jericho who climbed the sycamore tree (Luke 19:1–10).

41. *Homilies* 2.1.

42. *Recognitions* 3.71.

43. *Recognitions* 3.66.

44. *Ap Const* 7.46.

tries to subvert, we might immediately confute him. . . . I wish you the day after tomorrow to proceed to the Gentiles, and to follow in the footsteps of Simon, that you may inform me of all his proceedings.
—*Recognitions of Clement* 3.68

The first attempt of the false apostles was—as it turned out—their most successful. When Paul made his third journey through central Anatolia in AD 54 or AD 55, they followed hard on his heels. All that is known about this mission is contained in just one line. "He departed [from Antioch], and went all over the country of Galatia and Phrygia in order, strengthening all the disciples."[45] Paul inadvertently led the false apostles right to these churches, and some of them were swayed by the legalists. Paul and Timothy spent the next two years at Ephesus, where in AD 56 Paul wrote the Galatians. "I marvel that ye are *so soon* removed from him that called you into the grace of Christ unto another gospel."[46]

Much ink has been spilt over the location of these churches. They were not the saints in Iconium, Lystra, and Derbe that had accepted Paul and Barnabas on their first mission and rejoiced when Paul returned with the message from James. The Galatian schismatics seem to reside further west in what is known as the Turkish Lake District. Some of them had met Paul in the flesh, which leads us to speculate that Antioch of Pisidia was among the recipients of the Galatian letter.[47] Epaphras had preached in nearby Colosse, but it was after Paul had passed through the region, in the middle to late 50s.[48]

They next set their sights on the Corinthians. Paul had established the faith in Corinth during his first journey into Greece—in AD 51—and he ended up staying there a year and six months.[49] When he wrote his first epistle to the Corinthians in AD 57, there was some talk of circumcision and his rights as an apostle, but by and large he is giving normal pastoral advice. However, when Paul wrote the second letter less than a year later, he was forced to vigorously defend his doctrine and apostleship.[50] The false apostles had visited the Greek churches that summer and pressed their case.

---

45. Acts 18:23; also 19:1.

46. Galatians 1:6, emphasis mine.

47. "Ye know how through infirmity of the flesh I preached the gospel unto you at the first. And my temptation which was in my flesh ye despised not, nor rejected; but received me as an angel of God, even as Christ Jesus" (Galatians 4:13–14).

48. Colossians 1:7.

49. Acts 18:11.

50. 2 Corinthians 3:1–6; 11:1–12:19.

The false apostles asked the Corinthians to have Paul provide written confirmation of his backing by the Jerusalem leadership. Incredibly, a record of this has been captured in both the New Testament and the earliest writings of the Church. First, the perspective of the heretics.[51]

> Wherefore observe the greatest caution, that you believe no teacher, unless he brings from Jerusalem the testimonial of James the Lord's brother, or of whosoever may come after him. For no one, unless he has gone up thither, and there has been approved as a fit and faithful teacher for preaching the word of Christ—unless, I say, he brings a testimonial thence, is by any means to be received. But let neither prophet nor apostle be looked for by you at this time, besides us.
> —*Recognitions of Clement* 4.35

They were being deceitful. It is true that the Sanhedrin sent their written communiques to the Jews of the Diaspora by special messengers, the *Selihim*. But in lieu of that, Peter, James, and John had extended the right hand of fellowship to Paul, acknowledging his right to minister to the heathen.[52] The laying on of hands—known as *Semikhah*—was in fact the customary way to convey rabbinical authority.[53] The false apostles pounced on this, and pointed out that Paul could produce no such documentation.

We have Paul's defense in 2 Corinthians. "Do we begin to commend ourselves? Or need we, as some others, epistles of commendation to you, or letters of commendation from you?"[54] He pointed out that the ministration of the Spirit in their lives was better evidence of his apostleship than any letter of recommendation ever written. "Ye are our epistle written in our hearts, known and read of all men. Forasmuch as ye are manifestly declared to be the epistle of Christ ministered by us, written not with ink, but with the Spirit of the living God; not in tables of stones, but in fleshly tables of the heart."

The Torah-observant teachers also attacked his penchant for mystical visions and dreams. To be sure, Paul was vulnerable to these charges. His conversion on the way to Damascus was accompanied by a blinding light

---

51. The same tactic is found in the other branch of the Clementine literature. "Wherefore, above all, remember to shun apostle or teacher or prophet who does not first accurately compare his preaching with that of James [alternative translation: "... Unless he come to you with credentials of James ..."] who was called the brother of my Lord, and to whom was entrusted the administration of the church of the Hebrews in Jerusalem, and that even though he comes to you with witnesses" (*Homilies* 11.35).

52. Galatians 2:9.

53. 1 Timothy 4:14; 2 Timothy 1:16; Acts 6:6.

54. 2 Corinthians 3:1.

from heaven and the audible voice of the Lord.[55] In relating this to the Galatians, he told them he had not received the gospel from man, but by a direct revelation.[56] On another occasion—which Paul related to the Corinthian church—he had been raised up to the third heaven and heard unspeakable things.[57] All of this was fair game with which to discredit him.

Once again, we have a record from Paul's viewpoint and another from the perspective of the false apostles. Their arguments have been preserved in the *Homilies of Clement*. There are five full chapter in this book devoted to debunking visions as a means of acquiring spiritual insight.

> And Peter said: For your proposition is that one is better able to know more fully when he hears because of an apparition than when he hears with his own ears; but when you set about the matter, you were persuading us that he who hears through an apparition is surer than he who hears with his own ears. Finally, you alleged that, on this account, you knew more satisfactory the doctrines of Jesus than I do, because you heard His words through an apparition. . ... But he who trusts to apparition or vision or dream is insecure, for he does not know to whom he is trusting. For it is possible either that he may be an evil demon or a deceptive spirit, pretending in his speeches to be what he is not.
> —*Homilies of Clement* 17.14

Paul worked tirelessly to contain the heresy and keep it from spreading. He dispatched Titus to Crete to ordain solid elders and purge the churches of legalism."[58] Before his last trip to Greece, he left Timothy at Ephesus to guard the flock against "the teachers of the law."[59] Upon his return to Ephesus, he warned the elders against the "grievous wolves" which were headed their way.[60] According to the Book of Revelation, written about a decade

---

55. Acts 9:1–9.

56. Galatians 1:11–12.

57. 2 Corinthians 12:1–4.

58. "For there are many unruly and vain talkers and deceivers, especially they of the circumcision: whose mouths must be stopped, who subvert whole houses, teaching things which they ought not, for filthy lucre's sake . . . Wherefore rebuke them sharply, that they may be sound in the faith; not giving heed to Jewish fables, and commandments of men, that turn men from the truth" (Titus 1:10–14).

59. "Neither give heed to fables and endless genealogies, which minister questions, rather than godly edifying which is in faith: so do. Now the end of the commandment is charity out of a pure heart, and of a good conscience, and of faith unfeigned: From which some having swerved have turned aside unto vain jangling; desiring to be teachers of the law; understanding neither what they say nor whereof they affirm" (1 Timothy 1:4–7).

60. "For I know this, that after my departing shall grievous wolves enter in among you, not sparing the flock." (Acts 20:29).

later, Paul's efforts at Ephesus were ultimately successful. "Thou hast tried them which say they are apostles, and are not, and hast found them liars."[61]

The crisis could not have come at a worse time. Paul was imprisoned in Caesarea from AD 58 to AD 60 which was, in an interesting twist of irony, the hometown of Zacchaeus. After being taken to Rome, he remained in military custody until at least AD 62. Although he had extraordinary liberty for a prisoner—even to the extent of having his own rented house—it must have been a very frustrating time.[62] Paul knew exactly what was going on, but he was powerless to help out in person.

During his Roman imprisonment, Paul wrote to the Colossians and the neighboring churches of Laodicea and Hierapolis. These believers were located less than one hundred miles from the Galatian schismatics, and that gave him reason for concern. "For I would that ye knew what great conflict I have for you, and for them at Laodicea, and for as many as have not seen my face in the flesh."[63] He assured them they were complete in Christ, and there was nothing to be gained from the ceremonies of the Judaizers or the philosophy of the Greeks.[64]

The Date of the Schism

The New Testament does not tell us when or how they broke communion. Things were definitely coming to a head when Paul wrote to the Galatians in AD 56. Although nominally still in fellowship, they had started to observe the weekly Sabbath and the annual feasts.[65] The problem was uppermost in Paul's mind in all of the epistles he wrote in AD 57, including Romans, 1 Timothy, Titus, and 1 and 2 Corinthians. The apostle John, in the mid-60s, writes of an unspecified falling away in the *past* tense. "They went out from us, but they were not of us; for if they had been of us, they would no doubt have continued with us: but they went out, that they might be made manifest that they were not all of us."[66]

Relying on the limited Biblical evidence at our disposal, it is safe to say the final breach did not happen before AD 56. On the other hand, we

---

61. Revelation 2:2.
62. Acts 28:30.
63. Colossians 2:1.
64. Colossians 2:8; 2:16-17
65. "But now, after that ye have known God, or rather are known of God, how turn ye again to the weak and beggarly elements, whereunto ye desire again to be in bondage? Ye observe days, and months, and times, and years" (Galatians 4:9-10).
66. 1 John 2:19.

THE BACKGROUND OF THE GALATIAN HERESY 17

will adduce several lines of evidence below which will show they were on their own by AD 62. We thus have a set of bookends with which to bracket the date. We conclude that, after trying to influence the Christian movement for over a decade from the inside, the false apostles were on their own by AD 60.

The first century Catholics did not possess the Gospel of Luke, a fact which can help us date their departure. When Luke was in Rome, he wrote two manuscripts in rapid succession: The Gospel that goes under his name, and the Acts of the Apostles.[67] Acts brings the history of the apostles up to about AD 62, and the opening line tells us that the "former treatise"—the Gospel of Luke—had already been written. How much before is an open question, but presumably it was not more than a few months or a year. This provides us with a *terminus ad quem* for the publication of the third Gospel. The proto-Catholics were already out of fellowship when Luke published his Gospel in the early sixties.

> **Hegisippus**—A converted Jew who visited many of the Catholic congregations in the middle of the second century. He gathered up their oral traditions and set them down in a now-lost book, *The Memoirs*. Fortunately, the fourth century historian Eusebius preserved many passages in his *History of the Church*.

A terminus may also be deduced from the death of James, the Lord's brother. There are two accounts of his martyrdom extant. According to the historian Josephus, Ananus, the high priest, saw an opportunity to get rid of the Christian leader during a vacancy of the procuratorship after the death of Festus in AD 62. Ananus sentenced James and his companions to be stoned "as breakers of the law" before Festus's replacement arrived.[68] Josephus's testimony in this instance is particularly credible. It appears from the *Life of Flavius Josephus* that he lived in Jerusalem at the time, but whether he did or not, he personally knew many of the priests and politicians involved.

The second century version transmitted by the Catholic gadfly Hegisippus is absurd on its face. We are to believe that the priests asked James, the Lord's brother, to stand on the wall of the temple and tell the Passover crowd that Jesus was not the Messiah. When he declared that Jesus was sitting on the right hand of God, he was pushed from the heights and clubbed to death.[69] The Circumcision Party was thus outside the camp in AD 62—the year James was killed—or they would have known at least as much as Josephus.

---

67. Acts 1:1.
68. *Antiquities* 20.9.
69. *Eccl Hist* 2.23.

The Place of the Schism

There is no doubt where the heresy first took root and grew. The strongest evidence is Biblical, and it points us straight in the direction of central Anatolia. That is where the seeds of Jewish Christianity were first sown, and according to the Galatian epistle, they had been well received. We are told that some of the Galatian men were contemplating circumcision,[70] and the church had started to observe the Jewish holy days.[71] One of those festivals was a modified Passover which they held on the same day as the Jews—the 14th of Nisan.

> **Quartodecimans**—The proto-Catholics created a Christian Passover, which they observed on the same day as the Jewish festival. They borrowed the lunar-based formula from Moses; the evening of the first full moon after the vernal equinox. In the second century, the Roman church would always end the paschal fast on Sunday, and most of the churches followed their lead. Quartodeciman is the Latin word for "Fourteenthers."

This is significant because by the end of the second century, it had become standard throughout the Catholic world to observe Easter on Sunday—except in the heartland of Asia and Galatia. Those churches continued to observe the festival on the same day as Israel ate the lamb and bitter herbs. Polycrates, the bishop of Ephesus, wrote a brilliant defense of the paschal tradition which had passed down in his family for seven generations.[72] He names six churches which had never deviated from the 14th of Nisan observance: Ephesus, Smyrna, Hierapolis, Laodicea, Sardis, and Eumenia. These six cities form a long, narrow belt in western Turkey, fifty miles wide along the Aegean Sea and extending easterly up two river valleys, the Maeander and the Hermus, about one hundred fifty miles. This belt lies entirely within the Roman province of Asia, with the easterly-most city, Eumenia, near the border of Galatia.

> **Papias**—The bishop of Hierapolis, the holy city across the Lycus Valley from Colosse, in the early decades of the second century. Papias was the author of a five-part work entitled *The Exposition of the Sayings of the Lord*, fragments of which survive in Irenaeus and Eusebius. The work was probably a compilation of the oral traditions of the sectarians. Eusebius, who had read the book, judged Papias to have been "a man of low intelligence."

---

70. Galatians 5:3–6.
71. Galatians 4:10.
72. *Eccl Hist* 5.24.

Eumenia is now known as Civril. It lies about 75 miles east of Philadelphia and 75 miles northeast of the Hierapolis/Colosse/Laodicea triangle, both places which had been visited by the false apostles or been influenced by their doctrine before AD 70. Philadelphia had a "synagogue of Satan" back in New Testament days,[73] and Paul had to warn the Colossians about Jewish festivals.[74] Hierapolis and Laodicea were two of the Quartodeciman churches on Bishop Polycrates list, and Papias, the earliest Catholic elder whose writings are extant, lived above the gleaming white cliffs at Hierapolis.[75]

Forty miles away, at the very edge of the Asian-Galatian border, is the ancient city of Apamea—now known as Dinar.[76] Sitting astride the great east-west trade route, commanding the road to the prosperous Meander valley, it was one of the greatest cities in ancient Asia Minor. Apamea contained a sizable Jewish community, going back to BC 200 when Antioch the Great transplanted two thousand Jewish families to Phrygia.[77] These settlers prospered and grew so numerous that, in BC 62, the Roman consul seized almost sixteen lbs. of gold bound for Jerusalem.[78] The Babylonian Talmud writes disapprovingly how Hellenized and worldly this community had become over the centuries. "The wines and baths of Phrygia have separated the ten tribes from their brethren in Israel."[79]

Antioch of Pisidia was the scene of Paul's first mission in Galatia. William Ramsey speculated that Paul caught malaria in the coastal swamps and recuperated in the highlands of Antioch, which lies at an elevation of 3800'.[80] This is what lay behind Paul's words in Galatians 4:13. "As you know, it was because of an illness that I first preached the gospel to you, and even though my illness was a trial to you, you did not treat me with contempt or scorn. Instead, you welcomed me as if I were an angel of God, as if I were Christ Jesus himself."[81] Whether Ramsey's conjecture

---

73. Revelation 3:9.

74. Colossians 2:11–17.

75. Eumenia was the home of a unique inscription on many Christian (or Jewish-Christian) gravestones. The Eumenian formula says: "Thou shalt not wrong God." It is a warning to grave robbers couched in the language of the Ten Commandments.

76. A few miles east of Apamea, at the top of the hill before Apollonia, a boundary stone was found which marks the border between Asia and Galatia.

77. *Antiquities* 12.3.4.

78. Cicero, *Pro Flacco* 28.68.

79. b. *Shabbat* 147b.

80. *St. Paul the Traveller* p. 94.

81. Galatians 4:13–14 NIV. Paul's comment about them pulling out their eyes in verse 15 may refer to the effect of malaria on the eyes.

is true or not, these verses tell us that Paul personally knew some of the saints he was writing to.

If we continue further east, to Iconium and beyond, the paschal landscape changes dramatically. There is no indication the Catholics in that quarter had ever observed a 14th of Nisan Easter. The church at Iconium sent a bishop to Nicaea in AD 325, and he signed off on the Sunday Easter date along with the other 300 bishops.[82] The Catholicism which Gregory "the Wonder Worker" introduced to neighboring Cappadocia was also perfectly orthodox.[83] We have thus gone too far. We conclude that the primary recipients of Paul's epistle to the Galatians resided in the Turkish Lake District, from Antioch in Pisidia to the border town of Apamea.

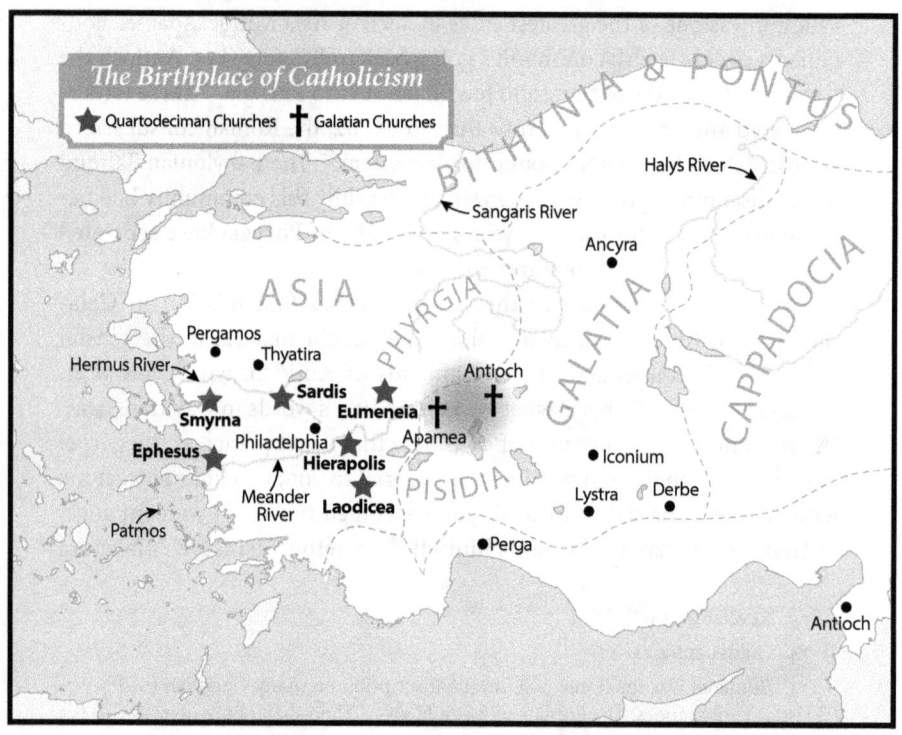

82. "The result was that they were not only united as concerning the faith, but the time for the celebration of the salutary feast of Easter was agreed on by all. Those points also which were sanctioned by the resolution of the whole body were committed to writing, and received the signature of each member" (*Life of Constantine* 3.14).

83. Gregory Thaumaturgis, who had studied under Origen in Palestine, brought Catholicism to Cappadocia circa AD 240. He was based in Caesarea Mazaca, modern-day Kayseri.

2

Founded on Fables

AD 60 to AD 80

*For we know that Simon and Cleobius, and their followers,
have compiled poisonous books
under the name of Christ and his apostles,
and do carry them about in order to deceive you.*

—APOSTOLIC CONSTITUTIONS 6.16

From AD 48 to AD 56, the Circumcision Party battled for the heart and soul of the Christian movement from the inside. They lost the backing of the apostles almost immediately at the Jerusalem council in AD 49. After establishing a single Torah-observant church in Galatia in AD 55, they found the door had been slammed shut in every other Pauline church. The Galatian success and the setbacks elsewhere led to a change in tactics.

They decided to separate and form their own church. They were so certain the apostles had taken a wrong turn in regards to the Law—one that Christ himself would have opposed—that they felt dutybound to rectify the mistake. These men truly believed the salvation of the world rested on their shoulders. "If they should be corrupted by any daring man, or be perverted by interpretations, as you have heard that some have already done, it will remain for those who really seek the truth to always wander in error."[1]

They then set about to manufacture fictitious letters and books that wove Peter, James and the false apostles into a believable historical narrative.[2] The apostle of the Gentiles–Paul–also had to be dealt with. After a decade of unsuccessfully trying to debate Paul, they decided to demonize him. Paul the apostle thus became Simon the Sorcerer, the blackest of false prophets.[3] The overall strategy was to clothe their Jewish doctrine with the cloak of apostolic authority, and it succeeded brilliantly. Because their first converts lived in isolated, remote villages, they did not realize the pseudo-apostles were actually adversaries of the apostles. They sincerely believed what they were taught, and passed it down to the generation that followed.

> **Irenaeus**—The bishop of Lyon, France in the last quarter of the second century. His work *Against Heresies* is a lengthy attack on Gnosticism and a primary source on Valentinus. Irenaeus pointed to the Roman succession list as proof of what is apostolic and true. A native of Asia Minor, he had been acquainted with Polycarp of Smyrna in his youth, supposedly a disciple of John.

In this way the loftiest, most glorious spiritual movement in man's history was hijacked by its foes. It must rank as the most successful religious fraud of all time. All of the surviving documentation tell us just how thoroughly the first generation of proto-Catholics had been taken in. Their descent from the apostles is taken for granted by all the Church Fathers of the second century.[4] The doctrine of apostolic succession, the ability to trace their lineage back to Peter and the apostles, became the cornerstone of the Catholic faith.

This insignificant sect evolved, spread across the Roman Empire and, 100 years later, gave themselves the grandiose name of *Ekklesia Katholika*, the Universal Church. By projecting the genuine history of the New

---

1. *Peter to James* 5.

2. Zacchaeus, the patriarch of the proto-Catholics, was the most likely author. We learn from *Recognitions* 1.17 that the *Preaching of Peter* was distributed from Caesarea, which just happens to be the hometown of Zacchaeus. "Whence, by his command, reducing into order what he had spoken unto me, I compiled a book concerning the true Prophet, and sent it to you from Caesarea by his command. For he said that he had received a command from you to send you every year an account of his sayings and doings." The *Preaching of Peter* demonstrates a detailed knowledge of the Mediterranean coastline, and this would also tally with a man from Caesarea.

3. This fictitious character was regarded by the Church as the fountainhead of all heresy well into the Middle Ages.

4. *Eccl Hist* 4.22; *Against Heresies* 3.3.1; *Prescrip* 32.1.

Testament forward, and intertwining it with the earliest stratum of Catholic writings, we will reconstruct the early, heretofore hidden years of the sect.

The Founding Charter

Every religious movement must have its own authoritative Scriptures, and the heresiarchs set about to prepare theirs. The initial canon of the sect consisted of the following books, all still extant in one form or another.

1. *The Epistle of Peter to James*—This letter legitimized the false apostles by providing them with links to James and the Jerusalem church. It provided the pseudo-apostles with the same documentation they had asked the Corinthian church to expect from Paul. In addition, this epistle authorizes the release of a new book to their flock, an alternate version of the Acts of the Apostles.

2. *The Preaching of Peter*—This pious novel was their alternate history of the apostolic period. Peter plays the leading role in spreading the gospel and Paul, under the pseudonym of Simon Magus, is the villain. Peter travels north up the Levantine coastline, preaching to crowds and debating Simon Magus at every turn. This lost work underlies two books which have survived, known as the *Recognitions of Clement* and the *Homilies of Clement*.

3. *The Teaching of the Lord through the Twelve Apostles to the Gentiles*—This work is usually known as the *Didache*, the Greek word for teaching. Addressed to the "Nations," or Gentiles, it established a Jewish form of Christianity in the Greco-Roman world completely apart from the Pauline tradition. It was their first manual of church order, and includes sample prayers, baptismal procedures, fasting guidelines, etc. Many of these practices are still regular fixtures of Roman Catholic and Orthodox piety.

4. *The Epistle of Clement to James*—This is the source of several key Catholic traditions, including what would become their marquee myth, the papacy of Peter. Simon Peter evangelizes some unspecified region "in the west" and ends up in Italy, where he becomes the first bishop of Rome. Peter then hand-picks Clement to succeed him, and bestows on his successors the power to "loose and bind."

The Epistle of Peter to James

The Epistle of Peter to James is a two-part work, with "Peter" dictating the first half and "James" issuing instructions in the second. In this extraordinary work we get to hear the heresiarchs speak in their own voice. It is the only text from the hands of the false apostles that has survive the centuries without being sanitized or cleaned up. The purpose of this exchange between Peter and James was to provide a believable backdrop for the introduction of a major new addition to their canon. The entire text has been reproduced in the addendum at the back of this book.

The first section purports to be a cover letter for an accompanying volume of sermons. This book is referred to six times as the "book of my preachings;" it is called *Clement's Epitome of the Popular Sermons of Peter* in another first century work.[5] The first and second century Catholics simply called it the *Preaching of Peter*.

It begins with Peter urging James to exercise extreme caution in distributing the new book. Peter is concerned because "the word of truth is being rent" by his adversary, who is easily discernable as Paul the apostle. "For some from among the Gentiles have rejected my legal preaching, attaching themselves to certain lawless and trifling preaching of the man who is my enemy." Note that Peter's doctrine is "legal" while his opponent's teaching is "lawless." He then launches into a broadside against this unnamed adversary who is establishing Christianity among the Gentiles outside of the Law.

> And these things some have attempted while I am still alive, to transform my words by certain various interpretations, *to the dissolution of the law*; as though I also were of such a mind, but did not freely proclaim it, which God forbid! *For such a thing would be to act in opposition to the law of God which was spoken by Moses,* and was borne witness to by our Lord in respect of its *eternal continuance*; for thus he spoke: 'The heavens and the earth shall pass away, but one jot or one tittle shall in no wise pass from the law.' And this He has said, that all things might come to pass. But these men professing, I know not how, to know my mind, undertake to explain my words, which they have heard of me, more intelligently than I who spoke them, telling their catechumens that this is my meaning, which indeed I never thought of. But if, while I am still alive, they dare thus to misrepresent me, how much more will those who shall come after me dare to do so!
>
> —*Epistle of Peter to James* 2, emphasis mine

---

5. *Clement to James* 20.

This, no doubt, helped the false apostles to sell their Torah-observance and legalism to an unsuspecting public.

The second half of the book is James' response. He has received the letter from Peter, read it to the elders of the church, and is going about to implement Peter's suggestions on disbursing the book. The elders of the movement were asked to guard the *Preaching of Peter* with a secrecy bordering on paranoia.

> Our Peter has strictly and becomingly charged us concerning the establishment of the truth, that we should not communicate the books of his preachings, which have been sent to us, to anyone at random, but to one who is good and religious, and who wishes to teach, and *who is circumcised*, and faithful. And these are not all to be committed to him at once; that, if he be found injudicious in the first, the others may not be entrusted to him. Wherefore let him be proved not less than six years.

The stipulation of circumcision should raise a red flag to anyone familiar with Christian theology. It was the battleground issue between the New Testament apostles and their most vocal opponents, the false apostles. The requirement to be "religious" can, in this context, only mean observant of the Law. This Christian sect was thus telling Gentiles they had to be circumcised and keep Torah, contrary to the doctrine of the apostles. The prospective teacher—which was an actual position in the first and second century church—was then taken to the waters of baptism, where he had to swear an extensive oath not to reveal the *Preaching of Peter* to outsiders. Part of this vow states:

> But even if it should ever seem to me that the books of the preachings given to me are not true, I shall not so communicate them, but shall give them back. And when I go abroad, I shall carry them with me, whatever of them I happen to possess. But if I be not minded to carry them about with me, I shall not suffer them to be in my house, but shall deposit them with my bishop.

This does not sound like the words of an apostle burning with zeal for the truth of the gospel! Instead, it sounds like someone who has just written a piece of fiction and is trying everything in his power to keep from being exposed.

The Preaching of Peter

The second book in the proto-Catholic Bible was the *Preaching of Peter*. It was introduced to the church membership shortly after AD 70 by the *Epistle of Peter to James*. We are certain of this date because the cessation of the temple sacrifice is mentioned more than once in the heavily-edited forms that have survived.[6] Its early origin is also seen in the fact that the Ebionites, the Palestinian branch of the movement, included this book among their sacred Scriptures.[7]

The Preaching of Peter is the proto-Catholic counterpart to the Acts of the Apostles. Peter was given roughly the same place in this literature that Paul occupies in the canonical New Testament. The first century proto-Catholics were taught that Peter, not Paul, carried the gospel of Jesus Christ to the Gentiles. The "Prince of the Apostles" was the heroic figure at the heart of their core myth, created completely independently of the New Testament.

The Preaching of Peter begins at Rome, where Clement, a philosophically-minded young man, hears Barnabas, a disciple of the Lord, and believes.[8] The two branches of the *Clementina* agree in placing this event during the ministry of Jesus. Clement follows Barnabas by ship to Caesarea, where he is introduced to Peter. The narrative then tracks Peter as he and Clement travel north up the eastern coastline of the Mediterranean, giving private lectures to his followers and engaging in public debates with Simon Magus. As they put words into Peter's mouth, we are treated to the raw, uncensored doctrine of the first century sectarians. At Antioch, Peter hears Clements' family history, meets a beggar lady, recognizes her as Clements' mother—hence the title "Recognitions"—and the family is reunited.

The Preaching of Peter is the ur-text—the lost literary ancestor—that underlies two extant books, the *Recognitions of Clement* and the *Homilies of Clement*. The original story was supposedly written by Clement, which explains why these books are known as the Clementines, the pseudo-Clementine writings, the *Clementina*, and the Clementine literature. Although they differ in many details, large portions of the two works are almost identical. They have a very complex textual history, comparable in many ways to an old house that has been remodeled, added onto, and repainted over the years. A couple of chronological markers point to a major rewrite around

---

6. *Recognitions* 1.39, *Homilies* 2.17.
7. *Panarion* 30.15.
8. *Recognitions* 1.7.

AD 150. The Gospel of John, which was just gaining acceptance in Catholic circles at that time, is cited rather timidly.[9]

The Clementine literature helps us to understand their tenacious attachment to several legends and characters not found in the New Testament. One of these is Simon the Magician. He was regarded by the Fathers of the Church as the father of all heresy, a sorcerer and master of black arts. Simon Magus was the proto-Catholic pseudonym for Paul the apostle, although his doctrine and personal history has been distorted beyond all recognition. We find in this caricature what the first generations of Catholics were taught about their great rival and nemesis.[10]

> And they told me that he makes statues walk, and that he rolls himself on the fire and is not burnt; and sometimes he flies; and he makes loaves of stones; he becomes a serpent; he transforms himself into a goat; he becomes two-faced; he changes himself into gold; he opens locked gates; he melts iron; at banquets he produces images of all manner of forms."
> —*Homilies of Clement* 2.32

Simon—like Paul—speaks against the Torah in numerous places, but the following passage makes the connection virtually undeniable. "Then after three days one of the brethren came to us from Gamaliel, whom we mentioned before, bringing us secret tidings that enemy had received a commission from Caiaphas, the high priest, that he should go arrest all who believed in Jesus, and should go to Damascus with his letters and that there also, he should make havoc among the faithful."[11] This is nothing but a thinly veiled allusion to Paul, prior to his conversion, making his way to Damascus.[12] The author was clearly conversant with the Acts of the Apostles, but in order for the deception to work, his intended readers had to be oblivious to it.

There is nothing new or novel about the identification of Simon with Saul of Tarsus. It was one of Ferdinand Baur's pet theories in the 1840s. The Tubingen School he founded posited an apostolic schism between Peter and Paul. The Petrine wing of the church became the Ebionites, who stayed faithful to their Jewish roots, while Paul was championed in the Gentile churches. According to Baur, the Jewish branch dominated the church for the first 100

---

9. The same verse, John 3:5, is found in both branches of the *Clementina* as well as another author of the period, Justin Martyr.
10. See *Recognitions* 2.9.
11. *Recognitions* 1.71.
12. Acts 9.

years, and the clash between the two branches of Christianity is expressed in the Clementine literature as the struggle between Peter and Simon.

Clement is another unscriptural character who harkens back to the *Preaching of Peter*.[13] Even though the *Preaching* was phased out in the second century, the ghost of Clement still roams the halls and corridors of the Vatican to this day. The huge body of forgeries attributed to Clement demonstrates the hold he has had on the Catholic mind. It gets even more absurd: in the Middle Ages, a total of thirteen popes and three anti-popes chose the pontifical name of Clement for their papacy.

The Barnabas of the *Clementina* has also cast a long shadow in the Roman church.[14] In the *Recognitions of Clement*, Barnabas was a "disciple of the Lord;" in Clement of Alexandria's *Stromata*, he is one of the seventy;[15] but in the *Gospel of Barnabas*, he has graduated to become one of the twelve apostles.[16] His name was later attached to the *Epistle of Barnabas* (AD 132) and the *Gospel of Barnabas* (circa AD 200). He has since merged into the Barnabas of the New Testament.

The *Ekklesia Katholika* severed all ties to the Clementine writings in the second century, even rewriting the *Preaching of Peter* into its present form. Nevertheless, we know that it was once part of their history because the characters and dogmas that originated in this literature have taken up permanent residence in the Church.

- Peter founded the church at Rome and served as its first bishop
- Peter founded the church at Antioch and served as its first bishop
- Zacchaeus was anointed the first bishop of Caesarea
- Clement, a fictional figure made up out of whole cloth, was originally designated the first bishop in the Roman succession after Peter. He is now regarded as the fourth pope.
- Simon the Magician was the father of Christian heresy
- The Barnabas of the *Clementina*

---

13. The canonical Clement who labored in the gospel is mentioned only once in the New Testament (Philippians 4:3). This was very late in the apostolic era, in the early 60's. The fictitious Clement of the *Preaching of Peter* was a Gentile, born in Rome, who heard the gospel while Jesus was still alive (*Recognitions* 1.1).

14. The Barnabas of the pseudo-Clementina is a completely different person than the Barnabas of the New Testament. The proto-Catholics did not use the Acts of the Apostles and created this fictional character for their own version of the apostolic epoch. Barnabas, Paul's first companion in the gospel, was a Levite from Cyprus (Acts 4:36).

15. *Stromata* 2.20.

16. *G Barnabas* 14.

There are several warnings in the Clementine literature against "false scriptures" and false chapters."[17] We believe the books they were trying to keep from their converts were the genuine writings of the apostles. The Acts of the Apostles would have been particularly enlightening to anyone raised on the *Preaching of Peter*. The following passage from the *Apostolic Constitutions* basically says as much.

> We have sent all these things to you, that ye may know our opinion; and that ye may not receive those books which obtain in our name, but are written by the ungodly. For ye are not to attend to the names of the apostles, but to the nature of the thing and their settled opinions. For we know that Simon and Cleobius, and their followers, have compiled poisonous books under the name of Christ and of His disciples, and do carry them about in order to deceive you ... .
> —*Apostolic Constitutions* 6.16

The Didache

One of the books in the proto-Catholic Bible was lost to the Christian world for hundreds of years. The recovery of this ancient work must rank as the greatest patristic find of all time. In 1873, the Orthodox bishop of Nicomedia, Philotheos Bryennios, discovered a manuscript in a monastery in Istanbul. The codex was dated AD 1056 by the scribe who penned it. It contained several early Catholic works, which he published, but tucked away inside, unnoticed for several years, was the *Didache*.

The *Didache* was their initial handbook of church order. It provides the clearest window we have to the early days of the movement. The *Didache* sets out regulations for fasting, baptism, and worship; provides them with templates for daily prayer and blessings for the Eucharistic meal; and it gives instructions to their (false) apostles and elders. The complete title, *The Teaching of the Lord through the Twelve Apostles to the Nations*, is revealing in itself. It tells us that these teachings were for the

---

17. "Simon, therefore, as I learn, intends to come into public, and to speak of those chapters against God that are added to the Scriptures, for the sake of temptation, that he may seduce as many wretched ones as he can from the love of God. For we not wish to say in public that these chapters were added to the Bible, since we should thereby perplex the unlearned multitudes, and so accomplish the purpose of this wicked Simon" (*Homilies* 2.39).

"If, therefore, some of the Scriptures are true and some are false, with good reason said our Master, 'Be ye good moneychangers,' inasmuch as in the Scriptures there are some true sayings and some spurious" (*Homilies* 2.51).

"Nations"—a Hebraism for Gentiles—and the use of this term betrays a Jewish hand behind the document.

The *Didache* as presently constituted should be dated around AD 90. We know it was within one generation of their founding—as some of the false apostles were still alive—but enough time had lapsed for them to discard circumcision.

The first five chapters are a moral tract known as the "Two Ways." Many authorities believe this section had its origin in the synagogues as an initiation catechism for Jewish proselytes. It was modified and included in the *Didache* to give their pagan converts an understanding of basic Judeo-Christian morality. The essence of the teaching is neatly captured in the opening line. "There are two ways, one of life and one of death; but there is a great difference between the two." The way of life consists of the Great Commandment (love of God and neighbor), the Golden Rule, the Ten Commandments, and extracts from the Sermon on the Mount.

Chapter 6 jumps right into their obligations under the Law. "If you are able to carry the full yoke of the Lord, you will be perfect; but if you are not able, do whatever you can." The key word here is "yoke," which was a common Hebrew idiom for the Law of Moses. Peter used the same expression at the apostolic council which decided on the obligations of *Goyim*: "Now therefore why tempt ye God, to put a yoke upon the neck of the disciples, which neither our fathers nor we were able to bear?"[18] Paul, writing to the Torah-observant Christians in Galatia, also employed it. "Stand fast therefore in the liberty wherewith Christ hath made us free, and be not entangled again with the yoke of bondage."[19] The sentence about carrying "the full yoke of the Lord" really makes no sense except as a redactor's seam. It sounds to our ear like a block of material has been removed here, perhaps relating to circumcision, and the editor attempted to smooth it over with the bland admonition to "do whatever you can."

The next sentence refers to *kashrut*, the Jewish dietary laws. "And concerning food, bear what thou art able. . ." Behind this brief pronouncement, we see another missing section of text. It perhaps covered the distinction between clean and unclean animals, forbade the eating of already dead or torn carcasses, discussed the humane (and kosher) method of slaughtering animals, etc.[20] The food regulations proved too cumbersome and too re-

---

18. Acts 15:10.

19. Galatians 5:1. It is also found in Jewish literature. "From whoever accepts upon himself the yoke of Torah do they remove the yoke of the state and the yoke of hard labor" (m. *Abot* 3.5a).

20. Perhaps it was similar to the meat restrictions enumerated in *Homilies of Clement* 7.8. "This is the service He has appointed: . . . . . . to abstain from the table of devils,

strictive to Gentiles not brought up under this kind of discipline, as the exhortation to "bear what thou able" implies. The dietary laws were scrubbed early on, and this reference and one in the *Gospel of Barnabas* are the only evidence we have of their existence in the Church.

Chapter 7 lays down regulations for baptism. "Baptize in the name of the Father, and of the Son, and of the Holy Spirit, in living water. But if thou have not living water, baptize into other water; and if thou canst not in cold, use warm. But if thou have not either, pour out water thrice upon the head. . ." The charge to use "living water" has a special meaning in rabbinic tradition. The *Mishnah* lists, in ascending order, "six grades among pools of water, each more excellent than the other."[21] Pond water, being stagnant, is at the bottom of the list, and living water—a Hebraism for fresh, flowing water—is at the top. The *Didache* states the preference for living water and then evaluates the suitable alternatives in descending order.

Chapter 7 continues: "Before the baptism, let the one who baptizes and the one to be baptized fast, and any others who are able to do so. And you shall require the one being baptized to fast for one or two days." The two-day delay—ostensibly for fasting—was needed to allow the pre-baptismal circumcision to heal. It was totally at odds with the practice of the apostles, who did not waste any time getting believers to the waters of baptism. The Ethiopian eunuch and the Philippian jailor were both baptized within hours of hearing the gospel. A confession of faith was all that was required by the servants of God.[22]

Chapter 8 begins with the law of fasting. They openly admit their bi-weekly fasting regulations came from the Pharisees, whom they call hypocrites. "But let not your fasts be with the hypocrites; for they fast on the second and fifth days of the week; but you shall fast on the fourth day and the day of preparation."[23] The Eastern Orthodox rites have never deviated from the Wednesday and Friday fast laid down by their forefathers. On the other hand, the Roman Catholics treat every Friday as a penitential day, denying themselves the pleasure of meat, but fasting per se is only required on Ash Wednesday and Good Friday.

The eighth chapter continues with instruction on prayer. The faithful were admonished to say the Lord's Prayer three time a day, the usual

---

that is, from food offered to idols, from dead carcasses, from animals which have been suffocated or caught by wild beasts, and from blood."

21. m. *Mikvaot* 1.1.

22. For examples of the authentic apostolic practice, see Acts 2:41, 8:36–39, 9:18, 10:47–48, 16:33, and 19:5.

23. The proud Pharisee in Luke 18:12 boasted that he was not as other men because, among other things, he fasted twice a week.

number of fixed prayers since the time of David.[24] The Jewish obligation to pray three times daily could, by the end of the first century, only be fulfilled by reciting the Eighteen Benedictions. The Lord's Prayer was given the same place in Catholic devotions as the Eighteen Benedictions held in the Hebrew liturgy. It was, as Tertullian put it, the "prescribed and regular" prayer.[25]

Chapters 9 and 10 contain instructions and sample table blessings for the Thanksgiving, the first century sacred meal that evolved into the Holy Eucharist. The first two prayers are simply a recasting of the standard Jewish blessings for bread and wine. The *berakah* pronounced over the cup—"Blessed art thou, O Lord our God, eternal King, Who creates the fruit of the vine"—became "We thank Thee, our Father, for the holy vine of David thy servant, which Thou madest known to us through Jesus Thy Servant; to Thee be the glory forever." Chapter 10 warehouses a Christianized version of the *Birkat Hamazon*, the main Jewish table grace, which was—and still is—said after the meal. *The Didache* instructed them to recite this prayer "after you are filled," leaving no doubt that the primitive Eucharist was an actual meal.

In Chapter 13, they reworked the Law of First Fruits to provide support for the false apostles. "Every first-fruit, therefore, of the products of the winepress and threshing floor, of oxen and of sheep, thou shalt take and give to the prophets, for they are your high priests. But if ye have not a prophet, give it to the poor. If thou makest a batch of dough, take the first fruit and give according to the commandment." One of the most important duties of the Jewish housewife was the dough offering. They were to set aside a small piece of dough every time they baked bread, and this was presented to the priests in due course. God's share—the *challah*—was generally understood to be about 1/24th of the kneaded dough.[26] The firstfruits are still collected by the Catholic Church; not in kind, but in money.

Chapter 15 deals with matters of administration. "Appoint, therefore, for yourselves, bishops and deacons . . . for they also render to you the service of prophets and teachers. Despise them not, therefore, for they are your honored ones, together with the prophets and teachers." The text of the *Didache* was redacted just as the false apostles were heading off into the sunset, and the elders were beginning to assume responsibility. Although the authority of the apostle class had waned, they still commanded considerable

---

24. Psalms 55:17; Daniel 6:10.
25. *On Prayer* 10.
26. m. *Hallah* 2.7.

respect within the community, especially among older believers. But the actual power was now wielded by the local elders.[27]

> **Clement of Alexandria**—The bishop of Alexandria and author at the end of the second century. Three of his complete works have survived, the most famous being the *Stromata* (ie, miscellanies or patchwork). He was a convert from paganism, and Greek philosophy is sprinkled throughout his books. His writings reflect the primitive canon of the Church, citing such works as the *Gospel of the Egyptians*, the *Tradition of Matthias*, the *Didache*, the *Shepherd*, and the *Epistle of Barnabas*.

It is often claimed that the *Didache* represents an isolated pocket of Jewish Christians or a minority faction in the backwaters of the primitive church. Not so. There is no doubt that it lay directly in the mainstream of historic Catholicism. The "Two Ways" section appears in the *Epistle of Barnabas*, sometimes almost word-for-word. Clement of Alexandria referred to it as "Scripture," and the Egyptian church was still using it as an instruction manual in the fourth century.[28] Three of the most influential church orders of the first centuries borrowed material from the *Didache*: the *Didascalia Apostolorum*, the *Apostolic Tradition*, and the *Apostolic Constitutions*. The mere fact they all drew water from the same well is proof positive they were from the same tradition.

The *Didache* does not cite Paul or contain even a particle of Pauline theology. This is surpassing strange when we consider that it was written to Gentiles, that Paul was the apostle to the Gentiles, and that he gave advice on many of the same matters. This "omission," if we may call it that, has long puzzled scholars, but it is exactly what we would expect. To the false apostles, Paul was a dangerous heretic; indeed, he was considered "the enemy." They would no more have quoted from Paul than from Satan himself. The *Didache* quotes liberally from the Gospel of Matthew, but never from the other twenty-six books of the New Testament.

---

27. The elder could, if necessary, place restrictions on the prophets as to how long they could stay and what they received for sustenance. If we read between the lines, we find there were abuses that had to be curbed. "And when the apostle goeth away, let him take nothing but bread until he lodgeth; but if he asks for money, he is a false prophet" . . . "And every prophet who ordereth a meal in the Spirit eateth not from it, except indeed he be a false prophet" . . . "But whoever saith in the Spirit, Give me money, or something else, ye shall not listen to him." The old order was still very much in evidence and honored, but the elders were now calling the shots.

28. *Stromata* 1.20; Athenasius, *39th Festal Letter*.

> **Didascalia Apostolorum**—Despite the title—*Teaching of the Apostles*—this work was actually compiled in the third century. It was an effort to bring the *Didache* up-to-date after the Church had accepted the New Testament. This church order lays out the responsibilities of bishops, priests, and deacons, discusses paschal customs, warns against the public baths, and derides whose who were still holding to the purity regulations. The *Didascalia* quotes extensively from the New Testament, but lacks Revelation, which is consistent with its Syrian origin.

The "apostles and prophets" mentioned in the *Didache* were obviously not in fellowship with Paul. They didn't use his epistles or employ his theology. Who were they? The only other such missionaries in the New Testament were the false apostles, the believing Pharisees who were pushing circumcision and Torah-observance on Gentiles. The *Didache* is thus the missing link which connects the heresy of Acts 15 with the beginnings of the *Ekklesia Katholika*.

The Epistle of Clement to James

The final member of the founding charter was the *Epistle of Clement to James*. It begins by exalting Peter above the other apostles. He was declared to be the "first of the apostles," the "first to whom the Father revealed the Son," the "called and elect," and the "excellent and approved disciple." Indeed, the very first sentence informs us that Peter was set apart to be "the foundation of the church." This would have been shocking news to Paul, who pointed to Christ as the only foundation of our faith.[29]

We are told that Peter had been sent to "enlighten the west" and that he had made it as far as Rome. Years have seemingly passed, and multitudes of Romans have been saved. Sensing he is close to death, Peter handpicks Clement to be his successor. The scene is carefully choreographed. Peter grabs Clements' hand, stands up in the midst of the congregation, and publicly endows him with the "chair of the teacher," which develops into the bishop's throne. Clement is granted the power to lose and bind, as Peter had. Clement initially declines the honor but, after hearing Peter's ringing endorsement, he reluctantly consents. Thus was born the myth of apostolic succession.

---

29. "For other foundation can no man lay than that is laid, which is Jesus Christ" (1 Corinthians 3:11).

Much of this letter is devoted to the duties of the bishop.[30] He is to join the youth in marriage, "anticipating the entanglements of youthful lust." Bishops were to act as parents to orphans. They were encouraged to be hospitable and frequent guests at dinner with their flock. They were to act as judges instead of taking disputes to the civil authorities. The business of the church is compared to the administration of a great ship, an analogy found again in the fourth century *Apostolic Constitutions*.[31]

Finally, a new book—*The Preaching of Peter*—is trumpeted. After Peter's death, Clement was instructed to send James an account of Peter's sermons and missionary activity. Clement signs off the *Epistle of Clement to James as follows*: "Where I, my Lord James, having promised as I was ordered, have not failed to write in books by chapters the greater part of his discourses in every city, which have already been written to you, and sent by himself for a token and thus I dispatch them to you, inscribing them "*Clements Epitome of the Popular Sermons of Peter.*"

---

30. This book ignores the counsel on bishops Paul gives the church in 1 Timothy 3 and Titus 1.

31. *Ap Const* 2.57.

3

Peter, the Bishop of Rome

> For we have not followed cunningly devised fables,
> when we made known unto you
> the power and coming of our Lord Jesus Christ,
> but were eyewitnesses of his majesty.
>
> —2 Peter 1:16

The most powerful and enduring myth ever created by the false apostles is that Peter was the first bishop of Rome and succeeded James as the head of the church. Billions of Catholics and Orthodox Christians have been taught—and fervently believe—that Peter established the visible Kingdom of God in the city of Rome. They have pinned their faith and hope of eternal salvation on this claim. But is it true?

What does the Bible and classical history tell us about first century Rome? It may have been the "strangers of Rome, Jews and proselytes," part of the crowd that witnessed the miracle of Pentecost in AD 30, which first carried the torch of faith to the capital.[1] The Roman church was therefore Jewish from its inception. Paul alludes to their background in the Law

---

1. Acts 2:10.

several times in his epistle to the Romans,[2] and this accords with the Acts of the Apostles, where Antioch had the distinction of being the first Gentile church.[3] However, by the time he wrote in AD 57, it had become a mixed church. "For I speak to you Gentiles, inasmuch as I am the apostle of the Gentiles, I magnify mine office..."[4]

The first Christians at Rome encountered a hostile political environment. Suetonius records the following about the reign of Tiberius Caesar, AD 14 to AD 37, when the church was first established. The saints were still classed and treated as Jews at this early stage.

> "He abolished foreign cults at Rome, particularly the Egyptian and Jewish, forcing all citizens who had embraced these superstitious faiths to burn their religious vestments and other accessories. Jews of military age were removed to unhealthy regions, on the pretext of drafting them into the army; those too old or too young to serve—including non-Jews who had adopted similar beliefs—were expelled from the City and threatened with slavery if they defied the order."
> —*Tiberius* 36

Cassius Dio provides some information from the beginning of Claudius' reign (AD 41 to AD 54) which may or may not be relevant. "When the Jews [of Rome] had again multiplied to the point where their numbers made it difficult to expel them from the city without a riot, he did not directly ban them but forbade them to gather together in accordance with their ancestral way of life."[5] The Roman synagogues were therefore closed in AD 41, but the Christians, with their little home gatherings, were probably left unmolested.

In AD 49, Claudius Caesar expelled all of the Jews living in Rome, including Priscilla and Aquila.[6] Suetonius's account of the matter tells us that the gospel of Jesus Christ had rent the Jewish community to the point they were causing civil disorder. "Since the Jews were continually making disturbances at the instigation of *Chrestus*, he expelled them from Rome."[7] By AD 57, Paul

---

2. "What shall we say then that Abraham our father, as pertaining to the flesh, hath found" (Romans 4:1)? "Know ye not, brethren, (for I speak to them that know the law,) how that the law hath dominion over a man as long as he liveth" (Romans 7:1)? See also Romans 14:2–17.

3. Acts 11:20–25.

4. Romans 11:13.

5. *History* 60.6.

6. Acts 18:2.

7. *Life of Claudius* 25.4.

could boast that their faith "was spoken of throughout the whole world."[8] He mentions two men and two women at the end of the Roman epistle who were laboring there in the Gospel.[9] Andronicus and Junio were probably the older servants of God in Italy, and quite possibly the founding apostles. That they had plenty to shepherd is certain: Tacitus speaks of "an immense multitude" of Christians who were tortured in the fall of AD 64.[10]

The Ministry of Peter

Where does Peter fit into this? The book of Acts provides us with periodic glimpses of his whereabouts for the first twenty years after Pentecost, and it was never at Rome. After the resurrection in AD 30, Peter, along with the other apostles, stayed in Jerusalem for several years. This period is covered from the beginning of Acts until chapter 7. In chapter 8, Peter and John follow Philip's mission into Samaria, in the geographic center of Israel. In the 9th chapter, we find Peter preaching in the coastal region directly west of Jerusalem: Lydda, Saron, and Joppa.[11] In the 10th chapter, Peter is led by the Spirit to Cornelius in Caesarea. All of this took place before Claudius Caesar acceded to the throne in AD 41.[12] In the 12th chapter, which was also "about that time," Herod tossed Peter into a Jerusalem prison.

In AD 45 or AD 46, the Christian leaders divided up the responsibilities of the ministry. The apostles did not claim a country for themselves—as asserted by Catholic tradition[13]—but they split the fields of labor along the Jew/Gentile divide. Peter, James and John agreed to shepherd the Jewish believers, and Paul was sent to the Gentiles.

> "But contrariwise, when they saw that the gospel of the uncircumcision was committed unto me, as the gospel of the circumcision was unto Peter; (For he that wrought effectually in Peter to the apostleship of the circumcision, the same was mighty in me toward the Gentiles:) And when James, Cephas, and John, who seemed to be pillars, perceived the grace that was given unto me, they gave to me and Barnabas the right hands of fellowship; that we should go unto the heathen, and they unto the circumcision."
> —Galatians 2:7–9

8. Romans 1:8.
9. Romans 16:7, 12.
10. Tacitus, *Annals* 15.44.
11. Acts 9:32, 35, 38.
12. Acts 11:28.
13. Syriac *Teaching* 1–10, *Acts of Thomas* 1.

There is nothing in this statement about Peter's oversight of the Roman church and no hint he was being sent there. Instead, he continued to minister to the sons and daughters of Abraham.

Peter may have elected to stay close to home for an entirely practical reason: he was a married man. We read in the synoptic Gospels that his mother-in-law got sick, and Jesus healed her with a touch of his hand.[14] Peter's wife was still alive when Paul wrote to the Corinthians in AD 57. "Have we not power to lead about a sister, a wife, as well as other apostles, and as the brethren of the Lord, and Cephas?"[15] We don't know the mechanics of this relationship, but it sounds like she accompanied Peter in the ministry. The early Catholics were aware that Peter had a wife, and we even catch a brief glimpse of her in the *Homilies of Clement*.[16] In the fourth century we are told that her name was Concordia, or Perpetua—take your pick—and they were blessed with a daughter named Petronilla.[17]

The year AD 48 again finds Peter in the holy city. From Jerusalem, he travels up the coastline to meet with Paul and the young Greek church at Antioch.[18] The following year the apostles and elders met at Jerusalem to decide the Gentile issue. Peter delivers what might be called the keynote address,[19] but it was James who made the final decision and dictated the letter to the Christians in Iconium, Derbe, and Lystra.

We are left in the dark for most of the 50s. The Acts of the Apostles focuses almost exclusively on Paul and his spectacular missions to the Greek world. We note that Paul wrote the passage about Peter's apostleship of the circumcision and his calling to the Gentiles in AD 56. Although he is describing events from 10 or 11 years before, there is no indication anything had changed. It is safe to presume that Peter was still ministering to his fellow countrymen in AD 56.

---

14. Matthew 8:14–15; Mark 1:29–31; Luke 4:38–39.

15. 1 Corinthians 9:5.

16. "Now at break of day Peter entered, and said, 'Clement, and his mother Mattidia, and my wife, must take their seats immediately on the wagon'" (*Homilies* 13.1). See also *Recognitions* 7.25; *Stromata* 7; *Eccl Hist* 3.30.

17. "Peter, in our presence thou hast made many blind to see and the deaf to hear and the lame to walk, and hast succored the weak and given them strength: but wherefore hast thou not succored thy daughter, the virgin, which grew up beautiful and hath believed in the name of God? For behold, her one side is wholly palsied, and she lieth there stretched out in the corner helpless" (*Acts of Peter* 1).

18. Galatians 2:11.

19. Acts 15:7–11.

Our best source on Simon Peter from AD 57 to AD 62 is the apostle Paul; not so much from what he says but from what he does not say. Although it is an argument from silence, it is, nevertheless, quite compelling.

In AD 57, Paul wrote the extant epistle to the Roman church. He addressed this letter to "all that be in Rome, beloved of God, called to be saints," not to the renowned apostle who supposedly sat on the bishop's throne. Peter is likewise missing from the main body of the letter and the extensive catalogue of names and personal salutations at the end. By my count, Paul greets 29 Christians who were living at Rome—many of them by name—but not Simon Peter.

In the last chapter of Acts, Paul appeals his case to Caesar and sails off to Rome. The brethren were so excited to finally see his face that they walked 30 or 40 miles to the Forum of Appius and the Three Taverns.[20] When the company arrives at Rome, Peter is not waiting at the gate to welcome him. In fact, we do not read of a glorious reunion between the two illustrious apostles at all—except in the apocryphal Catholic literature.

Paul subsequently spent two full years in Rome, under house arrest. He had tremendous liberty for a prisoner, receiving guests and openly preaching the Kingdom of God.[21] While waiting to be heard by Nero, Paul corresponded with churches and fellow-ministers by letter, five or six of which have been preserved in the New Testament. As was his practice, he passes along greetings from those in his immediate circle, but there is not a single salutation from Peter in any of the prison epistles. In AD 60 or AD 61, Paul wrote to the Colossian church. In chapter 4, he lists all of the Hebrew "co-workers for the Kingdom of God" who were with him.[22] Again, the fisherman from Galilee is nowhere to be found. It seems that every time the paper trail allows us to check on Peter, he is out of town.

---

20. Acts 28:15.

21. Acts 28:30, 31.

22. "My fellow prisoner Aristarchus sends you his greetings, as does Mark, the cousin of Barnabas. (You have received instructions about him; if he comes to you, welcome him.) Jesus, who is called Justus, also sends greetings. These are the only Jews among my co-workers for the kingdom of God, and they have proved a comfort to me" (Colossians 4:10–11 NIV).

Approx. Year	Peter's Location	Citation
30	Jerusalem	Acts 1:13–26
30	Jerusalem (Pentecost)	Acts 2:14–47
32	Jerusalem Temple	Acts 3:1–4:22
33	Jerusalem Temple	Acts 5:1–42
34	Jerusalem (Deacons)	Acts 6:2–7
35	Samaria	Acts 8:14–25
36	Jerusalem	Galatians 1:18
39	Lydda	Acts 9:32
39	Joppa	Acts 9:38–43
40	Caesarea	Acts 10
40	Jerusalem	Acts 11:2–18
45	Jerusalem prison	Acts 12:3–18
46	Jerusalem	Galatians 2:9
48	Antioch in Syria	Galatians 2:11–14
49	Jerusalem (Council on Gentiles)	Acts 15:7–11
56	Peter is designated the "apostle to the circumcision" in Galatians, no indication his ministry had ever changed	Galatians 2:7–8
58	Jerusalem (Paul's last visit)	Acts 21:18
63	"Babylon"	1 Peter 5:13

Is there any evidence in the New Testament—any at all—which would place Peter at Rome? There *may* be. It is possible that Peter fled to the city on the Tiber after James was stoned to death in AD 62. The only hint in the Bible is the cryptic greeting at the end of 1 Peter. "The church that is at Babylon, elected together with you, saluteth you; and so does Marcus my son."[23] Babylon, the ancient enemy of Israel, was often used in the first century as a cipher for Rome, the latest world power to persecute the people of God.[24] In the book of Revelation, John refers to Babylon as "that great city which reigneth over the kings of the earth."[25] In another passage, he makes the identification virtually certain. "The seven heads are seven mountains,

---

23. 1 Peter 5:13.

24. For other second and third century books which use Babylon to denote Rome, see *2 Baruch* 67.7 and *Sibylline Oracles* 5.215.

25. Revelation 17:18.

on which the woman sitteth."[26] Rome has been known as the city on seven hills since time immemorial.[27]

The little favor that Paul asks at the end of 2 Timothy lends support to this interpretation. "Only Luke is with me. Take Mark, and bring him with thee; for he is profitable to me for the ministry."[28] Here we have Timothy bringing Mark to Rome, and a bit later, Peter is writing from "Babylon" with Mark at his side. These two letters were written within a year or two of each other, so the chronology fits.

The Catholic Church understandably objects to being called the Whore of Babylon, the Scarlett Woman of Revelation 17. There is thus a certain irony in the fact that the only reference to Peter being at Rome is encapsulated in the word "Babylon." If Peter's euphemism at the end of 1 Peter doesn't mean Rome, there is absolutely nothing in the Scriptures which supports his presence there.

Apostolic Succession

The favorite argument used by the Church Fathers to prove God was on their side was apostolic succession. They used it freely in the first centuries to bludgeon their rivals and opponents over the head, and it remains the default argument to this day. There are three parts to this dogma. Peter was the first to sit on the *cathedra* at Rome, he was the head of the entire church, and he passed this authority down to those who followed in an unbroken chain of succession. We have examined the first claim and found it has no foundation in Scripture. But what about Peter's successors? Surely their names, order of service, and years in office would all be beyond doubt. As it turns out, even the most basic facts of the succession are wildly controversial, full of discrepancies and contradictions. Let's see if we can impose some order on this chaos.

The first century *Epistle of Clement to James* is the ultimate source of the succession myth. We are told that, before his death, Peter lays his hands on Clement in the midst of the congregation and entrusts him with the "chair of the teacher." He chooses Clement because "he has been with Peter from the beginning and he is worthy." Peter then bestows the "power of binding and loosing," which gives the holder of the seat at Rome the authority to

---

26. Revelation 17:9.

27. The Emperor Vespasian (reigned AD 69–79) minted a silver coin which shows a woman called Roma seated on seven hills. There is a suckling wolf at her side, a reference to the mythological origin of Rome.

28. 2 Timothy 4:11.

administer the church and settle doctrine. Up until the middle of the second century, Clement was the undisputed successor to Peter.

Tertullian, writing from the relative backwoods of North Africa circa AD 200, was one of the last holdouts for this line of succession. Clement still has the direct blessing and anointing of Peter.

> Let them [the heretics] produce the original records of their churches; let them unfold the roll of their bishops, running down in due succession from the beginning in such a manner that [their first] bishop shall be able to show for his ordainer and predecessor one of the apostles or an apostolic man, a man, moreover, who continued stedfast with the apostles. For this is the manner in which the apostolic churches transmit their registers: as the church of Smyrna, which records that Polycarp was placed therein by John; as also the church of Rome, *which makes Clement to have been ordained in like manner by Peter.*
> —On Prescription 32, emphasis mine

In the middle of the second century, Paul and his epistles were accepted by the Church and the succession was juggled around to reflect the new information. *The Teaching of Simon Cephas* (c. AD 160) and the *Martyrdom of Barsamya* (c. 240) now designate Ansus as Peter's direct successor.[29] No one knows where this man came from, but Ansus seems to have morphed into Lainus, the man we call Linus. Linus was one of the Roman saints who joined Paul in salutations at the end of 2 Timothy. The similarity in names was probably irresistible to someone trying to reconcile the conflicting accounts.

The Pauline material flooding the Church also breathed new life into the venerable name of Clement. The star of the *Preaching of Peter* turns into the man Paul mentioned briefly in his Epistle to the Philippians. "And I entreat thee also, true yokefellow, help those women which labored with me in the gospel, with Clement also. . . . ."[30] There is nothing in the New Testament which connects this Clement to Rome, but he quickly finds himself the fourth bishop of Rome.

The first testimony to the modern sequence is found in Irenaeus of Lyon. Closely allied with the progressive wing of the Church, he gives his

---

29. "This Barsamya, bishop of Edessa, who made a disciple of Sharbil, the priest of the same city, lived in the days of Fabianus, bishop of the city of Rome . . . . . . and Xystus received the ordination from Alexander; and Alexander received it from Evartis; and Evartis received it from Cletus; and Cletus received it from Anus; and Anus received it from Simon Cephas; and Simon Cephas received it from our Lord" (*Barsamya* Final Paragraph).

30. Philippians 4:3.

understanding of the Roman bishopric AD 185. Irenaeus admits that Linus was pulled from the newly-accepted letters of Paul.

> The blessed apostles [Peter and Paul] then, having founded and built up the Church [of Rome], committed into the hands of Linus the office of the episcopate. Of this Linus, Paul makes mention in the epistles to Timothy. To him succeeded Anacletus; and after him, in the third place from the apostles, Clement was allotted the bishopric.
> —*Against Heresies* 3.3.3

The following chart is the most ancient evidence of the Roman succession, along with their official position at the present. The lists have been arranged in ascending chronological order. We do not find any real consistency, which is to say, we are not on firm ground historically, until we reach the fifth name around the turn of the first century. The first four, at the least, are suspect. They are nothing more than a name embellished with a pious legend. Clement seems to wall off the historic figures from the legendary ones, and Evaristus was probably the first man to actually sit on the Roman *cathedra*.

Clement to James	Teaching of Simon Cephas	Irenaeus	Tertullian	Hippolytus	Martyrdom of Barsamya	Vatican at Present
AD 80	AD 160	AD 185	AD 200	AD 225	AD 240	AD 2020
Peter	Peter	Peter	Peter	Peter	Peter	Peter
Clement	Ansus or Isus	Linus	Clement	Linus	Ansus	Linus
		Anacletus		Clement	Cletus	Anacletus
		Clement		Cletus	Evartis	Clement
		Evaristus			Alexander	Evaristus

In 1947, the Vatican felt it necessary to revisit the foundation of their faith, the Roman succession. Until then, Cletus had been considered the third bishop after Peter, and Anacletus was fifth in the line of succession. After 1900 years, though, it had finally become clear that Cletus and Anacletus were one and the same person. It had somehow escaped their attention all those years. So poor Cletus was eliminated, his paper existence and good name rubbed out just as easily as they had been created in the first place.[31]

---

31. The *Liber Pontificalis* presents Cletus and Anecletus as two separate and distinct individuals. This sixth century list of popes gives Peter a 25 year papacy, followed by Linus (11 years), Cletus (7 years), Clement (9 years), Anecletus (12 years), and then Evaristus. We are told that Cletus was a Roman from the district of Vicus Patricius, the

Peter's Acts in Rome and Martyrdom

Apocryphal tales about Peter's tenure in Rome sprang up like weeds after a summer rain. *The Teaching of Simon Cephas* takes off right where the *Homilies of Clement* ends. "In the third year of Claudius Caesar (AD 44) Simon Cephus departed from Antioch to go to Rome." The whole city turns out to adore Peter. They fetch Simon the Sorcerer, and the two contenders have a public showdown in the forum. Simon fails in an attempt to raise a man from the dead but, after Peter invokes the name of Christ, the man rises off the bier. This work asserts that Peter served "in the rank of Superintendent of Rulers for 25 years," an odd turn of phrase for the first pope. We learn that Peter is executed the year Nero is overthrown—AD 68—which is indeed about 25 years.

The seminal myth of Peter's martyrdom has been preserved in the Syriac *Teaching of the Apostles*. "And Nero Caesar dispatched Simon Cephas with the sword in the city of Rome."[32] This is what Catholics were taught until the middle of the second century. However, once they got their hands on the Gospel of John, a more sensational death was constructed for Peter. The first appearance of the replacement myth is found in the *Teaching of Simon Cephas in Rome* (c. AD 160). "Caesar had commanded that Simon should be crucified with his head downward, as he himself had requested."[33] This story was echoed by multiple sources later in the second century, and it has become the accepted tradition of the Church.[34] The *Teaching of Simon Cephas* also switches which of the apostles gets the sword. It is now Paul who gets beheaded, not Peter, and this has also become the received tradition.

One of those sources is the *Acts of Peter*, which collected all of the martyrdom stories and stitched them together. Written late in the second century, it is one of the earliest of the so-called apocryphal Acts, what most of us would call a tall tale. At the end, Peter beseeches his executioner to crucify him upside-down.[35] In chapter 35, we find the introduction of the *Quo Vadis* legend. In this touching bit of fiction, Peter is fleeing Rome for

---

son of a certain Emilianus. Anecletus was declared to be a Greek from Athens, the son of an Anthiocus.

The fourth century *Liberian Catalogue* is also certain they were two different men, but they followed each other in this account. Peter is assigned a 25 year papacy, Linus 12 years, Clement almost 10 years, Cletus 6 years, Anacletus 12 years, Aristus 13 years, and Alexander 11 years.

32. Final sentence.
33. *Simon Cephas* 6.
34. *Acts of Peter* 37; *Prescrip* 36; *Eccl Hist* 3.1.
35. *Acts of Peter* 37.

his life, is met by the Lord who asks "Where are you going," (*Quo Vadis*) and Peter, understanding his fate, returns to face execution.

All we actually know about Peter's last days is contained in just two short passages of Scripture. In John 21:18, the Lord told Simon that he would need to be dressed and cared for in his old age. "Verily, verily, I say unto thee, When thou wast young, thou girdest thyself, and walkedst whither thou wouldest: but when thou shalt be old, thou shalt stretch forth thy hands, and another shall gird thee, and carry thee whither thou wouldest not." Peter would, when he got old, need to stretch out his arms to have someone else put on his robe. The other verse is in Peter's second epistle. Simon is nearing the end of the journey and, like many elderly people, is anticipating his demise. "Knowing that shortly I must put off this my tabernacle, even as our Lord Jesus Christ hath shown me."[36] This matter-of-fact statement sounds more like a man resigned to aging or a terminal illness than someone facing the horrors of crucifixion.

---

36. 2 Peter 1:14.

4

The Teaching Develops and Spreads

AD 60 to AD 150

As the true Prophet has told us,
a false prophet must first come from some deceiver;
and then, in like manner, after the removal of the holy place,
the true Gospel must be secretly sent abroad
for the rectification of the heresies that shall be.

—Homilies of Clement 2.17

Our first post-separation glimpse of the new sect comes from the book of Revelation. It would therefore be extremely useful to know when John was on the isle of Patmos "for the word of God and the testimony of Jesus Christ."[1] The issue has never been satisfactorily resolved, but there are only two serious contenders. John either had the vision shortly after the death of Nero, in AD 69, or it was at the latter end of Domitian's reign in AD 95. After analyzing all of the evidence at the back of the book (p. 184), we conclude that the facts are best explained by a provenance in the late sixties.

In John's messages to the seven churches of Asia, he glances twice at the proto-Catholics. Here are his observations on the church at Smyrna. "I know the blasphemy of them which say they are Jews, but are not, but are

---

1. Revelation 1:9.

the synagogue of Satan."[2] To the church at Philadelphia he wrote: "Behold, I will make them of the synagogue of Satan, which say they are Jews, and are not, but lie; behold, I will make them to come and worship before thy feet, and to know I have loved thee."[3] When the apostle John looked into the camp of the legalists, this is what he saw: Gentiles who were acting like Jews. It is a concise but very accurate description of the sectarians.

The proto-Catholics did not amount to much in AD 69. They were just another Christian offshoot—along with the Nicolaitans and the Balaamites—and they did not weigh any heavier on John's mind. He connects them with just two cities, Smyrna and Philadelphia, although there were others further east beyond the provincial border in Galatia. From Smyrna, the false apostles had travelled fifty miles down the coastline to the magnificent capital of Asia. The saints at Ephesus weighed their message in the balance and found them wanting. "Thou hast tried them which say they are apostles and are not, and hast found them liars."[4] This leads us to believe that, by AD 69, the sectarians had not yet spread far from their place of incubation in the Turkish Lake District of Galatia. They had reached the Aegean Sea on the west, but no further.

What were relations like between the Pauline churches and the schismatics? There seems to have been some ill feelings for a while, at least in Smyrna. "I know the blasphemy [the reviling or slander] of them which say they are Jews, and are not, but are the synagogue of Satan."[5] The false apostles initially took a conciliatory stance toward those whom they regarded as deceived. The following passage from the *Apostolic Constitutions* is surely from this era. "But whosoever comes to you, let him first be examined, and then received: for ye have understanding, and are able to know the right hand from the left, and to distinguish false teachers from true teachers. But when a teacher comes to you, supply him with what he wants with all readiness. And even when a false teacher comes, you shall give him for his necessity, but shall not receive his error. Nor indeed may ye pray together with him, lest ye be polluted as well as he."[6] The apostle John took a harder line in the churches he was responsible for. "If there come any unto you, and bring not this doctrine, receive him not into your house, neither bid him God speed: For he that biddeth him God speed is partaker of his evil deeds."[7]

2. Revelation 2.9.
3. Revelation 3.9.
4. Revelation 2:2.
5. Revelation 2.9.
6. *Ap Const* 7.28 .
7. 2 John 10–11.

Thus, there was some limited contact between the two fellowships for a few years. However, the memory of the "other Christians" did not pass beyond the first generation and it certainly did not leave Asia Minor. The length of time it took for some of the apostolic writings to make their way into Catholic hands tells us how little communication there was after the passage of a decade or two.

The Early Transformation of Doctrine

The doctrine of the new sect underwent a rapid transformation in the seventh and eighth decades of the first century. There were several contributing factors, all abetted by the fact they were still small enough to change direction easily. The destruction of the temple just ten years after the founding shook their faith in the sacrificial cult. This was followed by a tsunami of anti-Semitic sentiment that swept through the empire after the Judaean conflict ended in AD 72. The crushing defeat of the Hebrew people, the humiliating procession at Rome, and the appearance of massive numbers of Jews in the slave markets all worked to deprive Judaism of its former mystique.[8] It was not a good time to be promoting anything tainted by Moses.

After the war, the Emperor Vespasian appropriated the temple tax, which had formerly been voluntarily paid by Jewish men over the age of twenty, as a form of war reparations. A new tax, the *Fiscus Judaicus*, was levied on all Jews; men, women and children.[9] When his son Domitian was elevated to the throne in AD 81, he expanded the tax and ruthlessly enforced payment. "Domitian's agents collected the tax on Jews with a peculiar lack of mercy; and took proceedings not only against those who kept their Jewish origin a secret to avoid the tax, but against those who lived as Jews without professing Judaism."[10] A circumcised, Sabbath-keeping Christian would definitely have been at risk under Domitian.

The demographics of the young sect also played a role in the reshaping of doctrine. The original band of false apostles were all Jewish, although a couple of names on the Clementine roster appear to be Greek. Within thirty years or so, all of them had settled down or passed on, the founder died, and control of the church passed into the hands of the elders. These men were Gentiles, now on their own without any further influence from the Jewish

---

8. "Now the number of those that were carried captive during this whole war was collected to be ninety-seven thousand, as was the number of those that perished during the whole siege eleven hundred thousand (1,100,000)" (*Wars* 6.9.3).

9. *Wars* 7.6.

10. Suetonius, *Domitian* 12.2.

homeland. Their theology responded, and the more demanding *mitzvahs* (commandments), like circumcision and the dietary laws, were tossed overboard. The proto-Catholic ship did not gain momentum until it was refitted to be more accommodating to Gentiles.

Circumcision was one of the first *mitzvahs* to be dropped. Its quick demise was perhaps inevitable given the spirit of the times and the stiff headwind they ran into. After AD 72, circumcision became the ultimate test to determine who was liable to pay the *Fiscus Judaicus*. The practice thereafter carried a financial penalty with it. Suetonius continued the previous quotation as follows: "As a boy, I remember once attending a crowded courtroom where the procurator had a ninety-year old man stripped to establish whether or not he had been circumcised."[11] Suetonius was born in AD 69, and would have been a boy in the late seventies.

As if this were not enough, there were also strong cultural biases against the practice. In the Hellenic world, where the beauty of the human body was greatly admired, circumcision was considered barbaric and aesthetically disfiguring. The Greeks, who exercised naked in the gymnasium, looked down with scorn on any form of bodily mutilation. The natural reluctance to undergo such a painful procedure, combined with financial disincentives and cultural disdain, all combined to doom the practice early on.

The only overt mention of circumcision in the founding documents was in the *Epistle of Peter to Clement*. Circumcision was one of the criteria for gaining access to the most secret of their Scriptures, the *Preaching of Peter*. They put these words into the mouth of James, the same man who decided in Acts 15 not to burden Gentiles with the Law. "Our Peter has strictly and becomingly charged us concerning the establishment of the truth, that we should not communicate the books of his preachings, which have been sent to us, to anyone at random, but to one who is good, and religious, and who wishes to teach, and *who is circumcised*, and faithful." Taking the step of circumcision was a huge commitment, but it gave one admission into the sect and its inner circle. Only the select few who were elevated to teacher status were entrusted with a copy of the book.

Although circumcision was phased out in the first century, a vestige still lives on in the language of the Church. In Judaism, circumcision is known as "the seal," a sign literally written in human flesh to mark the covenant God had made with Abraham. This is implicit in the blessing given at the *Brit Milah* ceremony on the eighth day. "Blessed be He who sanctified His beloved from the womb, and put His ordinance upon his flesh, and His

---

11. The Nazis of the Third Reich also used this technique to flush out suspected Jews.

offering with the sign of a holy covenant."[12] Paul also alludes to the connection between circumcision and the seal when he writes of Abraham. "And he received the sign of circumcision, a *seal* of the righteousness of the faith which he had yet being uncircumcised: that he might be the father of all them that believe, though they be not circumcised; that righteousness might be imputed unto them also."[13]

When circumcision and sacrifices were discarded, the nomenclature of "the seal" was applied to immersion—the only part of the three-step conversion ritual that remained. This tradition goes clear back to the first century, as illustrated by the *Recognitions of Clement*. "Now God has ordered everyone who worships Him to be sealed by baptism."[14] The mid-second century *Shepherd of Hermas* records: "Before a man bears the name of the Son of God, he is dead; but when he receives the seal, he lays aside his deadness, and receives life. The seal, then, is the water: they descend into the water dead, and they arise alive."[15]

Baptism is never spoken of as the seal in the New Testament. Instead, Pauline Christians were sealed by the anointing of the Holy Spirit. "In whom also after that ye believed, ye were sealed with that Holy Spirit of promise, which is the earnest of our inheritance until the redemption of the purchased possession . . .."[16]

The Jewish dietary laws—known as *kashrut*—also had a short life in the sect.[17] The saints in Colossae, those closest to the proto-Catholic heartland, had been exposed to the doctrine of the Galatian schismatics. Paul's council to them includes a glance at the food laws. "Let no man therefore judge you in meat, or in drink, or in respect of a holyday, or of the new moon, or of the Sabbath day."[18] The *Didache* tells us that the food regulations were little more than a memory by AD 90. "And concerning food, bear what thou art able."[19]

12. Donin, *To Be a Jew*, 275.

13. Romans 4:11, emphasis mine.

14. *Recognitions* 6.

15. *Shepherd*, Similitude 9.16. "And they entreated him that they might also receive the seal of baptism, and they said to him: As our souls are at ease, and as we are earnest about God, give us the seal; for we have heard thee say that the God whom thou proclaims recognizes his own sheep through his seal" (*Acts of Thomas* 2.26–27).

16. Ephesians 1:13–14, see also 4:30; 2 Corinthians 1:22.

17. The word kosher is derived from *kashrut*.

18. Colossians 2:16.

19. *Didache* 6. For a full discussion of Paul's views on *kashrut*, see Romans 14. He sums it up in verse 17: "For the kingdom of heaven is not meat or drink, but righteousness, and peace, and joy in the Holy Spirit."

How did the sectarians intellectually justify the radical transformation of doctrine? People in general are resistant to change, and they do not like their deepest beliefs and convictions challenged. The answer is provided by the *Epistle of Barnabas*. We learn that a literal observance of Torah was allegorized away early in the second century by a highly symbolic method of biblical interpretation.

The *Epistle of Barnabas* was written very close to AD 132. The sixteenth chapter refers to the temple being pulled down and rebuilt by their enemies. In AD 130, the Emperor Hadrian laid the foundations of a temple to Zeus in the holy city, which triggered the Bar Kokhba Rebellion. This work is anonymous, despite the attribution in the title to the Clementine Barnabas. The actual author—a self-proclaimed teacher of the sect—stated that his purpose in writing was to "perfect the knowledge" of his brethren. The knowledge he was so anxious to impart was an allegorical way of interpreting the Law.

Pseudo-Barnabas delights in deriving simple moral lessons from the Hebrew Scriptures. Circumcision was no mere cutting away of the flesh, but it was a matter of hearing with faith and understanding. What a revelation that would have been to Pauline Christians![20] The true fast was not to put on sackcloth and ashes, but it was to "loose the bands of iniquity, undo heavy burdens, let the oppressed go free, feeding the hungry."[21] The Sabbath was to be understood in light of the Psalmist, who proclaimed that a day is as a thousand years. The eighth day is a figure of the new creation and, in the meantime, it is the day on which Jesus rose from the dead. The food laws were also to be understood figuratively. Pork had been forbidden to teach them not to forget the Lord in good times and then cry out—like pigs—when hungry. The *Epistle of Barnabas* was considered quasi-canonical for years, filling the theological niche that the letters of Paul would later provide.

The proto-Catholics Spread

The movement got off to a slow start. The proto-Catholics were confined to western Asia Minor for the first thirty or thirty-five years, with only a minor outlier in Syria and a few disciples in Israel. The churches of proconsular Asia and Galatia dominated the sect for the first 100 years. Smyrna, home

---

20. "In whom also ye are circumcised with the circumcision made without hands, in putting off the body of the sins of the flesh by the circumcision of Christ" (Colossians 2:11).

21. He was citing Isaiah 58:6.

THE TEACHING DEVELOPS AND SPREADS

to one of their earliest congregations in AD 69, was the "Vatican" of the movement until Rome's ascendency in the middle of the second century.[22]

The Torah-observant teachers developed a small following in Palestine. Later called Ebionites, the Hebrew converts did not evolve along with the Gentile branch of the sect but remained faithful to their Jewish roots. Irenaeus (c. 185) sketches out their doctrine in a few broad strokes.

> Those who are called Ebionites agree that the world was made by God; but their opinions with respect to the Lord are similar those of Cerinthus and Carpocrates [ie, they were adoptionists denying the divinity of Christ]. They use the Gospel according to Matthew only, and repudiate the apostle Paul, maintaining he was an apostate from the Law. As to the prophetical writings, they endeavor to expound them in a somewhat singular manner: they practice circumcision, persevere in the observance of those customs which are enjoined by the Law, and are so Judaic in their style of life that they even adore Jerusalem as if it were the house of God.
> —*Against Heresies* 1.26.2

> **Hippolytus**—An influential Roman theologian, teacher, and author early in the third century. Hippolytus was a voluminous writer, including a primer on heresy called *The Refutation of all Heresies*, and he most likely authored *The Apostolic Traditions*. He was an ardent supporter of the Gospel and Revelation of John, both still controversial, and championed the Logos Christology found in John's writings.

Hippolytus (c. 225) shines a ray of light into this dark age of church history. He reports that, about the year AD 100, a Syrian holy man named Elchasai received a profound revelation from an immense angel.[23] He took the message into Mesopotamia, and met with some success. Was Elchasai assuming the mantle of the false apostles, men he had known and respected in his youth? He taught such standard Judeo-Christian fare as circumcision, daily ablutions, the Sabbath, praying toward Jerusalem, an adoptionist Christology, and a reverence for the apostle Peter.[24] Elchasai's mission had far-reaching consequences. It is known that the third century prophet Mani was brought up in a strict Jewish-Christian sect in southern

---

22. Revelation 2:9.
23. *Refutation* 9.8–12.
24. *Eccl Hist* 6.38; *Panarion* 19.3.

Iraq, and the *Cologne Mani Codex* explicitly states that Elchasai was "the founder" of their law.[25]

In AD 112, Pliny the Younger was governor of Bithynia and Pontus, the Roman provinces which ran easterly from Constantinople along the southern shore of the Black Sea. Among his correspondence to Emperor Trajan was a letter seeking council on the legal status of Christians. He paints a picture of an incredible number of believers, although whether they were Catholic or Christian is an open question.

> Others, those names were given to me by an informer, first admitted the charge and then denied it; they said that they had ceased to be Christians two or more years previous, and some of them even twenty years ago. They all did reverence to your statue and the images of the gods in the same way as the others, and reviled the name of Christ. They also declared that the sum total of their guilt or error amounted to no more than this: they had met regularly before dawn on a fixed day[26] to chant verses alternately amongst themselves in honor of Christ as to a god, and also to bind themselves by oath, not for any criminal purpose, but to abstain from theft, robbery, and adultery, to commit no breach of trust, and not to deny a deposit when called upon to restore it. After this ceremony it had been their custom to disperse and reassemble later to take food of an ordinary, harmless kind; but they had in fact given up this practice since my edict, issued on your instruction, which banned all political societies . . .
>
> The question seems to me to be worthy of your consideration, especially in view of the number of persons endangered; for a great many individuals of every age and class, both men and women, are being brought to trial, and this is likely to continue. It is not only the towns, but villages and rural districts too which are infected through contact with this wretched cult. I think though that it is still possible for it to be checked and directed to better ends, for there is no doubt that people have begun to throng the temples which had been almost entirely deserted for a long time, the sacred rites which had been allowed to lapse are being performed again, and the flesh of sacrificial victims is on sale everywhere, though up until recently scarcely anyone could be found to buy it.
>
> —*Pliny Letter to Trajan No. 96*

---

25. See *On the Origin of His Body*.
26. Before the reign of Constantine, Sunday was an ordinary work day.

Rome was their first big step away from the Asian homeland, a decade or so before the turn of the first century. In their marquee myth, Peter established the church at Rome in the third year of Claudius Caesar, or AD 44.[27] We covered the overwhelming witness of Scripture to the contrary in the previous chapter. The first three or four names in the Roman succession are complete fiction, their terms of office spliced together from tradition, and their accomplishments mere legend. There is not an ounce of truth to any of it.

The proto-Catholics may have made a high-level convert inside the Roman court. In AD 95, the Emperor Domitian's cousin Flavius Clemens and his wife Domitilla were accused of "atheism, for which offence a number of others also, who had been carried away into Jewish customs, were condemned, some to death, others to confiscation of property."[28] Clemens was executed, and his wife was exiled. What is puzzling about this incident is that, if Jewish, they had done nothing wrong under Roman law. Judaism was a legally recognized religion throughout most of the imperial period; indeed, Jews had been accorded special privileges. The charge of "atheism" was usually levied against illicit cults like Christianity. It may be, as the historian Suetonius believed, that Domitian used the accusation to cloak his suspicion members of the ruling family were plotting against him.[29] Or it may be that Flavius Clemens and Domitilla had embraced a variety of Christianity which practiced "Jewish customs."

If the idea that the cream of Roman society would embrace this "wretched cult" seems far-fetched—and admittedly it does—there is some supporting evidence. The entrance to the oldest Catholic burial ground in Rome, the Cemetery of Domitilla, lies on the ancestral lands of the Flavian family. An inscription bearing Domitilla's name is still visible at the foot of the entrance stairway. The oldest stratum of burial chambers inside the catacomb is pagan, as one would expect, but late in the second century they were surrounded by Christian burials. The emperor Nerva—who succeeded Domitian—"released such as were on trial for treason and restored the exiles."[30] Presumable the proclamation included Domitilla; the noble lady got her property back, and her heirs donated the land to the church.

The origin of the Greek churches has been lost in the mists of time, but they were probably colonized by way of Rome. The Greeks have never

27. *Simon Cephas* 6.
28. Cassius Dio, *History of Rome* 67.14.
29. "The occasion of Domitian's murder was that he had executed, on some trivial pretext, his own extremely stupid cousin, Flavius Clemens" (Suetonius, *Domitian* 15).
30. Cassius Dio, *History of Rome* 68.1.

observed the fourteenth of Nisan *Pascha*—eliminating a direct lineage from Asia Minor—and the long-winded letter known as *1 Clement* hints at a special and even paternal relationship between Rome and Corinth. The overall tone is that of a parent giving counsel to his children. The young Corinthian church was experiencing a leadership crisis, and the mother church was helping them sort it out. *First Clement* is traditionally dated AD 95—for absolutely no compelling reason—but we believe it belongs to the middle of the second century. The first solid landmark we come to in the Balkans is the open letter Quadratus addressed to Hadrian, emperor from AD 117 to AD 138.[31] A founding date of AD 120 to AD 125 best fits the meager evidence.

The proto-Catholics did not get established in Palestine until the Bar Kokhba rebellion. After the Romans recaptured Jerusalem in AD 70, the Tenth Legion was permanently garrisoned near the tower of David, and the holy city lay in ruins for sixty years. The string of fifteen bishops in Jerusalem between the two insurrections, as reported by the historian Eusebius, is a historical impossibility.[32]

> **Justin Martyr**—A prominent teacher and apologist who resided in Rome in the middle of the second century. He taught from his house, which was located "above a man named Martin, near the Timiotinian Bath." Justin wore the philosopher's cloak and extolled Christianity as the "true philosophy." He wrote extensively, but only three works have survived: *1* and *2 Apology*, and the *Dialogue with Trypho*. He was the last of the Catholic Fathers not to acknowledge Paul or cite the Pauline epistles.

In AD 130, Hadrian decided to rebuild Jerusalem as a Roman *colonia*, and to compound the blunder, he made circumcision a capital crime. The result was the bloody Bar Kokhba uprising. When it ended in AD 135, Hadrian concluded that Judaism was simply incompatible with Roman civilization. He therefore purged the land of its Jewish inhabitants and repopulated it with foreign settlers. Jews were even banned from the holy city upon pain of death. The first Catholics rode in with the waves of these colonists and, according to Eusebius, settled in the coastal cities of Caesarea, Ptolemais (Acre), and Tyre.[33] A satire by Lucian, *The Death of Peregrinus*, which lampoons the Cynic philosopher, tells of his opportunistic conversion to Christianity in Palestine about AD 155.

The Egyptian church was also founded in the years following Bar Kokhba. Justin Martyr relates an incident that took place in Alexandria sometime

---

31. *Eccl Hist* 4.3.
32. *Eccl Hist* 4.5.
33. *Eccl Hist* 5.23.

in the 140s. A young and overly-zealous member of the church petitioned the governor for permission to make himself a eunuch, which was denied.[34] One of the first Catholic teachers on the Nile, Pantaenus, was nicknamed the "Sicilian Bee," which may tell us something of his country of origin.

The Roman province of Proconsular Africa received the Catholic gospel between AD 160 and AD 170, where it quickly spread. The *Acts of the Scillitan Martyrs* records the legal proceedings of twelve Christians who were tried and convicted in Scilla—now Kassarine, Tunisia—in AD 180. The Roman prosecutor asked what was in their satchel, and their spokesman replied, "books and letters of Paul, a righteous man." The first Latin Father of the Church—Tertullian—wrote voluminously from Carthage between AD 190 and AD 215.[35]

Catholic missionaries reached France in the middle of the second century. Lugdunum—now known as Lyon—was the administrative center of Roman Gaul and a substantial city of some 50,000 souls. The church at Lyon favored the new Roman theology, an indication that their teachers were part of the Roman occupation, but most of its members came from Asia Minor. The Galatians were the easterly-most branch of the Celts, the same ethnic stock as the Gaul's of France. *The Martyrs of Lyon and Vienne*, a martyrology dated AD 177, provides valuable background on the formation of the Church in Roman Gaul. After a gruesome display of public torture, the survivors sent an account of their sufferings back to their brethren in Anatolia. We learn that several of these martyrs had been born in Asia or Phrygia. Their Gallic tormentors were trying to stamp out what they called a "foreign and new religion" which, from their perspective, was certainly the case.[36]

> **Eusebius**—A prolific writer, Eusebius is best known for his *History of the Church*. His extensive use of primary sources and citations makes him particularly useful. Eusebius was the bishop of Caesarea from c. AD 315 to AD 335 and, in this capacity, attended the Council of Nicaea AD 325.

Catholicism was surprisingly slow to reach the northern and eastern reaches of the fertile crescent. Edessa was their initial beachhead to the region. It was also the myth-making capital of the east—almost rivaling Rome in the west—and so facts must be carefully separated from fiction. The royal

---

34. *1 Apo* 29. Oddly enough, Origen, the bishop of Alexandria at the beginning of the third century, also castrated himself (*Eccl Hist* 6.8). He did it from a literal reading of Matthew 19:12.

35. Tertullian tells us the Scillitan martyrs were the first Christians executed in Africa. "Vigellius Saturninus, who first here used the sword against us, lost his eyesight" (*To Scapula* 3).

36. *Eccl Hist* 5.1.

archives of this frontier city were said to contain a two-way correspondence between King Abgar V and Jesus Christ, which Eusebius, gullible as always, passes along without comment.[37] The Diatessaron was their first Gospel text, which is a strong dating indicator.[38]

Tatian—a student of Justin Martyr—compiled the Diatessaron in Rome and was excommunicated for his efforts. In AD 172, the native Assyrian packed his bags and went home. A confidant of the Edessene royal court named Bardaisan befriended Tatian, got a copy of the Syriac-language Gospel, and carried it to Edessa. The king was among the first to convert. King Abgar VIII reigned from AD 177 to AD 212, the last in a long line of rulers bearing that name. Bardaisan's *Book of Laws* states: "In Syria and Edessa, men used to part with their manhood in honor of [the god] Tharatha; but when King Abgar became a believer, he commanded that everyone that did so should have his hand cut off. From that day until now, no one does so in the country of Edessa." The sign of the cross replaced the symbol of Baal on his coinage, and in AD 201 the Edessene church, the first Christian chapel known to history, was flooded by the Daisan River.[39]

The northeast corner of the Roman Empire—more or less the eastern half of modern Turkey—was a polyglot of tongues and dialects. This linguistic barrier served as a powerful deterrent to outside missionaries. When Paul and Barnabas reached Lystra, which is in central Anatolia, the townsmen understood them in Greek but spoke the Lycaonian language among themselves.[40] Peter addressed his first epistle to the saints in Cappadocia—among other places—but it would take Catholic missionaries another 200 years to penetrate this far into the interior. Gregory Thaumaturgis is credited with extending the faith south from Pontus into Cappadocia around AD 240.[41] An Armenian nobleman, also named Gregory, studied Christianity in Cappadocian Caesarea and introduced it to his homeland late in the third century.[42] Armenia was the first country to officially make Catholicism the state religion—some say in AD 301 and others in AD 311—anticipating the conversion of the Roman empire by many decades.

---

37. *Eccl Hist* 1.13.
38. *Eccl Hist* 5.23.
39. See *Chronicle of Edessa*.
40. Acts 14:11.
41. Tertullian mentions the presence of Christians in Cappadocia c. AD 210, but the Roman province then included what we now call Pontus (*To Scapula* 3). Under Trajan (AD 98 to AD 117), maritime Pontus was joined with inland Cappadocia to become the imperial province of Cappadocia.
42. Modern Kayseri, Turkey.

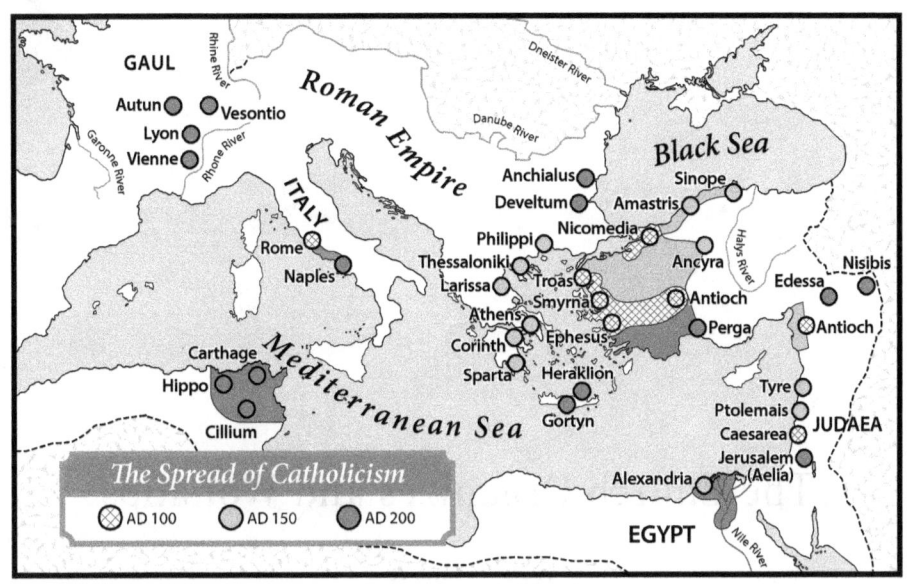

5

The Church Organizes and Worships

AD 60 to AD 150

> Elect, therefore, for yourselves,
> bishops and deacons worthy of the Lord, men meek,
> and not lovers of money, and truthful, and proved;
> for they also render to you the service of prophets and teachers.
>
> —DIDACHE 15

The primitive Catholic community was organized along the same lines as the New Testament fellowship. At the top, directing the church, was a class of preachers modeled after the ministry Christ had ordained. They referred to themselves as "apostles" or "prophets." Below them were the elders of the local congregations, who cared for the flock in the absence of the apostles.[1]

The authority of the new sect was initially vested in the pseudo-apostles. This was a copycat ministry that went forth the same way as the Twelve and the Seventy. "But concerning the apostles and prophets, according to the decree of the Gospel, thus do."[2] Their homeless lifestyle is hinted at by the *Recognitions of Clement*.

---

1. The office of the presbytery was created by the twelve apostles to help them care for the flock, and the proto-Catholics found them equally indispensable.
2. *Didache* 11.

> Be ye constant in hearing the word; that at the end of that time [three months], if any are able and willing to follow us, they may do so, if duty will admit of it. And when I say if duty will admit, I mean that no one by his departure must sadden anyone who ought not to be saddened, as by leaving parents who ought not to be left, or a faithful wife, or any other person to whom he is bound to afford comfort for God's sake.
> —*Recognitions of Clement* 3.72

Both the *Homilies* and the *Recognitions of Clement* boast of recruiting from Paul's ministerial staff. "But whereas we were his fellow laborers at the first, so long as he did such things without doing wrong to the interests of religion [i.e., the Law]; now that he has madly begun to attempt to deceive those who are religious [Torah observant], we have withdrawn from him."[3]

The *Didache* provides us with a brief glimpse into this rival ministry at the end of its short existence.

> Let every apostle who comes to you be received as the Lord. But he shall not remain more than one day. However, if necessary, let him remain a second day. But if he stays for three, he is a false prophet. And when the apostle departs, let him take only enough bread to last until he reaches shelter; if he asks for money, he is a false prophet."
> —*Didache* 11

The aging pseudo-apostles were no longer engaged in mission work. Every provision had been made for them to settle down, and within one generation, all had done so. "But every true prophet that willeth to abide among you is worthy of his support. So also a true teacher is himself worthy, as the workman, of his support. Every first-fruit, therefore, of the products of wine-press and threshing-floor, of oxen and of sheep, thou shalt take and give to the prophets, for they are your high priests."[4]

The second office were the leaders of the local congregations, known by the quaint title of "rulers" or "guides" in the primitive church. "After the death of the apostles, there were Guides and Rulers in the churches . . ."[5] In the following passage, Peter is bestowing the office on Zacchaeus, who displays his

---

3. *Homilies* 2.75. Also, *Recognitions* 2.1. "Then Niceta and Aquila, who had formerly been disciples of Simon [Paul], and were converted to the faith of Christ under the teaching of Zacchaeus. . .."

4. *Didache* 13.

5. Syriac *Teaching*; "and he (Peter) served there in the rank of the Superintendent of Rulers twenty-five years." (*Simon Cephas*); "We will all die with Barsamya, who is our teacher and guide." (*Barsamya* 3); "art thou Barsamya, who hast been made ruler and guide of the people of the Christians?" (*Barsamya* 7); See also *Did Apost* 15, *Addaeus*.

usual false humility. "But Zacchaeus, falling at his feet, begged that he would permit him to decline the rulership; promising at the same time, and saying, Whatever it behooves the ruler to do, I will do; only grant me not to have this name: for I am afraid of assuming the name of the rulership, for it teems with bitter envy and danger."[6] The title and duties of this office were derived from the head official in the synagogue, known as elders or rulers.[7]

The rulers of the synagogues not only led congregational prayers and Torah readings, but they also provided and maintained the place of worship. The *Ekklesia Katholika* did not have public buildings to gather in until the third century, so the elders provided their homes for this purpose. "And they assembled themselves day and night in the house of Narcissus the presbyter. And Peter discoursed unto them from the scriptures of the prophets and of those things which our Lord Jesus Christ had wrought both in word and in deeds."[8]

The first Catholic rulers/elders were appointed by the false apostles. However, once all of the pseudo-apostles had passed away or settled down, the elders were then selected by the congregation.[9] Paul viewed the unmooring of the eldership from the authority of the apostles as a dangerous step. "For the time will come when they will not endure sound doctrine; but after their own lusts shall they heap to themselves teachers, having itching ears."[10] After the demise of the false apostles, these men were the only authority in the loosely-affiliated home churches for several generations.

The office of the bishop was constituted when they grew numerous enough to have several assemblies in one town. There had to be someone with the authority to settle disputes and coordinate church business, and we deduce that, in Syria at least, this man was called the ruler. "Let there be a Ruler over the elders who are in the villages, and let him be recognized as head of them all, at whose hand all of them shall be required . . ."[11]

---

6. *Homilies* 3.63.

7. Mark 5:22–38; Luke 13:14; Acts 13:15; 18:8.

8. *Acts of Peter* 13.

9. "Elect, therefore, for yourselves, bishops and deacons worthy of the Lord, men meek, and not lovers of money, and truthful, and proved; for they also render to you the service of prophets and teachers" (*Didache* 15).

10. 2 Timothy 4:3.

11. Syriac *Teaching* 24.

The Rites of Prayer and Worship

The Catholics of the early centuries gathered for prayer twice a day, six days of the week. The Jews attended synagogue three times daily in Jesus' time, but the evening prayer was ruled optional after the destruction of the temple. The great repository of the ancient church, the *Apostolic Constitutions*, thus says: "Assemble yourselves together every day, morning and evening, singing psalms and praying in the Lord's house; in the morning saying the sixty-second Psalm, and in the evening the hundred and fortieth, but principally on the Sabbath day."[12] The *Apostolic Tradition* (c. AD 215) stresses the morning obligation in numerous passages, but it never speaks of assembling again after work.[13] It appears the evening service had been dropped at the latter end of the second century.

> Syriac *Teaching of the Apostles*—This book purports to be the instructions of the apostles on the day of Pentecost. As each apostle heard in a different language, they understood where the Spirit was sending them to preach. It then launches into 27 canons of church law, which Paul and Timothy supposedly deliver to the churches, and ends with a list showing the countries which each apostle evangelized. The work is an odd mosaic of Catholic legend mixed with the canonical Acts, suggesting a composition date between AD 180 and AD 200.

The Psalter was the heart and soul of their weekday prayers. This was a direct carryover of the "Morning Psalms" of the Hebrew liturgy, Psalms 145 to 150, which were recited every morning before the Eighteen Benedictions. The Syriac *Teaching of the Apostles* thus instructs: "In the service of the Church repeat ye the praises of David day by day."[14] The Latin liturgy still concludes the morning office of prayer—known as Lauds—with Psalms 148, 149, and 150. The term springs from the frequent expressions of praise—or "lauds"—found in these verses. Psalms 148 begins, "Praise ye the Lord. Praise ye the Lord from the heavens: praise him in the heights. Praise ye him, all his angels: praise ye him, all his hosts. . ."

The prayer practices of the sectarians came from the Jewish side of the family. The Catholic liturgy was a reformulation of the Eighteen Benedictions, the great liturgical prayer of the synagogue. They prayed standing, a practice that has survived in many of the high churches.[15] They faced

---

12. *Ap Const* 2.59. "And seek out day by day the faces of the saints, in order that you may rest upon their words" (*Didache* 4).
13. *Ap Trad* 31.2; 33; 35.2-3.
14. Syriac *Teaching* 19.
15. "And when thou prayest, thou shalt not be as the hypocrites are: for they love to

toward the east, just as the Eighteen Blessings are directed toward Jerusalem and the Temple Mount.[16] They prayed with their arms uplifted, their hands outstretched, and their palms forward.[17] The *orante* position, as it is known, is traceable to the priestly blessing in the temple, and it is widely depicted in early Catholic art. The men prayed with their heads uncovered—the custom of ancient Israel until Talmudic times—while the women veiled themselves. Paul, the ex-Pharisee, taught this as well. "Every man praying or prophesying, having his head covered, dishonoureth his head."[18] For women, Paul declared that their long hair was a sufficient covering or veil.[19] For a few years, the proto-Catholics even laid on *tefillin*, a practice which has left a quaint little custom in its wake.

Tefillin, the phylacteries of the New Testament, are worn by pious men at morning prayers.[20] Square little black boxes attached to a base, the *tefillin* are bound by thongs onto the inside of the left bicep and the top of the forehead. These two leather cubes contain thin strips of parchment inscribed with four passages of Torah.[21] Devout Jews would often emboss the Hebrew letter *Shin*—meaning *Shaddai* or God—on the case of the head-*tefillin*. The proto-Catholics changed this to the first letter of the word Christ, which is *Chi*, or X, in Greek. When the use of *tefillin* was discontinued, they retained the custom of signing the cross on their foreheads where the head-*tefillin* used to be.

> **Tertullian**—The first of the Latin Fathers, and perhaps the most interesting to read. Tertullian hailed from Carthage in North Africa, the country now known as Tunisia. He wrote over thirty extant works on a wide variety of Christian topics. Most of his output can be placed in the period AD 200 to AD 215. Tertullian was the first to use the Latin term *Trinitas* and attempt a rigorous definition.

---

pray standing in the synagogues and in the corners of the streets, that they may be seen of men" (Matthew 6:5).

16. "The apostles therefore appointed: Pray ye toward the east, because 'as the lightening which lighteth from the east and is seen even to the west, so shall the coming of the Son of Man be . . . .'" (Syriac *Teaching* 1).

17. 1 *Clement* 2; Tertullian *Apology* 30. This was also the practice of the New Testament church. "I will therefore that men pray everywhere, lifting up holy hands, without wrath and doubting" (1 Timothy 2:8).

18. 1 Corinthians 11:4.

19. "But if a woman have long hair, it is a glory to her: for her hair is given her for a covering [or veil]" (1 Corinthians 11:15).

20. This *mitzvah* is found in Deuteronomy 6:8. "Thou shalt bind them for a sign upon thine hand, and they shall be as frontlets between thine eyes."

21. Deut 6:4–9; 11:13–21; Exod 13:1–10, 13–16.

Tertullian, writing around AD 200, tells us what a slavish superstition it developed into. "At every forward step and movement, at every going in or out, when we put on our clothes and shoes, when we bathe, when we sit at table, when we light the lamps, on couch, on seat, in all the ordinary actions of daily life, we trace upon the forehead the sign."[22] The constant signing was believed to protect them from Satan. "And when tempted always reverently seal thy forehead (with the sign of the cross). For this sign of the Passion is displayed and made manifest against the devil if thou makest it in faith, not in order that thou mayest be seen of men, but by thy knowledge putting it forward as a shield. If indeed the adversary, seeing the power of the Spirit outwardly displayed in the image of baptism, he takes to flight trembling, not at thy striking him but at thy breathing [upon him]."[23]

> **The Mishnah**—After the loss of the Temple, two disastrous wars, and expulsion from the holy city, the leading rabbis felt the need to preserve their oral traditions. So, at the beginning of the third century, they compiled the key legal rulings of the sages. This was done in Galilee, where most of the Jews lived after Bar Kokhba. They organized this voluminous material by dividing it into six orders, which were further subdivided into 63 tractates. The Mishnah is thus cited by name and tractate. This six-part structure became the template for all of the Talmudic literature which followed.

The Breviary—now called the Liturgy of the Hours—was derived from the Hebrew convention of praying at the cardinal points of the day. The first generation of Catholics were taught to recite the Lord's Prayer three times daily.[24] This threefold pattern of daily prayer had been a fixture of Judaism since the time of David.[25] The Jewish disciples continued the practice out of lifelong habit—Peter went up to the housetop to pray "about the sixth hour"—but it was never taught to Gentile Christians.[26] The course of daily prayer prescribed by the Roman Church still includes Terce, Sext, and None, the Latin words for three, six and nine, respectively.

The proto-Catholics continued the Jewish custom of *nelilat yadayim*—ritual hand-washing—before approaching God in prayer. The *Apostolic Tradition* (c. AD 215) speaks of washing hands before the first prayer in the

---

22. *On the Crown* 3.
23. *Ap Trad* 37.
24. *Didache* 8.
25. Psalms 55:17; Luke 1:10 The Mishnah gives the range of acceptable times for the three prayers. "The morning prayer [may be recited] until midday. R. Judah says, 'Until the fourth hour.' The afternoon prayer [may be recited] until the evening. R Judah says, 'Until mid-afternoon.' The evening prayer has no fixed [time]" (*Berakhot* 4.1).
26. Acts 10:9.

morning and again after getting up at midnight to pray.[27] Tertullian heaps scorn upon the practice and puzzles over its origin. "These are the true purities; not those which most are superstitiously careful about, taking water at every prayer, even when they are coming from a bath of the whole body."[28]

Sunday was the highlight of the liturgical week. Most of the components of this service were borrowed from the synagogues, perhaps the thought in John's mind when he called them "synagogues of Satan."[29] The home where they gathered for worship was called "the place of instruction," clearly derived from the "House of Learning" or *Beit Midrash* in Hebrew.[30] First century synagogues were segregated, with separate sections for men and women, and the proto-Catholics also segregated their assemblies.[31] Catholic women covered their heads with a scarf; married Jewish women wore a head covering at synagogue.[32] The elder of each congregation was given the honor of a special high-backed chair called "the chair of the teacher," or *kathedra* in Greek.[33] This corresponds to Moses' seat in the synagogues.[34]

The service began by reading "the memoirs of the apostles and the writings of the prophets," to use Justin Martyr's memorable phrase.[35] The Christian lection is a direct carryover of the Torah readings on Sabbath and festival days. The Jews stand respectfully when the Torah scroll is brought up for reading and again when it is returned to the ark. Catholics were likewise instructed to rise and stand reverently during the gospel portion. "At the conclusion of the other scriptures let the Gospel be read, as being the seal of all the scriptures; and let the people listen to it standing upon their feet."[36] The deacon would then stand and ask that quarrelling brethren reconcile.[37] The congregation would rise together for common prayer, which also came

---

27. "And let every faithful man and woman, when they rise from sleep at dawn, before they undertake any work, wash their hands and pray to God, and so let them go to work." "And at midnight, rise and wash thy hands with water and pray" (*Ap Trad* 35).

28. *On Prayer* 13.

29. Revelation 2:9; 3:9.

30. These were the study halls where Torah was taught, often situated in or adjacent to a synagogue.

31. *Ap Trad* 18.2.

32. *Ap Trad* 18.5.

33. *Clement to James* 19.

34. Matthew 23:2. A cathedral is now the principle church of a diocese, the one which houses the bishop's throne and acts as the seat of administration.

35. *1 Apology* 67.

36. Syriac *Teaching* 8.

37. *Didache* 14. This was done in accordance with Matthew 5:23–24.

from Jewish precedents. The central liturgy of the synagogue—the Eighteen Benedictions—is recited while standing, and for this reason is often called the *Amidah*, which literally means "standing."[38] The kiss of peace followed common prayer.[39]

At this point, the catechumens were dismissed and the faithful were summoned to the "divine table."[40] The Latin word for dismissed—*missa*—has become the colloquial name for the entire service: Mass. Only the spiritually mature members, those who had been regenerated in the waters of baptism, were invited to this banquet. The sacred meal was served by deacons, who mixed the wine and set plates of bread, fish, and fruit on the table. The baptized members would then recline together and enjoy "the communion of the table."[41] After the elder recited the blessing for the bread and broke the loaf, the meal got underway.[42] We will cover this first century institution and its evolution into the Eucharist in chapter 7.

Synagogue Blessings Become the Catholic Liturgy

The central prayer of the synagogue liturgy is the Eighteen Benedictions, or *Shemoneh Esrei* in Hebrew. It is also called the *Amidah* ("Standing") because it is recited while standing and sometimes the *HaTefilah* ("The Prayer") because the obligation to pray can only be fulfilled by its recitation. The *Shemoneh Esrei* is a long, flowing tapestry of nineteen fixed prayers and petitions.[43] Although it did not crystallize into its present form until the end of the first century, most of the material would have been intimately familiar to the false apostles. They prepared a Christian liturgy based upon the Eighteen Benedictions but rewritten entirely in terms of the New Covenant. These reformulated prayers became the first Catholic liturgy.

The first century revisers focused on a subset of the *Shemoneh Esrei* known as the Seven Benedictions. On Shabbat, New Moons, and festival days, the Eighteen Benedictions are shortened to make room for the Torah lesson. The thirteen middle blessings are dropped and replaced by a prayer which

---

38. The Lord refers to this custom in Matthew 6:5.
39. *1 Apo* 65.
40. *Recognitions* 10.72.
41. *Recognitions* 7.36.
42. The ritual blessings used on this occasion for the bread and cup have been preserved in *Didache* 9, and the meal concluded with the table grace recorded in *Didache* 10.
43. An additional curse against "Nazarenes and heretics" was added late in the first century, making a total of 19 blessings. It is now the Twelfth Blessing. The designation of "18 Benedictions" was so entrenched that it was not changed.

affirms the sanctity of the day, the *Kedushat hayom*.[44] This same collection of seven prayers, all dressed up in Christian terminology, can still be found in Book 7 of the *Apostolic Constitutions*. It is the Catholic version of the Seven Benedictions. Not only do we find the same topics in the same order, but the Christianized *Kedushat hayom* lies between the retooled third and sixteenth blessings, precisely where a knowledgeable and skilled liturgist would place it.

The Third Blessing of the *Amidah* is known as "Holiness." If the *Amidah* is repeated by the prayer leader, the congregation rises after the second blessing to recite a special prayer, the *Kedushah*. It is the chorus of the angels surrounding the throne of God in the prophetic visions of Isaiah and Ezekiel. "Holy, Holy, Holy is the Lord of Hosts: the whole earth is full of His glory (Isaiah 6:3) followed by "Blessed be the glory of the Lord from his place" (Ezekiel 3:12). In the *Amidah*, these two verses serve to introduce a short declaration of God's holiness. Sure enough, book 7 of the *Apostolic Constitutions* contains both of these elements, the *Kedushah* and the sentence proclaiming God's holiness. The first line of the *Kedushah* became the Sanctus of the Roman rite and the Trisagion of the Orthodox liturgy.

A comparison of the Seven Blessings with the liturgical prayers in *Apostolic Constitutions* 7 leaves little doubt they were the original prototypes. However, we must keep in mind that even the earliest of the extant Catholic prayers are generations removed from the *Amidah* of Paul's day, and they had been Christianized and expanded considerably in the interim.

- **First Blessing** ("Fathers") became *Apostolic Constitutions* 7.33
- **Second Blessing** ("God's Power") became *Apostolic Constitutions* 7.34 and the first five lines of 7.35
- **Third Blessing** ("Holiness of God") became the rest of *Apostolic Constitutions* 7.35.
- **The Sanctity of the Day** (*Kedushat hayom*) became *Apostolic Constitutions* 7.36
- **Fifteenth Blessing** ("Blessing of David") became the first line of *Apostolic Constitutions* 7.37
- **Sixteenth** ("Hear our Prayer") and **Seventeenth Blessing** ("Worship") became the balance of *Apostolic Constitutions* 7.37. The petition to "Hear our voice" and "accept our prayers" of the 16th Benediction became "do thou, O Lord God, accept the prayers which proceed from the lips of Thy people which are of the Gentiles." The petition to receive

---

44. "On the Sabbath and on festivals and on the Day of Atonement, one recites Seven and recites the sanctification of the day in the middle" (t. *Berakhot* 3.12a).

the "offerings of Israel" in the 17th Blessing became an enumeration of the righteous Hebrews God had accepted. This section concludes with: "Now also do Thou receive the prayers of Thy people which are offered to Thee with knowledge, through Christ in the Spirit."

- **Blessing No.18** ("Thanksgiving") became *Apostolic Constitutions* 7.38

We can examine the evidence for ourselves. The complete text of the First Benediction and about one-half of the Catholic version from *Apostolic Constitutions* 7.33 are shown below in parallel columns. This particular blessing is known as *Abot*, meaning Fathers.

First Blessing of the Amidah	Apostolic Constitutions 7.33
"Blessed art Thou, Lord our God and God of our fathers, God of Abraham, God of Isaac, and God of Jacob. The great, mighty, and awesome God, God Supreme, who extends loving kindness and is Master of all, Who remembers the gracious deeds of our forefathers, and who will bring a Redeemer with love to their children's children for His name's sake. King, Helper, Savior and Protector. Blessed art Thou, Lord, Protector of Abraham."[45]	"Our eternal Savior, the King of gods, who alone art almighty, and the Lord, the God of all beings, and the God of our holy and blameless fathers, and of those before us; the God of Abraham, and of Isaac, and of Jacob; who art merciful and compassionate, long suffering, and abundant in mercy..." "For from that truth which was in our forefather Abraham, when he changed his way Thou didst guide him by a vision, and didst teach him what kind of state this world is; and knowledge went before his faith, and faith was the consequence of his knowledge; and the covenant did follow after his faith. For thou saidest: 'I will make thy seed as the stars of heaven, and as the sand which is by the seashore.' Moreover, when thou hast given him Isaac, and knewest him to be like him in his mode of life, Thou wast then called his God, saying: 'I will be a God to thee, and to thy seed after thee.' And when our father Jacob was sent into Mesopotamia, Thou showedst him Christ, and by him speakest, saying: 'Behold, I am with thee, and I will increase thee, and multiply thee exceedingly.' And so spakest Thou to Moses, Thy faithful and holy servant, at the vision of the bush: 'I am He that is; this is my name for ever, and my memorial for generations of generations.' O Thou great protector of the posterity of Abraham, Thou art blessed forever."

---

45. Donin, *To Pray as a Jew* p. 77

The patrimony of the Christian prayer is beyond doubt. We find the same exact themes—with only minor exceptions—in the same exact sequence as the First Blessing. There are also remarkable similarities in word selection and phraseology.

- The "God of our fathers" vs. the "God of our holy and blameless fathers."
- The "God of Abraham, of Isaac, and Jacob" vs. the "God of Abraham, and of Isaac, and of Jacob."
- "Who extends loving kindness" vs. "who art merciful and compassionate, long suffering, and abundant in mercy."
- The Hebrew Blessing speaks of the promise to bring a redeemer to their children's children. The Catholic prayer expands this line into a recounting of the promises made to the four Patriarchs regarding their seed.
- For "His Name's sake" vs. "this is my name forever."
- The "Protector of Abraham" vs. the "great protector of the posterity of Abraham."
- "Blessed art thou, Lord" vs. "Thou art blessed forever."

The Jewish Roots of Catholic Baptism

Baptism was the gateway sacrament of the sectarians. The founders deliberately chose the tripartite conversion ritual of the Jewish proselyte—circumcision, immersion, and sacrifice—over the immersion-baptism of the apostles. The reason, of course, was the Law. As the rite that symbolized the acceptance and obligation of Torah, circumcision was the doctrinal battleground of the New Testament. The *Apostolic Tradition* (c. AD 215) contains the fullest account extant of the early ritual, and it is still possible to see the outline of the old proselyte initiation under the third century rubrics. The whole schema is based on a baptism at daybreak on Easter Sunday.

The baptismal candidates would wash themselves on Thursday of Holy Week, and fast all day Friday and Saturday. A pre-baptismal fast of one or two days goes all the way back to the beginning of the sect.[46] The underlying reason for the short delay is found in the Babylonian Talmud: "He is to be circumcised, and *when healed*, brought immediately to baptism."[47] Assuming there is no infection or hemorrhaging, it takes thirty-six to forty-eight hours

---

46. *Homilies* 13.9; *Didache* 7.
47. b. *Yebamoth* 47, emphasis mine.

for the incision to fully heal.[48] Then, on the evening prior to Easter, the catechumens would kneel in front of the bishop, who exorcised the evil spirits by breathing on their faces and sealing their foreheads, ears, and noses. The seal of confirmation is a living linguistic reminder of what used to fit into this time slot. Circumcision was the *seal* of the Abrahamic covenant.

The all-night vigil which followed was spent "studying the scriptures and instructing them." According to the Babylonian Talmud, Jewish proselytes were to be coached prior to immersion in "the lighter and weightier commandments; and informed as to the sins regarding the corner of the field, the forgotten sheaf, the gleaning, and the tithe for the poor."[49] They had to be immersed in Torah before they were immersed in water. The Catholic teachers adopted this rule. "Let him, therefore, who is to be taught the truth in regard to piety be instructed before his baptism."[50]

The next morning, at the water's edge, they were asked to "put off their clothes" and "stand in the water naked." The Catholics of the first centuries were baptized entirely naked, but we should keep in mind that the ceremony was performed at the break of dawn. The parallel instructions in the Syrian *Didascalia Apostolorum* indicate that the practice was universal and not limited to Rome.[51] The women were even required to take off their jewelry and rings. "And last the women, who shall all have loosed their hair and laid aside the gold ornaments which they were wearing. Let no one go down to the water having an alien object with them." This custom is traceable to the rabbinic principle that, when immersing in a mikveh, "no separating element shall intervene between the water and the body."[52] Both ribbons and knotted hair, which prevent water from reaching the individual hair strands,

---

48. "And unto Hamor and unto Shechem his son hearkened all that went out of the gate of his city; and every male was circumcised, all that went out of the gate of his city. And it came to pass on the third day, *when they were sore*, that two of the sons of Jacob, Simeon and Levi, Dinah's brethren, took each man his sword, and came upon the city boldly, and slew all the males" (Genesis 34:24–25, emphasis mine).

49. b. *Yebamoth* 47.

50. *Ap Const* 7.39. In the *Recognitions*, they have Peter making an exception to the rule. "Otherwise she must have been instructed and taught many days before she could have been baptized" (7.34).

51. "When women go down into the water, those who go down into the water ought to be anointed by a deaconess with the oil of anointing; and where there is no woman at hand, and especially no deaconess, he who baptizes must of necessity anoint her who is being baptized. But where there is a woman, and especially a deaconess, *it is not fitting that women should be seen by men*. But with the imposition of hand do thou anoint the head only... let a woman deacon, as we have already said, anoint the women" (*Did Apost* 16, emphasis mine).

52. b. *Kerithoth* 82a.

were considered a *chatzitzah*, or barrier.[53] The instruction to "loose the hair" makes perfect sense in this light.

After renouncing Satan, the candidates were turned to face the rising sun, where they made a profession to do God's will. Once in the water, they were again turned and baptized facing toward the east. This eastern orientation is classically Jewish. The People of the Covenant have prayed toward Jerusalem since the first temple was built and, in the Diaspora, this generally meant toward the east. Synagogues are deliberately laid out so that "the doors of synagogues open only eastward," and Torah scrolls are stored along the eastern wall."[54] Catholics have always prayed toward the east,[55] and their church buildings are oriented on an east-west axis.[56]

The baptismal candidates brought an offering—usually bread—for the meal which followed baptism. This was a replacement for the first sacrifice made by Jewish converts after immersion.[57] The bread was their contribution to the sacred banquet, which they were now qualified to participate in. We know what happens next from only one source, the *Homilies of Clement*.[58] At this meal, the elder would tear the loaf, sprinkle salt on a piece, and hand it to the newly-baptized member. The salt here is very significant. Salt always had to accompany bread or grain offerings in the temple, and the salting of the bread tells us this was intended to be an offering. "And every oblation of thy meat (i.e., meal) offering shalt thou season with salt; neither shall thou suffer the salt of the covenant of thy God to be lacking from thy meat offering: with all thine offerings thou shalt offer salt."[59]

Their baptismal theology was solidly anchored in the sacrificial system of Moses and Aaron. Just as rabbinical Judaism substituted liturgical prayer for the blood of bulls and goats, so the proto-Catholics replaced the temple sacrifices with baptism. This doctrine is explicitly stated in the *Recognitions of Clement*.

53. "These interpose on man: . . . and the ribbons which are on the heads of girls" (m. *Mikvaot* 9.1a).

54. t. *Megillah* 3.22.

55. Tertullian, *Apology* 16; *Stromata* 7.

56. "And for the presbyters let there be assigned a place in the eastern part of the house; and let the bishop's throne be set in their midst, and let the presbyters sit with him. And again, let the laymen sit in another part of the house toward the east. For so it should be, that in the eastern part of the house the presbyters sit with the bishops, and next the laymen, and then the women that when you stand up to pray, the rulers may stand first, and after them the laymen, and then the women also. For it is required that you pray toward the east. . ." (*Did Apost* 12).

57. b. Kerithoth 8b–9a.

58. *Homilies* 14.1.

59. Leviticus 2:13.

But when the time began to draw near that what was wanting in the Mosaic institutions should be supplied, as we have said, and that the Prophet should appear, of whom he had foretold that He should warn them by the mercy of God to cease from sacrificing; lest haply they might suppose that on the cessation of sacrifice there was no remission of sins for them, He instituted baptism by water amongst them, in which they might be absolved from all their sins on the invocation of His name.
—*Recognitions of Clement* 1.39

Nothing could be further from the teaching of the apostles. They unequivocally pointed to Christ as God's complete and perfect provision for sin. "In whom we have redemption through his blood, the forgiveness of sins, according to the riches of his grace."[60] Peter's expression of this doctrine has been fashioned into one of the most beloved hymns of redemption. "Forasmuch as ye know that ye were not redeemed with corruptible things, as gold and silver. . .but with the precious blood of Christ, as of a lamb without blemish and without spot. . ."[61]

The Roman church now teaches that baptism is required to blot out original sin, but in the first centuries, baptism was believed to banish evil spirits and demons. It was essentially what we would call an exorcism; indeed, the oil with which they were anointed was called the "oil of exorcism."[62] Exorcism by adjuration was a popular Jewish superstition in those days, playing off the reverence and power accorded to the name of God.[63] This doctrine is clearly spelled out in the *Recognitions of Clement*. "But in the present life, washing in a flowing river, or fountain, or even in the sea, with the thrice-blessed invocation, you shall not only be able to drive away the spirits which lurk in you; but yourselves no longer sinning, and undoubtingly believing God, you shall drive out evil spirits and dire demons, with terrible diseases, from others."[64]

The pre-baptismal rites focused heavily on releasing the candidate from the power of Satan. In the *Apostolic Tradition*, an exorcism was done

60. Ephesians 1:7; see also Colossians 1:13–14; 1 John 1:7.
61. 1 Peter 1:18–19.
62. *Ap Trad* 21.
63. See Acts 19:13–16; Antiquities 8.2.5.
64. *Homilies* 9.8. "Everyone who has at any time worshiped idols, and has adored those whom the pagans call gods, or has eaten of the things sacrificed to them, is not without an unclean spirit; for he has become the guest of demons, and has been partaker with that demon of which he has formed the image in his mind, either through fear or love. And by these means he is not free from an unclean spirit, and therefore needs the purification of baptism, that the unclean spirit may go out of him" (*Recognitions* 2.71).

during the fasting period and then again on Easter Sunday, culminating in a formal renunciation at the water's edge. "And when the presbyter takes hold of each one of those who are baptized, let him renounce saying, 'I renounce thee, Satan, and all thy service and all thy works.' And when he has said this, let him anoint him with the oil of exorcism, saying: Let all evil spirits depart far from thee."[65] A three-fold repudiation of Satan, known as the baptismal vows, still lives on in the high Christian churches.

We are now at a place where we can compare the rulings of the rabbis, the customs of the early Catholics, and the teachings of the apostles. The derivation of many common Catholic practices from Jewish sources is readily seen by comparing the first and second columns. To see how far this diverges from the New Testament model, the corresponding teaching of the apostles is provided in the third column.

Law of Moses, Jewish Tradition	Early Catholic Practice	New Testament Christianity
Eighteen Benedictions recited in the synagogues	Synagogue blessings were rewritten to become the liturgy of the church	No known liturgy; prayed extemporaneously
Pharisees observed Levitical washings taken from temple service	Washed hands before meals, before prayers, and after sleeping	Did not adopt hand-washing rituals
Pharisees observed the Levitical purity code	Couples separated during menstruation, washed after sex, churching of women after childbirth	Sex restricted to marriage, menstruation and childbirth were not considered unclean
Jews observed annual feasts and holy days	Gentile believers observe church or liturgical calendar	Gentile believers did not observe Jewish calendar
Pesah was the highlight of the annual calendar	Observed Passover, which evolved into Easter	Passover meal became the apostolic breaking of bread
Pharisees fasted twice/week and Day of Atonement	Fasted twice weekly and six days before Passover	Gentile believers were not taught set days of fasting
Prayed daily at the third, sixth, and ninth hours	Taught to pray at the third, sixth, and ninth hours	Gentiles were not taught to pray at set times
Jews had three-step conversion ritual	Adopted three-step Jewish proselyte ritual	Baptism consisted solely of immersion
Prayed facing the Temple	Prayed facing the east	Prayed to Father in heaven

---

65. *Ap Trad* 21.

6

The Fathers of Uncleanness

> Now ye are clean through the word
> which I have spoken unto you
>
> —JOHN 15:3

The Jews were heirs to a curious set of taboos known as the purity laws. These complex regulations were tightly woven into the fabric of their daily lives. Some of them were actual *mitzvahs*—commandments of God—and these were honored and respected by the Lord. But others were merely traditions of men, the rulings of prominent rabbis and sages. Jesus strenuously objected to the man-made rules, and we often read of him sparring with the Pharisees over their application.

Moses set down the primary causes of impurity—the Fathers of Uncleanness—in the middle chapters of Leviticus and Numbers 19. They are known collectively as the laws of separation because they demarcate the clean from the unclean. It should be made clear that ritual impurity is not the same as sin. A menstruant, for example, is considered unclean, even though she has not violated any commandment. As a general rule, sin can only be atoned by blood or sacrifice while uncleanness is rectified by a process which usually involves washing and the passage of time. The subject is so vast and complex that an entire division of the Talmud—one out of six—is devoted to purities.

The false apostles, with their Pharisaic background, wholeheartedly embraced the purity code. The agents that trigger ritual uncleanness are listed below. Many are liquids and, in an interesting bit of symmetry, the process that deactivates uncleanness also involves a liquid: water. There is an abundance of patristic evidence that the early Catholics observed the first two, a reference here and there to the second two, and no evidence whatsoever for the last one.

1. Bodily fluids, especially blood, menstrual discharge, or semen—Leviticus 15
2. The birth of a child, with its attendant bleeding—Leviticus 12
3. Contact with a human corpse, bones, or graveyards—Numbers 19
4. The bodies of unclean animals, insects, and lizards—Leviticus 11
5. Leprosy and other skin diseases—Leviticus 13–14

Moses implicitly taught that uncleanness was contagious. The *Mishnah* recognizes five gradations in the Fathers of Uncleanness (the primary generators), depending how the impurity is transmitted, how long it lasts, and if it can be passed along.[1] Uncleanness can be spread by direct physical contact, by entering an enclosed space or in the case of the most virulent—a corpse—merely by overshadowing.[2] For a *Niddah* (menstruant), a woman in her cycle would be the Father of Uncleanness. If someone touched her or sat on her couch, they would be rendered unclean at the second remove. To become ritually pure, they would need to wash their clothes, bathe, and they were not purified until the setting of the sun. The degree of defilement grows less potent with each step away from the primary generator.

Jesus of Nazareth transcended the purity laws. One time in Galilee he reached out to touch a leper, and "immediately his leprosy was cleansed."[3] In a pericope shared by three of the Gospels, Jesus was summoned to Jairus' house and, on the way, a woman with an issue of blood touched his garment and was healed. When he arrived at the house, he took the dead maiden by the hand, and she arose. Both the bleeding woman and the corpse should have made Jesus unclean.[4] But instead of transmitting impurity to him, they were healed and made whole.

---

1. m. *Kelim* 1.
2. "Then said Haggai, if one that is unclean by a dead body touch one of these, shall it be unclean? And the priests answered, it shall be unclean" (Haggai 2:13).
3. Matthew 8:3.
4. Matthew 9:18–26; Mark 5:22–43; Luke 8:41–56.

Family purity is the category of Jewish law which deals with menstruation and marital relations. According to Leviticus 15:19, a woman was unclean for seven days following the first appearance of her menses. The sages extended this by seven clean days and added a ritual bath to the process. A *Niddah* would immerse herself in a mikveh pool on the evening of the twelfth day before the couple could resume normal life. Marital relations during her separation were strictly forbidden. It was an extremely serious offence, the penalty for which was to be "cut off from the commonwealth of Israel."[5]

The false apostles and their protégé took this teaching seriously. The importance of menstrual separation is repeatedly emphasized throughout the *Homilies of Clement*.[6]

> However, it is necessary to add something to these things which has not community with man, but is peculiar to the worship of God. I mean purification, not approaching to a man's own wife when she is in separation, for so the Law of God commands.
> —*Homilies of Clement* 11.28

> But who is there to whom it is not manifest that it is better not to have intercourse with a woman in her separation, but purified and washed. And also after copulation, it is proper to wash.
> —*Homilies of Clement* 11.30

These practices lingered in the *Ekklesia Katholika* for centuries. Even in progressive Rome, the issue of bathing after marital relations was still being discussed in the third century. "He who has used marriage is not defiled; for those who are washed have no need to wash again, for they are pure."[7] In Syria, the old customs may have persisted up until the fourth century. "An husband, therefore, and a wife, when they company together in lawful

---

5. Leviticus 20:18. The *Mishnah* tells us what being cut off meant. "On account of three transgressions do women die in childbirth: because they are not meticulous in the laws of (1) menstrual separation, (2) in [those covering] the dough offering, and (3) in [those covering] the kindling of a lamp [for the Shabbath]" (m. *Shabbat* 2.6).

6. "But when through carelessness they neglected the observation of the proper times, when the sons in succession cohabiting through ignorance at times when they ought not, place their children under innumerable afflictions. . .and in truth, such afflictions arise because of ignorance; as, for instance, by not knowing when one ought to cohabit with his wife, as if she be pure from her discharge" (*Homilies* 19.22).

"To abstain from the table of devils, that is, from food offered to idols, from dead carcasses, from animals which have been suffocated or caught by wild beasts, and from blood; not to live any longer impurely; to wash after intercourse; that the women on their part should keep the law of purification" (*Homilies* 7.8).

7. *Ap Trad* 36.10.

marriage, and rise from one another, may pray without any observations, and without washing are clean."[8]

The doctrine of uncleanness continued to manifest itself in the sacraments of the church. A woman in her menses was barred from the baptismal font. "And let those who are to be baptized be instructed to wash and cleanse themselves on the fifth day of the week. And if any women be menstruous, she shall be put aside and baptized another day."[9] They were also denied the sacrament of communion. "Concerning menstruous women, whether they ought to enter the temple of God while in such a state, I think it superfluous even to put the question. For, I opine, not even they themselves, being faithful and pious, would dare when in this state either to approach the Holy Table or to touch the body and blood of Christ."[10] The same letter addresses the uncleanness brought about by a wet dream. "They who have had involuntary nocturnal pollutions are at their own discretion [whether to receive communion or not]."[11]

The eastern churches have never strayed far from the ancient landmarks. The Russian Orthodox Church reluctantly permits a menstruant to attend Mass, but they are asked not to take communion, touch the communion bread, kiss the icons, or drink holy water. Presumably a mere touch would defile the holiness of those sacred objects. Greek Orthodox priests also counsel women not to communicate during their period.

The bleeding brought on by childbirth would also render a woman *niddah*. An Israeli woman was ritually unclean for seven days after the birth of a son and unclean "in the blood of her purification" for an additional thirty-three days.[12] After the forty days had passed, she would bring a lamb to the priests at the door of the temple.[13] This ceremony surfaces in Catholic tradition as the "Purification of Women after Childbirth before the Door of the Church." Forty days after giving birth, a Catholic mother would go to the porch of the church and kneel down in prayer.[14] Being ritually unclean, she had to wait for the blessing of the priest before being allowed back into the church, which blessing is called "The Churching of Women." She was then expected to produce an offering and resume communicating.

---

8. *Ap Const* 6.29.
9. *Ap Trad* 20.5–6.
10. *Dionysius to Basilides* 2.
11. *Dionysius to Basilides* 4.
12. Leviticus 12:2–4.
13. Leviticus 12:6.

14. In later years, a special pew for these women was reserved just inside the door of the church.

The purity regulations also prohibited contact with dead bodies. We know the proto-Catholics believed such—at least for a while—because an entire chapter of the *Apostolic Constitutions* argues that you are not defiled by touching a corpse. Reading between the lines, it appears that some traditional believers still believed in corpse contamination while the Church as a whole had moved beyond it.

> Do not therefore keep any such observances about legal and natural purgations, as thinking you are defiled by them. Neither do you seek after Jewish separations, or perpetual washings, or purifications upon the touch of a dead body... Whence you also, O bishops and the rest, who without such observances touch the departed, ye ought not to think yourselves defiled.
> —*Apostolic Constitutions* 6.30

Jesus ignored this prohibition when he raised the ruler's daughter from the dead. "But when the people were put forth, he went in, and took her by the hand, and the maid arose."[15] The Son of man was immune from corpse uncleanness.

Peter and Table Fellowship

The oral law developed its own code of purity. One of the core doctrines of the Pharisees is that Levitical purity was not just for the priesthood, but it was destined for all Israel. "If ye will obey my voice indeed, and keep my covenant, then ye shall be a peculiar treasure unto me above all people: for all the earth is mine: and *ye shall be unto me a kingdom of priests, and an holy nation.*"[16] The Pharisees took these words to heart, and sought to live like priests and Levites in the temple. Eating, and everything associated with it, became a sacred act with its own set of regulations. A man's house became the temple of God, the kitchen table was the holy altar, and ordinary food was treated as the priestly portion of the offerings. Therefore, as the priests would carefully wash in the brazen laver before approaching the altar, so the "Separated Ones" would cleanse their hands before eating.[17]

---

15. Matthew 9:25, emphasis mine.

16. Exodus 19:5-6, emphasis mine.

17. "Thou shalt also make a laver of brass, and his foot also of brass, to wash withal: and thou shalt put it between the tabernacle of the congregation and the altar, and thou shalt put water therein. For Aaron and his sons shall wash their hand and their feet thereat: when they go into the tabernacle of the congregation, they shall wash with water..." (Exodus 30:18-20).

As the Levites scrubbed the sacred vessels in the sanctuary, so the Pharisees would wash their cups and pots at home.[18]

The Lord did not validate the ritual washing of hands or scrubbing of pots because of their human origin:

> And when they saw some of his disciples eat bread with defiled, that is to say, with unwashen, hands, they found fault. For the Pharisees, and all the Jews, except they wash their hands oft, eat not, holding the traditions of the elders. And when they come from the market, except they wash, they eat not. And many other things there be, which they have received to hold, as the washing of cups, and pots, brazen vessels, and of tables. Then the Pharisees and scribes asked him, 'Why walk not thy disciples according to the tradition of the elders, but eat bread with unwashen hands?' He answered and said unto them. . . 'Howbeit in vain do they worship me, teaching for doctrines the commandments of men. For laying aside the commandment of God, ye hold the tradition of men, as the washing of pots and cups: and many other such like things ye do.' And he said unto them, 'Full well ye reject the commandment of God, that ye may keep your own tradition.'
> —Mark 7:2–9

This doctrine made it impossible for Pharisees to eat at the same table with Gentiles or even the unwashed masses of Israel.[19] It would be like shaking hands with Typhoid Mary, something you would want to avoid at all costs. What the Pharisees applied to the uncircumcised and the unclean, the proto-Catholics applied to the unbaptized. Catechumens and hearers were not allowed to join in table fellowship with the rest of the church until they had taken the step of baptism.

The Peter of the *Clementina* articulates this fundamental teaching on many occasions.[20]

---

18. "The clay pot the meat (sin offering) is cooked in must be broken; but if it is cooked in a bronze pot, the pot is to be scoured and rinsed with water" (Leviticus 6:28 NIV).

19. t. *Demai* 2.2.

20. "When he had thus spoken, he [Peter] retired to take food along with his friends; but he ordered me to eat by myself; and after the meal, when he had sung praise to God and given thanks, he rendered to me an account of this proceeding, and added 'May the Lord grant to thee to be made like us in all things that, receiving baptism, thou mayest be able to meet with us at the same table'" (*Recognitions* 1.19).

"Let no one of you therefore be saddened at being separated from eating with us, for everyone ought to observe that it is for just so long a time as he pleases. For he who wishes soon to be baptized is separated but for a little time, but he for a longer [time] who wishes to be baptized later. Everyone therefore has it in his own power to demand

But this also we observe, not to have a common table with Gentiles unless when they believe, and on the reception of the truth, are baptized, and consecrated by a certain threefold invocation of the blessed Name; and then we eat with them.
—*Recognitions of Clement* 7.29

Nor do we take our food from the same table as Gentiles, inasmuch as we cannot eat along with them, because they live impurely. But when we have persuaded them to have true thoughts, and to follow a right course of action, and have baptized them with a thrice blessed invocation, then we dwell with them. For not even if it were our father, or mother, or wife, or child, or brother, or any other one having a claim by nature on our affection, can we venture to take our meals with him; for our religion compels us to make a distinction.
—*Homilies of Clement* 13.4

The real Peter, the one we read about in the New Testament, had been led to exactly the opposite conclusion. It was Simon Peter to whom God gave the revelation of the clean and unclean animals. "Ye know how that it is an unlawful thing for a man that is a Jew to keep company, or come unto one of another nation; but God hath showed me that I should not call any man common or unclean."[21] However, when Peter went to inspect the Gentile church at Antioch, he still felt the full force and fury of the old tradition. "But when Peter was come to Antioch, I withstood him to the face, because he was to be blamed. For before that certain came from James, he did eat with the Gentiles; but when they were come, he withdrew and separated himself, fearing them which were of the circumcision."[22] But the following year, at the Jerusalem council, Peter helped guide the apostles into accepting Gentiles as equal brothers in Christ.

Jesus had no qualms about eating with sinners and social outcasts. In the fifth chapter of Luke, he answered his critics with the observation that these were the very people who needed help. "But their scribes and Pharisees murmured against his disciples, saying, Why do ye eat and drink with publicans and sinners? And Jesus answering said unto them, They that are whole need not a physician; but they that are sick."[23] He ran into the same

---

a shorter or a longer time for his repentance; and therefore it lies with you, when you wish it, to come to our table; and not with us, who are not permitted to take food with anyone who has not been baptized" (*Recognitions* 2.72).

21. Acts 10:28.
22. Galatians 2:11–13.
23. Luke 5:30–32.

self-righteous attitude a couple of chapters later. A Pharisee invited Jesus to his home for supper, and a sinner woman showed up and anointed his feet. The Pharisee thought within himself that a real prophet would know and avoid such an unclean woman. But Jesus reproved the Pharisee—not the woman—comparing her love and care for him with his neglect as a host.[24] Finally, in the fifteenth chapter, he responded to their hardness of heart with three parables: The Parable of the Lost Sheep, the Missing Coin, and the Prodigal Son. He was trying to get them to grasp the value of a single repentant soul.

We have seen how the proto-Catholics embraced the purity code of Moses and the Pharisaic ban on eating with Gentiles. We will discover in the next chapter that the doctrine of table separation gave rise to the two-part structure of the Mass.

---

24. Luke 7:36–50.

7

The Primitive Eucharistic Meal

AD 70 to AD 140

> When ye come together therefore into one place,
> this is *not* to eat the Lord's supper,
> for in eating one taketh before other his own supper:
> and one is hungry, and another is drunken.
>
> —1 Corinthians 11:20–21, emphasis mine

The spotlight in this chapter will be on the centerpiece of Catholic religiosity and devotion, the Eucharist. The historical roots of this rite are not as straightforward as it might seem. We are, after all, examining an apostate sect, not the church familiar to us from the New Testament. While the earliest stages of its evolution are concealed by a lack of documentation, there is still enough linguistic and structural evidence for us to connect the dots.

By the beginning of the Christian era, the common meal had been elevated to a semi-sacred status in Jewish life. The Pharisees had introduced hand-washing and other temple rites to the domestic table, and every mealtime act, no matter how minor, had been invested with religious significance. One of these was a short little ritual involving bread that kicked off every communal or family meal, a custom that the Lord himself followed. "It came to pass, as he sat at meat with them, he took bread, and blessed it, and brake, and gave to them"[1] Because of this custom, a common Hebrew idiom for eating together or sharing a meal was to "break bread."[2]

The bread-breaking ritual consisted of four consecutive steps performed in rapid succession. The host would:

1. Take the bread and hold it in his hands
2. Recite a blessing over the bread
3. Break or tear it into pieces
4. Distribute a piece to each guest

The dining furniture of the Mediterranean civilizations are as foreign to us as their table manners. The dining room of the upper-class Roman family was called the *triclinium*, named for the three couches that furnished the room. These couches faced inward upon three sides of a square, leaving the front open for serving. In the center stood an elevated table upon which household slaves would place the food and beverages. Each couch supported a large, stuffed cushion, wide enough to accommodate three recumbent diners. In polite society, diners would recline on their left elbow, which rested on a pillow, and eat with their right hand. The host reclined on the left couch, and in the place of greatest access and proximity, the guest of honor faced him on the middle couch.[3] The guests were arranged further to the right by decreasing rank and social status, while the family members lounged behind the host on the left couch. At the Last Supper, Jesus served as host, and John, who was "leaning on Jesus' bosom," reclined next to him on the left cushion.[4]

The First Century Thanksgiving Meal

In the 1940s, the Anglican priest Gregory Dix wrote an influential book on the origins of the Catholic Eucharist, *The Shape of the Liturgy*. He noted that the only unchanging constant of the Eucharist down through the ages

---

1. Luke 24:30. We find the same sequence at the miracle of the loaves and fishes. "And he commanded the multitude to sit down on the grass, and took the five loaves, and the two fishes, and looking up to heaven, he blessed, and brake, and gave the loaves to his disciples, and the disciples to the multitude" (Matthew 14:19). Again at the Last Supper. "And as they were eating, Jesus took bread, and blessed it, and brake it, and gave it to the disciples, and said, Take, eat; this is my body" (Matthew 26:26).

2. Acts 2:46; 20:11; 27:35.

3. The Tosefta explains the protocol: "When there are three couches, the greatest [in importance] reclines at the head of the middle [couch]" (t. *Berakhot* 5.5).

4. John 13:23–25.

has been the arrangement of its constituent parts, what we might call its external structure. While the language of the liturgy, the thing which is *said*, has never ceased to evolve, the core of the rite, the thing which is *done*, has remained remarkably stable. He pointed out that the Lord used seven separate acts when he instituted the New Covenant Breaking of Bread.[5]

1. Jesus took bread
2. Broke it
3. Gave thanks over it
4. Gave it to his disciples
5. He took the cup
6. Gave thanks
7. Gave it to the disciples

By way of contrast, the ritual used by the *Ekklesia Katholika*, from the first century until the present, from the Euphrates River to the Atlantic Ocean, has always consisted of just four steps. These are:

1. The offertory
2. The prayer
3. The fraction
4. The distribution

The Catholic Eucharist was not patterned after the breaking of bread and taking of the cup at the Last Supper. No, it had an altogether different origin. Dom Dix deduced from the four-step structure that it originated as a first century Jewish meal. As we will see, the evidence fully confirms Gregory Dix's brilliant insight.

Feasting—with the joy and personal bonding it brings—played a large role in all of the Hebrew holy days. Even an ordinary Sabbath concluded with the *Oneg*, an informal time of socializing with refreshments after the service. The false apostles felt a commemoration of the Lord's death deserved no less, and so they ended the Scripture reading and communal prayers on Sunday with a sacred meal. It was known in the first century simply as the "Thanksgiving," or *Eucharistia* in Greek. We will call it the primitive thanksgiving meal to differentiate it from the sacramental Eucharist it developed into.

---

5. *Shape*, 48.

The thanksgiving meal goes back to the founding of the sect. The *Didache* contains instructions which point us in the direction of a meal, but it requires some knowledge of Jewish table customs to decipher.

> But every Lord's day do ye gather yourselves together, and break bread, and give thanksgiving after having after having confessed your transgressions, that your sacrifice may be pure.
> —*Didache* 14

Let's pull this sentence apart line by line. They "broke bread," meaning they shared a meal together, and then they "gave thanksgiving," meaning they recited the customary blessing after eating. The main table blessing was, in fact, recited at the conclusion of the meal. The "sacrifice" in this context was the food on the table. The Pharisees viewed food as an offering, and when accompanied by the proper blessing and confession, they trusted it was a "pure" sacrifice, acceptable to God.

Serving meals was normally the responsibility of household servants, but at the sacred banquet, those duties were assigned to the deacons (*diakonos*, meaning servant). Like Stephen and his fellows who distributed food to the poor widows,[6] the first Catholic deacons were little more than table attendants and waiters. They set the table, brought the food offerings to the dining room, mixed the wine, and cleaned up afterwards. With the demise of the primitive thanksgiving meal, the deaconate has become little more than a training ground for the priesthood.

The table blessings for the sacred meal have been warehoused in the *Didache*. Chapter 9 contains the two most common mealtime blessings, those for bread and wine. The first *berakah* was for the cup. As a symbol of joy and good cheer, the rabbis made extensive use of wine in their rituals. Every person at the table would recite this blessing for his or herself before the meal began. The second blessing was for the bread, and it was delivered by the host on behalf of the whole company. If this blessing was recited at the beginning of the meal, it would suffice for all of the food which followed, except wine and fresh fruit, which have their own blessings.

Chapter 10 contains the reformulated Grace after Meal, the main Jewish table blessing. This prayer is required if bread or cereal grains in any form are consumed. A meal—as opposed to a mere snack—is defined by the presence of bread. Known as the *Birkat Hamazon*, this blessing is recited after everyone has finished eating. The specific language of the *Didache* leaves little doubt this was an actual meal and not a symbolic sacrament. "But after ye are *filled*, thus give thanks." Peter gives the same blessings over the food

---

6. Acts 6:1–6.

followed by a thanksgiving in the *Homilies of Clement*. "And having blessed the food, and having given thanks *after being satisfied*. . ."[7] Again, as in the *Didache*, the main table grace was delivered after they had given the blessing for bread and eaten the bounty of the table.

The summons to recite the *Birkat Hamazon* was also incorporated into the primitive thanksgiving meal. When three or more adults are dining together and must say grace, the host issues a formal invitation to pray and those at the table give their assent. Known as the *Birkat Zimun*, the summons is phrased in a slightly different manner according to the number of people at the table. According to the *Mishnah*, they had a standard formulation for three, ten, 100, 1,000, and 10,000 people.[8] This shows up in the Mass as the pre-Eucharistic dialogue between the priest and the congregants. The declaration of the priest, "Let us give thanks unto the Lord our God," is phrased in precisely the same language employed by the rabbis when one hundred persons are present, except the *Birkat Zimun* has "bless" in the Jewish manner instead of the Christianized "give thanks." The Hebrew invitation simply says, "Let us bless the Lord our God."

A formal Jewish feast was preceded by an extensive bout of preliminary rituals, and many of these made it into the eucharistic meal. They washed their hands by pouring water over one hand and then the other. The deacons mixed the wine with water. The wines of ancient times were not the quality of modern vintages, and they were often diluted with water to make them less potent.[9] The Jews incorporated the act of mixing the cup into their mealtime rituals, and the *Mishnah* recounts several rabbinic disputes over matters of procedure.[10]

After the preliminaries were over, the meal began with the breaking of bread. The host would hold the bread in his hands, recite the blessing, tear off a piece, and one-by-one hand it to each person at the table. This ritual in its entirety was incorporated into the primitive eucharistic meal and from there it passed to the sacramental Eucharist. *The four actions of the Catholic Eucharist—the offertory, the prayer, the fraction, and communion—are nothing other than the four steps of the Hebrew bread blessing ritual.*

---

7. *Homilies* 1.22, emphasis mine.

8. m. *Berakhot* 7.3.

9. The Greeks and Romans often added honey to improve the flavor.

10. "They do not recite the blessing over wine until one puts water into it—the words of R. Eliezer. But (other sages) say, They even recite the blessing (beforehand)" (m. *Berakhot* 7.5d, e). "The House of Shammai say, They wash the hands and then mix the cup. But the House of Hillel say, They mix the cup and then wash the hands" (m. *Berakhot* 8.2). The Hillelites and the Sammaites were the two principal schools of the Pharisees.

The Four Steps of the Primitive Thanksgiving Meal

The sacred meal—and later the Holy Eucharist—began with the offertory. The original offerings of the first and early second centuries were the bread, wine, cheese, fruit, and fish which the congregants brought for the potluck-style meal. This food was deemed to be an *offering* to God, in accordance with the doctrine of the Pharisees, and eating was considered a holy act. The food was carried in the woven baskets depicted in banqueting scenes on catacomb walls. These baskets were deposited on a special table at the back of the assembly room until needed.

Two different customs developed to get the food offering—later the sacraments—from the back of the room to the banqueting table or altar. In the east, the laity brought their oblation to a designated table before the service began. Then, after the Gospel portion was read, the offerings were taken up to the front in a resplendent ceremony known as the Great Entrance. In a solemn procession, beginning with torches and candles, a deacon held the sacred bread high above his head, followed by a priest with the chalice. In the west, the laity has always made the offerings themselves at the chancel rail, laying the bread on a linen cloth and pouring the wine into a silver cup. Gregory Dix threw down the gauntlet to some aspiring liturgist to explain what lay behind the divergence in custom.[11] It may be no more complicated than this: in the Levant, the first century deacons were responsible to bring the baskets of food to the table, while in Rome, the congregants carried the baskets themselves.

A passage from the *Didascalia Apostolorum* brings us back tantalizingly close to those days. "But of the deacons, let one stand continually by the oblations of the Eucharist and let another stand without by the door and observe them that come in. And afterwards, when you offer, let them minister together in the church."[12] It has been customary since ancient times to collect alms at this time, and consequently the offertory has become a euphemism for the collection of money.

The second act of the bread-breaking ritual was the blessing. After all of the guests were seated at the table, the Jewish head of house would recite the blessing over the bread, the Hebrew *Hamotzi*. "Blessed art Thou, Lord our God, King of the universe, who brings forth bread from the earth."[13] While they had still the primitive Thanksgiving meal, the proto-Catholics

---

11. *Shape*, 121.
12. *Did Apost* 12.
13. Donin, *To be a Jew*, 168.

would recite the spiritualized Christian version. We know the exact wording from the *Didache*:

> We thank Thee, our Father, for the life and knowledge which Thou made known to us through Jesus Thy Servant; to Thee be the glory forever. Even as this broken bread was scattered over the hills, and was gathered together and became one, so let Thy Church be gathered together from the ends of the earth into Thy kingdom; for Thine is the glory and the power through Jesus Christ forever.
> —*Didache* 9

The third step in the bread ritual was the fraction. This was the physical tearing or breaking of the loaf, and it marked the beginning of the meal proper.[14] It was an expected courtesy for each diner to take a piece of bread from the host. This rubric was incorporated into the sacred banquet and from there made its way to the liturgical Eucharist. Tertullian, writing around AD 200, drives the point home. "We take also, in congregations before daybreak, and from the hand of none but the presidents, the sacrament of the Eucharist. . ."[15] We observe the continuance of this practice today when the officiating priest places the wafer in the hand or on the tongue of the communicants.

Communion, the culmination of the four-step ritual, was the sacred meal itself. The *Recognitions of Clement* speaks explicitly of the baptized enjoying "the communion of the table."[16] The parallel passage in the *Homilies* describes the scene in greater detail, beginning with the breaking of bread, the blessing, the distribution, and finally concluding with the meal.

> Peter came several hours after, and breaking the bread after thanksgiving, and putting salt upon it, he gave it first to our mother and, after her, to us her sons. And thus we took food along with her and blessed God."
> —*Homilies of Clement* 14

It was their first food of the day and, indeed, of the week. "The faithful shall be careful to partake of the Eucharist before eating anything else."[17]

---

14. "R. Simeon b. Gamaliel says, Pieces [of bread] serve as an important sign for the guests. Whenever the guests see the pieces [being brought out], they know that something else [some other course] is to follow them" (m. *Berakhot* 7).

15. *On the Crown* 3.

16. *Recognitions* 7.36.

17. *Ap Trad* 36.

Pious Jews, on the Sabbath, are careful not to eat before morning prayers,[18] and the proto-Catholics transferred this rule to the first day of the week. The Eastern Orthodox are still careful not to eat or drink on Sunday mornings before receiving the sacraments.

The Thanksgiving Meal becomes the Liturgical Eucharist

The primitive thanksgiving meal gave rise to two Catholic institutions: the Holy Eucharist of the Mass and the *agape,* or love feast. Gregory Dix believed the sacramental Eucharist had been detached from the sacred supper by the first generation of apostles, but the same chain of evidence leads us into the early years of the second century.[19] The first century *Didache* unquestioningly refers to a formalized meal of some kind. Then, as we move into the second century, the Catholic authors have almost nothing to say about the subject. The literary record is a blank slate.

Pliny's letter to Trajan (c. AD 112) may be the smoking gun we are looking for. His knowledge of Christians came solely from interrogations and torture, and is therefore biased and thin.

> After this ceremony [the Sunday morning service] it had been their custom to disperse and reassemble later to take food of an ordinary, harmless kind; but they had in fact given up this practice since my edict, issued on your instruction, which banned all political societies . . . . .
> —*Pliny Letter to Trajan No. 96*

Christianity was not yet recognized as a legal religion in AD 112, but it was still classed in the more nefarious category of a political society. Participating in politics was dangerous business to the Roman authorities. Perhaps the Catholic elders considered it less of a risk to abbreviate the meal to just bread and wine—and shorten the service—or perhaps it was just a desire to better line up with the Gospel account. It seems unlikely that, if the Bithynians had just eaten the primitive thanksgiving meal, they would reassemble later to eat another fellowship meal. Pliny's account makes more sense if they had just participated in a quick ritual of bread and wine, and then got together later to eat an "ordinary" meal.

---

18. The rabbis taught that our spiritual devotion to God should come before our physical needs (j. *Berakhot* 10b).

19. *Shape,* 101.

The first liturgical Eucharist we come across in the Fathers is the *First Apology* of Justin Martyr, and it can be dated very close to AD 150.[20] We can thus place the beginning of the sacramental Eucharist around AD 110 in Asia and perhaps a bit later in Rome.

The new Eucharistic rite took the four-action shape of the bread ritual and reassembled its component parts. The summons to say table grace became the dialogue between priest and congregation. The offertory was restricted to just bread and wine. The blessing over the bread was jettisoned and replaced by the main table grace, which they formerly recited after the meal. The fraction was still the breaking of the bread, and communion became the reception of the bread and cup from the hand of the presbyter.

The Source of the Eucharistic Prayer

The invocation over the sacramental Eucharist was taken from the last of the Hebrew table blessing, the one recited after the meal. The *Birkat Hamazon* is by far the longest of the mealtime blessings, taking two or three minutes to complete. The outline of this prayer was framed by the words of Moses. "When thou hast eaten and art full, then thou shalt bless the Lord thy God for the good land which he hath given thee."[21] It is the only blessing expressly commanded by Torah and therefore occupies a special place of honor in Jewish ritual. They discharged this obligation by blessing 1) the food, and 2) the land, and 3) Jerusalem and the Sanctuary. A fourth benediction was added after the Great Jewish War.

The Eucharistic prayer of the primitive church contained the same series of three thanksgivings as the original "Three Blessings," as it was called in the Talmud, but the material was recast in a Christian mold. The revised table grace has passed into Catholic usage as the "Eucharist," which is simply the Greek word for thanksgiving (*Eucharistia*). Let us view the text of the first century Thanksgiving from *Didache* 10 alongside the modern Jewish Grace after Meal.[22] We have underscored, italicized, and bolded the portions of the two prayers which show the closest correspondence.

---

20. *1 Apology* 65, 66.

21. Deuteronomy 8:10.

22. The *Birkat Hamazon* has been taken from Hayim Donin's *To Pray as a Jew*, 289–93.

Birkat Hamazon	Didache 10
First Blessing: "Blessed art Thou, Lord our God, King of the universe, who in His goodness, grace, loving kindness, and mercy, nourishes the whole world. He gives food to all flesh, for His loving kindness is everlasting. In His great goodness, we have never lacked for food; may we never lack for food <u>for the sake of His great Name</u>. For he nourishes and sustains all. He does good to all, and prepares food **for all his creatures that He created.** *Blessed art Thou, Lord, who provides food for all.*"	"We thank Thee, holy Father, for Thy holy name which Thou didst cause to tabernacle in our hearts, and for the knowledge and faith and immortality which Thou madest known to us through Jesus Thy Servant; to Thee be the glory forever. **Thou, Master almighty, didst create all things** <u>for Thy name's sake</u>; *Thou gavest food and drink to men for enjoyment,*
Second Blessing: "<u>**We thank Thee, Lord our God, for the desirable, good and spacious land**</u> that Thou gave our forefathers as a heritage; for having brought us out of the land of Egypt and redeemed us from slavery; for Thy covenant that Thou sealed in our flesh; for Thy Torah which Thou taught us and Thy statues which Thou made known to us; for the life, the grace and loving kindness that Thou has bestowed on us; and for the food with which Thou constantly feed and sustain us every day, at all times and in every hour. **For everything, Lord our God, we thank Thee and bless Thee;** <u>may Thy name be blessed in the mouth of every living creature at all times and for all time</u>; as it is written: 'When you have eaten and are satisfied, you shall bless the Lord your God for the good land that He has given you.' Blessed art Thou, Lord, for the land and for the food."	<u>**that they might give thanks to Thee**</u>; <u>but to us Thou didst freely give spiritual food and drink and life eternal through Thy Servant.</u> **Before all things we thank Thee that Thou art mighty;** <u>to Thee be the glory forever.</u>

Third Blessing: "Be merciful, Lord our God, to Thy people Israel, to Thy city, Jerusalem, and to Zion, the dwelling place of Thy glory, *to the royal House of David,* Thine anointed, and to the great and holy Temple that was called by Thy name. Our God, our Father, tend us, feed us, sustain us, maintain us, and comfort us. <u>Grant us speedy relief, Lord our God, from all our troubles</u>. And please, Lord our God, let us not need other people's gifts or loans, but only Thy filled and open hand, holy and bountiful. So that we may not ever be shamed or humiliated. **Rebuild Jerusalem, the holy city,** soon in our days. Blessed art Thou, Lord, who in His mercy builds Jerusalem. Amen."	Remember, Lord, Thy Church, <u>To deliver it from all evil</u> and to make it perfect in Thy love, and **gather it from the four winds**, sanctified for Thy kingdom which Thou hast prepared for it; for Thine is the power and the glory forever. Let grace come, and let this world pass away. *Hosanna to the God (Son) of David!"*

There are marked similarities, both in subject matter and actual verbiage, between the two prayers. In the first benediction, we find that the proto-Catholics were not as profuse in praising God for feeding the world as the rabbis. Instead, they focused on the spiritual blessings of the indwelling Name, knowledge, and faith; contrasting the "everlasting" kindness of God in providing for his creation with the "immortality" they had received in Jesus. Both prayers touch on the themes of creation and the Name, and the "food for all His creatures that He created" was changed to "food and drink to men for enjoyment."

In the second blessing, gratitude for giving their forefathers the land of Israel, Torah, circumcision, and food for themselves became appreciation for the "spiritual food and drink and eternal life" freely given through Christ. Both prayers go on to offer an explicit expression of gratitude: "For everything, Lord our God, we thank Thee" became "Before all things we thank Thee."

In the third blessing, the lengthy petition to be merciful to Israel, Jerusalem, Zion, and the holy temple became a simple request to remember the church. Both benedictions refer to David, but the emphasis has shifted from a restoration of the Davidic Kingdom to the purification of the Kingdom of God. The request to rebuild the Holy City was converted into a petition for the ingathering of the holy church. "Grant us speedy relief from all our troubles" was transformed into the request from the Lord's Prayer to "deliver us from all evil."

We have provided six lines of evidence for the theory that a sacred banquet—now discontinued—underlies the Catholic Eucharist. It is astounding to think that the nucleus of the present Mass was born of a simple Jewish supper, but this fact explains much of the terminology and structure of the rite. Let us recap the evidence:

- The four-step structure of the Catholic rite has no foundation in Scripture, but instead represents the normal progression of the Hebrew bread blessing ritual. It was the unanimous testimony of the three evangelists and Paul that Jesus used seven separate acts at the last supper.
- The technical term "Eucharist" has no basis in Scripture. It is clearly derived from the Jewish Grace after Meal, which was known as the Thanksgiving, or *Eucharistia* in Greek. The apostles almost always referred to the New Covenant rite as the "Breaking of Bread" and connected the word "thanksgiving" with mealtime prayers.[23]
- The Catholic Eucharistic prayer was patterned after the *Birkat Hamazon*. Why use a mealtime blessing if it was not an actual meal?
- The *Didache* supplies separate blessings for bread and wine, and instructs them to say the main table grace after they are satiated, all of which accords with normal mealtime customs. The word "filled" in the *Didache* points to an actual meal, not a ceremony.
- The dialogue preceding the Eucharist is clearly derived from the Hebrew invitation to say grace. It cannot be a coincidence that this dialogue is framed in almost exactly the same language as the Jewish *Birkat Zumun*. As Gregory Dix observed, this fact alone would be enough to identify the Christian Eucharistic prayer with the *Birkat Hamazon*.[24]
- The Pharisaic prohibition against eating with the uncircumcised became the Catholic rule forbidding the unbaptized to sup with the baptized. The catechumens were dismissed (Latin *missa*) before the primitive thanksgiving banquet and later before the liturgical Eucharist.

---

23. "Forbidding to marry, and commanding to abstain from meats, which God hath created to be received *with thanksgiving* of them which believe and know the truth. For every creature of God is good, and nothing to be refused, if it is received *with thanksgiving*, for it is sanctified by the word of God and prayer" (1 Timothy 4:3–5, emphasis mine).

24. *Shape*, 127.

The Lord's Supper

The *agape* or, as it was usually called, the Lord's Supper, was not the apostolic love-feast celebrated by Peter and Jude.[25] It was, instead, what remained of the primitive thanksgiving meal after the liturgical elements had been extracted. The bread ritual at the beginning of the banquet was combined with the cup of blessing and the Grace after Meal to form the sacramental Eucharist. Everything that lay between—basically the meal—became the *agape*.

The Lord's Supper remained a corporate affair of the church. They were held under the auspices of an elder or bishop, and the rule that barred catechumens from eating with the baptized was observed. It was a solemn occasion, eaten in silence unless the presbyter expounded on the Scriptures or asked someone to sing.[26] Everyone at the table received bread from the elder, as they had at the primitive thanksgiving meal, but this was "blessed bread," carefully distinguished in their minds from the bread of the Eucharist. The *Apostolic Tradition* explains the difference. "And they shall take from the hand of the bishop one piece of a loaf before each takes his own bread, for this is 'blessed' bread, but it is not the Eucharist as is the Body of the Lord."[27]

We can hardly do better than to quote Tertullian at this point. He is taking great pains in this passage to emphasize that the Lord's Supper is a religious gathering and not an occasion for debauchery.

> The participants, before reclining, first taste of prayer to God. As much is eaten as satisfies the cravings of hunger; as much is drunk as befits the chaste. They say it is enough, as those who remember that even during the night they have to worship God; they talk as those who know that the Lord is one of their auditors. After manual ablution, and the bringing in of lights, each [or perhaps "one"] is asked to stand forth and sing, as he can, a hymn to God—either one from the holy scriptures or one of his own composing—a proof of the measure of our drinking. As the feast commenced with pray, so with prayer it is closed.[28]
>
> —*First Apology* 39

25. 2 Peter 2:13; Jude 12.

26. The tractate *Derekh Eretz* gives the following rule governing formal Jewish meals. "It is forbidden to talk during the meal, lest the food be swallowed the wrong way."

27. *Ap Trad* 26.

28. We know the exact wording of the concluding prayer. It is an abridgement of the Grace after Meal. "Thou art blessed, O Lord, who nourished me from my youth, who givest food to all flesh. Fill our hearts with joy and gladness, that having always what is sufficient for us, we may abound unto every good work, in Christ Jesus our Lord, through whom glory, honor, and power to Thee forever. Amen" (*Ap Con* 7.49).

A painting of the Lord's Supper—known as the Breaking of Bread—has been preserved in the Catacomb of Priscilla. It lies directly above a *triclinium* chamber carved out of the rock, couches and all. This is one of the oldest catacombs in Rome, and the so-called Greek chapel, where the *Fractio Panis* fresco was found, belongs to its earliest phase. Even the fact that the inscriptions are in Greek attest to its high antiquity. The mural, which dates from the second half of the second century, was miraculously preserved by a thick crust of stalactites until they were removed by chemical reagents in 1893.

The fresco shows six men and a veiled woman behind a table, reclining on sloped couches. The diners rest on their left arms and reach for food with their right. The presiding elder, a bearded man, is sitting upright in the place of the host on the left. His arms are stretched out straight, holding a small loaf, and his head is thrown back, depicting the recitation of the blessing over the bread.[29] There is a round table in the foreground set with a two-handled cup—used in the hand-washing ritual—a plate with five loaves of bread, and another with two fishes. The five loaves and two fishes connect the supper with the miracle of the loaves.[30] Several large wicker baskets of bread are sitting on each side of the table.

29. The elevation of the bread, an act that regained significance in medieval times, derived from the raising of the *matzah* at the Passover supper.

30. Matthew 14:19.

8

The Introduction and Acceptance of Paul

AD 144 to AD 155

> Just as our dear brother Paul
> also wrote to you with the wisdom that God gave him....
> His letters contain some things that are hard to understand,
> which ignorant and unstable people distort,
> as they do the other Scriptures, to their own destruction.
>
> —2 Peter 3:15–16 NIV

The *Ekklesia Katholika* began as a curious blend of Palestinian Christianity and Pharisaic Judaism. Zacchaeus the founder spent the decade of the sixties writing their faux Scriptures and laying the foundation of the sect. Some of the more burdensome obligations—like circumcision and the dietary laws—were discarded in the seventies and eighties. They continued to inch away from the Law and move closer to the theology of Paul, but he was still unknown to the sectarians. They justified the shift in doctrine by taking refuge in symbolism and allegory. The catalyst which finally brought Paul out into the open was a reformer named Marcion.

Marcion was born and raised in Sinope, a thriving Greek settlement on the southern shore of the Black Sea.[1] The town has a beautiful natural harbor and, in antiquity, it was the foremost port on the *Pontus Euxinus*. Marcion became a ship owner and, by all accounts, a wealthy merchant.[2] His father was the elder of the local Catholic congregation, and it is safe to assume they gathered for worship in his home. He was thus brought up in the sect and thoroughly versed in its Scriptures, doctrine, and traditions. The leading authority on Marcion, Adolf von Harnack, believed that Marcion and his family must have come out of Judaism, so thoroughly Jewish was his exegesis of the Hebrew Scriptures.[3] Harnack did not realize that Marcion was simply a typical Catholic of that era.

Sometime in the 130s, Marcion stumbled across a collection of Paul's epistles in his home town. We can only speculate where he found them, but there is no compelling reason to look elsewhere. If there was any place where Pauline Christians were thick on the ground, it was Asia Minor.[4] Peter had addressed his first epistle to "the strangers scattered throughout Pontus, Galatia..." clear back in the sixth decade of the first century, and the Roman administrator Pliny tells us how numerous Christians had become by AD 112.[5]

Reading Paul was, for Marcion, a life-altering experience, and he began to see the gospel in an entirely new light. Martin Luther would have the same epiphany 1400 years later. One fact was glaringly obvious: The Christianity he grew up believing had no connection with the Pauline missions. The friends he worshipped with had never seen Paul's writings or even heard the name of the apostle. It was all very unsettling, and Marcion couldn't help wondering where they fit in.

The key that unlocked the puzzle was the epistle to the Galatians. After reading Galatians—and 2 Corinthians—Marcion was able to correctly guess some of the history of the New Testament. The message of Jesus Christ had been corrupted by "false apostles and Jewish evangelists" and only Paul, who had received a direct revelation from God, had grasped the spiritual essence of the gospel. Even the twelve apostles had not made a complete break with their Jewish heritage. "For [they maintain] that the apostles intermingled

---

1. *Against Marcion* 1.1.
2. *Against Marcion* 3.6.
3. *Marcion*, p. 15.
4. One of Paul's closest helpers in the gospel, Aquila, was a native of Pontus (Acts 18:2–3).
5. 1 Peter 1:1; *Pliny Letter No. 96*.

the things of the law with the words of the Savior."[6] This makes little sense to us today, knowing the decision that was reached in Acts 15, but Marcion had never seen the Acts of the Apostles. He saw himself as a reformer, restoring Gentile Christianity to the purity of its Pauline foundation. "For they allege that Marcion did not so much innovate on the rule [of faith] by his separation of the law and gospel, as to restore it after it had been previously adulterated."[7]

Marcion set down his theology in a little work Tertullian called the *Antitheses* (meaning contradictions).[8] This book contrasted, in a point-by-point fashion, the commandments of the Law with the precepts of the gospel. The following are typical examples of Marcion's contradictions. While Moses had legislated an eye for an eye; Christ advocated unconditional forgiveness. Joshua had conquered Canaan with violence and cruelty; Christ stressed mercy and compassion. Elisha had children eaten by bears; Christ said, "Let the little children come unto me." Marcion rejected the orthodox tendency to allegorize the Hebrew Scriptures, insisting what was written must stand on its own merits. One only needs to read Papias, the *Epistle of Barnabas*, the *Shepherd of Hermas*, or even Justin Martyr to see why he took this position. The use of allegory by Catholic apologists had reached utterly preposterous proportions by the second quarter of the second century. Marcion could not reconcile the two covenants and insisting that the God of Israel could not possibly be the Father of Jesus Christ, he rejected all thirty-nine books of the Old Testament.

Marcion's Bible consisted of two parts: Gospel and Apostle. The *Apostolicon* was a collection of the following ten epistles of Paul: Galatians, Romans, 1 and 2 Corinthians, 1 and 2 Thessalonians, Colossians, Philippians, Philemon and Ephesians. Marcion carefully combed through these letters and removed anything that pertained to the old covenant. The three pastoral epistles—1 and 2 Timothy, and Titus—were probably never seen by Marcion, and his followers added them later to the *Apostolikon*.

Marcion then turned his attention to the Gospel. He sought to reestablish the authentic text of the Gospel, which had also been Judaized and corrupted. He chose the Gospel of Luke, probably because Luke was a Gentile and the evangelist most closely associated with Paul.[9] The Gospel of John, arguably the least friendly to the Jews, might have been more logical, but it was not known to him. Matthew, the traditional Gospel of the

6. *Against Heresies* 3.2.2.
7. *Against Marcion* 1.20.
8. *Against Marcion* 4.1.
9. *Against Marcion* 4.2.

proto-Catholics and the one he grew up with, would have been irredeemably polluted. Marcion used both the pen and the eraser in editing and emending.[10] He removed the opening chapters relating to the birth and infancy of Jesus, all references to the Hebrew prophets or Messianic testimonia, and every place where Jesus participated in the Passover or showed respect to the Law.

Marcion journeyed to Ephesus—the Vatican of that era—where he was given a hearing and rebuffed. Around AD 140, he sailed on to Rome.[11] Marcion spent the first few years in Rome writing the *Antithesis*[12] and preparing the *Evangelicon* and the *Apostolikon*. He made a large financial contribution to the church, and gained respect by the force of his intellect and personal piety. He then asked Pius, the bishop of Rome, for a formal hearing.

In AD 144, Marcion stood before a gathering of the Roman presbyters and took as his point of departure the Parable of the Good and Corrupt Tree. "For a good tree bringeth forth not corrupt fruit; neither doth a corrupt tree bring forth good fruit."[13] By his analysis, the God of creation and Abraham was the corrupt tree, and the Father of Jesus Christ was the good tree. His listeners must have been in shock! He was attacking the very foundation of their faith, slandering Moses, and separating Christ from the Law and Prophets. Marcion was sharply rejected, expelled from fellowship, and his 200,000 sesterces returned. The year of his excommunication is unusually secure for this nebulous period of church history. It was burned into the memory of the Marcionites as the beginning of their reformed church.[14]

The Church Responds to Paul

This was the first time Paul had been openly debated in Catholic circles. We have no record of their initial response, but we can guess. Justin Martyr,

---

10. Tertullian had a picturesque way of describing the emendations and deletions: "What Pontic mouse ever had such gnawing powers as he who has gnawed the Gospels to pieces" (*Against Marcion* 1.1)?

11. *Against Marcion* 1.19 According to Tertullian, Marcion was a heretic in the era of Antoninus Pius, who began to reign in AD 138.

12. Although the *Antithesis* is a lost work, we do know the opening line. "O wonder beyond wonders, rapture, power, and amazement is it, that one can say nothing at all about the gospel, nor even conceive of it, nor compare it with anything."

13. This statement is found in both the traditional Gospel of the sectarians (Matthew 7:17) and the new Gospel favored by Marcion (Luke 6:43).

14. "Now, from Tiberius to Antoninus Pius there are about 115 years and 6½ months. Just such an interval do they place between Christ and Marcion" (*Against Marcion* 1.19).

an orthodox teacher living in Rome, wrote about the extraordinary success of the Marcionites a few years after the excommunication. "And he, by the aid of the devils, has caused many of every nation to speak blasphemies."[15] Tertullian confirmed the phenomenal growth of the sect fifty years later. "Marcion's heretical teaching has filled the whole world."[16] Such was the power of Paul's spirituality. The Roman presbyters themselves saw the passion aroused in their own congregations by the Apostle. After reading the *Didache*, the *Epistle of Barnabas*, and the other literature of the second century church, it is not difficult to see why. They are dry and lifeless compared to the magnificent language and brilliant insights of Paul.

Admiration for the new apostle spread like wildfire. One of the most interesting epigraphic monuments of the ancient Church is the Epitaph of Abercius. The author was the bishop of Hieropolis—to be distinguished from Hierapolis—and he had travelled the length of the empire to confirm his faith.[17] At the age of seventy-two, sometime late in the reign of Marcus Aurelius (AD 161 to AD 180), he wrote his own epitaph.

> The citizen of an eminent city, this monument I made
> whilst still living, that there I might have in time a resting place for my body.
> My name is Abercius, the disciple of the holy shepherd
> who feeds his flocks of sheep on the mountains and in the plains,
> who has great eyes that see everywhere.
> This shepherd taught me the Book worthy of belief.
> It is he who sent me to Rome to behold the royal majesty
> and to see the queen arrayed in golden vestments and golden sandals.
> There also I saw the people famous for their seal.
> And I saw the plains of Syria and all its cities, and also Nisibis
> when I crossed the Euphrates. Everywhere I met brethren in agreement,
> having Paul [as my companion] . . . . .

The grassroots enthusiasm generated by Paul is also highlighted in the following incident. An Asian presbyter got so carried away with passion for the apostle that he composed an apocryphal tale in his honor. *The Acts of Paul and Thecla*, as it is known, embellished the Iconium mission with details of a beautiful virgin, her conversion, and her steadfastness. After being removed from office, the man admitted he did it "out of love for Paul" and to "augment Paul's fame. A date of AD 180 cannot be far off the mark.[18]

15. *1 Apology* 26.
16. *Against Marcion* 5.19.
17. Avircius Marcellus is mentioned by Eusebius in his *History of the Church* 5.16.3.
18. Tertullian, *On Baptism* 17. Tertullian wrote around AD 200, which provides us with a *terminus ad quem* for the *Acts of Paul and Thecla*.

The presbyter even provided the Catholic world with a physical description of their new celebrity. "And he saw Paul coming, a man small in size, baldheaded, bandy-legged, well-built, with eyebrows meeting, rather long-nosed, full of grace."

The Acts of the Scillitan Martyrs describes the trial and execution of twelve Christians in modern Tunisia. It is a court record dated July 19, AD 180. During the proceedings, the Christians were asked what was in their bag. Speratus told the proconsul that it contained "Books and letters of Paul, a righteous man." Would the "books of Paul" be the Acts of the Apostles?

How do we know Marcion was the source of the Pauline corpus? It turns out that he left his literary fingerprints on the letters in the form of a distinctive prologue. These short introductions are known as the Marcionite or Old Latin prologues because they were still attached to the epistles in the fourth century Latin translation, the Vulgate. They all follow the same basic outline. The prologues begin by giving the nationality of the recipients, notes they had received the gospel from Paul, declares they had been let astray by false apostles, and concludes by giving the place of composition. The preface to the Galatian letter is typical of them all.

> The Galatians are Greeks. They accepted the word of truth first from the apostle, but after his departure were tempted by false apostles to turn to the law and circumcision. These the apostle recalls to the faith of the truth, writing to them from Ephesus.

The first Catholics to handle these letters, not being familiar with the material, did not recognize the heading for what they were. Consequently, when they made copies for neighboring congregations, they were careful to duplicate them exactly as they had received them, headings and all. The prologues tell us not only *where* they got the epistles, but also *when* they entered the Catholic canon.

The prologues have long been held to be Marcionite in origin because of their *content*. The Pauline churches had been seduced by pseudo-apostles preaching the Law and circumcision. But there is another, even more compelling, reason. The *order* of Paul's letters to the churches, as understood by the author of the headings, happens to be the same order they are found in the *Apostolikon*. Statistically speaking, the odds of this being a coincidence are close to zero.

Paul is Examined—AD 144 to 155

Marcion was not the only one to possess the riches of Paul. We know the Egyptian Gnostics had several of his epistles in the early decades of the second century. Hippolytus, in his *Refutation of all Heresies*, has preserved excerpts from the writings of Basilides, a renowned Alexandrian theologian who taught "in the time of Hadrian," AD 117 to AD 138. Basilides was conversant with at least four of Paul's epistles: 1 Corinthians, 2 Corinthians, Romans, and Ephesians.[19]

One passage in particular—1 Corinthians 2:9—shows up in an astonishing number of Catholic and Gnostic manuscripts. "But as it is written, eye hath not seen, nor ear heard, neither have entered into the heart of man, the things which God hath prepared for them that love him." In 1945, fifty-two scrolls were discovered in an earthenware jar near the village of Nag Hammadi in Upper Egypt. They were written in Coptic, the language of Egyptian Christianity. The texts included the *Gospel of Thomas*, the *Acts of Peter*, the *Dialogue of the Saviour*, and the *Prayer of the Apostle Paul*, all of which contain variants of this saying.[20]

> **1 Clement**—An anonymous letter sent from the Roman church to their Greek compatriots at Corinth. It was occasioned by a leadership crisis, and the mother church, called "ancient," was offering advice to the young congregation at Corinth. It is dated from a mention of "sudden and repeated calamities"—taken to mean a persecution under Domitian—but it fits far better with literature in the middle of the second century. 1 Clement was considered quasi-canonical and read in the churches for centuries.

The Catholic Fathers of the 140s and 150s were also partial to this passage. It is cited in the *Memoirs* of Hegisippus, *1 Clement*, *2 Clement*, the *Martyrdom of Polycarp*, and the prefix to the Ethiopic version of the *Epistle of the Apostles*. Not one of them credits Paul as the source. The *Clementine Homilies* was redacted during this time into something like its present form. The editor includes the following statement in a debate between Clement and Appion. "For it has been well said *by someone*, 'Evil communications corrupt good manners.'"[21] That *someone*, of course, was Paul. This direct citation of 1 Corinthians 15:33 was not attributed to the blessed apostle; no, it was cited anonymously.

---

19. *Refutation* 7.13–15.

20. The verse is also cited in the Book of Baruch, the Acts of the Holy Apostle Thomas, and the Manichaen Fragment M 789 from Turfan.

21. *Homilies* 4.24.

This perfectly illustrates how Paul was treated between the expulsion of Marcion AD 144 and his admittance to the canon circa AD 155. He was *persona non grata* for the entire decade. The literature written during this period shows a reoccurring pattern of citing Paul's epistles and appropriating his theology, but without acknowledging his authorship. You could say that Paul had made it to the door, but he had not yet been invited into the church.

The *First Epistle of Clement* was written at the end of the transitional period. Paul is twice mentioned by name, but only one of his epistles, 1 Corinthians, is cited as Scripture. Nevertheless, the author uses Pauline imagery, metaphors and language at least half a dozen times without naming the source. In chapter 34, we find the newly popular verse from 1 Corinthians: "Eye hath not seen, nor ear heard . . . . . ." In chapter 47, they are admonished to "Take up *the* epistle of the blessed apostle Paul," undoubtedly referring to 1 Corinthians but indicating they were not aware of the second letter to the Corinthians. The author was familiar with the Roman epistle as well.

> **Ignatius and his epistles**—The most controversial figure in the entire field of patristics is Ignatius. He was allegedly the bishop of Antioch around the turn of the first century, but his seven letters do not appear in the literature until AD 155. The storyline is that he was arrested by the Romans, is being taken to Rome for trial, and along the way he writes to six churches and one fellow bishop. The letters are a steady stream of clichés, mixed metaphors, and silly symbolism. Pseudo-Ignatius tries to mimic Paul and sound profound, but he lacks the intellect to pull it off. The letters are plagued with anachronisms, which betray their mid-second century origin.

The seven Ignatian letters were also written in that uneasy decade after Marcion's excommunication. The author's command of the Pauline corpus was astonishingly thin. Pseudo-Ignatius was very conversant with 1 Corinthians and quotes from it liberally, but he never credits Paul. Some scholars make the case that he also knew Ephesians and Romans, but it's weak. Paul is mentioned by name in just two passages of Ignatius. In the *Epistle of Ignatius to the Ephesians*, he writes: "You are initiates of the same mysteries as our saintly and renowned Paul of blessed memory (may I be found to have walked in his footsteps when I come to God!), who has remembered you in Christ Jesus in every one of his letters."[22] In actual fact, Paul did not mention the Ephesians "in every one of his letters," but the statement would make more sense if they only had a couple of Paul's epistles.

Not everyone in Rome got on board the Pauline express. Certainly Pius, the bishop who presided over Marcion's hearing, did not favor the

---

22. *Ig to Eph* 12.

questionable new books, and acceptance of Paul was never going to happen on his watch. Pius held the reins of power until his death in AD 155, which turns out to be a key date in the whole transition.[23] Even Justin Martyr, surely one of the more progressive Catholics of that era, does not explicitly quote from the Apostle to the Gentiles. Living at Rome, he would have seen the whole drama play out before his very eyes.

We may also count Hegesippus among the Catholic literati who did not join the reformation. The sixth century writer Stephanus Gobarus has preserved a fragment of the second century historian.

> The good things prepared for the righteous, eye has not seen nor ear has heard nor have they entered into the human heart. Hegisippus, an ancient writer who belonged to the apostolic age, says in the fifth book of his *Memoirs*, on what basis I do not know: "This is said in a twisted manner, and those who use this saying are liars, since both the Holy Scriptures and the Lord said, 'Blessed are your eyes, which see, and your ears, which hear.'"
> —Photius, *Bibliotheca* codex 232

The passage he had trouble with is our old friend 1 Corinthians 2:9, although the first and third sentences have been transposed. Hegesippus strenuously objects to those who accept this verse—and by extension its author—because in his mind it contradicts the words of Jesus from the rock-solid Gospel of Matthew. He had some harsh words for those who used this saying—meaning Paul's supporters. He called them "liars."

Polycarp Gives the Imprimatur

The leading Christian clergyman in the middle of the second century was Polycarp of Smyrna. There is no exact modern equivalent of his spiritual position inasmuch as ecclesiastical authority was more personal and less institutional in AD 150. Nevertheless, the eighty-year old bishop commanded great respect in the Catholic world and his words carried enormous weight. Polycarp derived his preeminence from great age, his eldership of Smyrna—the historic hub of the movement—and from his alleged relationship with

---

23. We note that Pius' brother wrote the *Shepherd of Hermas* between AD 145 and AD 150, and it does not display the slightest knowledge of Paul. This religious allegory follows Hermas, a freed slave, as he is led through five visions and given 12 mandates of conduct. The book is a call to repentance, and emphasizes morality over theology. Deemed to be almost canonical and read in some of the churches, it was one of the most popular books in Christendom for centuries.

the apostle John. He was martyred in AD 156, and the mob looking on was heard to shout: "This is the teacher of Asia, the father of the Christians."[24]

> **Polycarp**—The Catholic bishop of Smyrna in the middle years of the second century. He is the key link in one of the chains of apostolic succession. Only one of his writings has survived, along with an account of his martyrdom in AD 156. His *Epistle to the Philippians* is a confusing jumble of short citations, including extracts from almost all of Paul's letters. As the *de facto* leader of the Church, Polycarp was signaling his endorsement of the Apostle and, sure enough, after AD 155, Paul shows up everywhere.

This background is necessary to an understanding of the epistle he sent to the Philippian Catholics around AD 155. This letter—*Polycarp's Epistle to the Philippians*—has no discernable purpose except to signal his endorsement of Paul. Twice he calls him "blessed." All of Marcion's *Apostolikon* is represented in this little missive except Colossians and Philemon, and it contains the first patristic citations of 1 and 2 Timothy. He quotes or alludes to the Pauline corpus no less than twenty times, and many of these citations are clumsy, barely fitting the context. He finally comes out toward the end of the letter and flatly declares one of Paul's sayings to be Scripture. "For I trust that ye are well versed in the sacred scriptures, and that nothing is hid from you; but to me this privilege is not yet granted. It is declared then in these *scriptures*, 'Be ye angry, and sin not,' and 'Let not the sun go down upon your wrath.'"[25]

What Polycarp designates as "Scripture" are the two parts of Ephesians 4:26. In the first half of that verse, Paul loosely paraphrases the Septuagint rendering of Psalms 4:4. When he said that they were "well versed in the Scriptures" and "nothing was hid from them," Polycarp was making sure they got the subtle message. The new Epistle to the Ephesians was to be considered just as inspired and canonical as the old, venerated book of Psalms.

That same year, AD 155, Polycarp traveled to Rome to meet with his counterpart in the capital. We cannot help but wonder if the aged Polycarp did not offer some guidance and counsel to Ancetus, the young man who had just been installed as bishop. We know they discussed the differences in their Easter observances, and it is easy to speculate that Polycarp put his weight behind the growing chorus of Paulinists. Possibly Polycarp had been waiting for new, like-minded leadership in Rome before publicly voicing his support. The Roman church had inspected the letters for a full decade by this time, and many of her brightest minds had cited them anonymously.

---

24. *Mar Polycarp* 12.
25. *Polycarp to Phil* 12, emphasis mine.

Polycarp now validates them with his stamp of approval. We could say that the official acceptance of Paul by the *Ekklesia Katholika* began that year.

Polycarp also began to connect the Catholic communities in Greece and Asia Minor to the New Testament churches planted by Paul. Enough time had lapsed since the Catholics had established a church at Philippi that he could assert the following without raising any eyebrows. "But I have neither seen nor heard of any such thing among you, in the midst of whom the blessed Paul labored, and who are commended in the beginning of his epistle."[26] Although Polycarp pretends they were the fruit of Paul's labor and acquainted with his apostolic letter, he unwittingly lets the cat out of the bag. "He, when among you, accurately and steadfastly taught the word of truth in the presence of those who were then alive. And when absent from you, he wrote you a letter, which, if you carefully study, you will find to be the means of building you up in that faith which has been given you." This is terribly awkward language for those who, if they actually were the planting of Paul, would have known that letter from beginning to end.

Is it realistic—or even possible—for a sect that started out so virulently opposed to Paul to reverse itself so quickly? An example pulled from more recent times proves that it is. Joseph Smith, the Mormon prophet, secretly began to take "celestial wives" early in the 1840s, but it was not pronounced an official doctrine of the movement until 1852. It was greatly resisted at first, and many Latter Day Saints left the fold. Nevertheless, a plurality of wives quickly became one of the distinctive tenets of the new American sect. Just a few decades later, because of continual troubles with the law and a desire for statehood, they began to back away from the practice. In 1890, President Wilford Woodruff published a manifesto repudiating plural marriage, and the Saints began to censure members who did not fall in line. They have been outspoken in their opposition ever since, even providing legal assistance to prosecute fundamentalists still living the Principle, as they call it. The Mormons thus managed to move into and out of a very controversial teaching within a span of only 50 years.

---

26. *Polycarp to Phil* 3.

9

The Evolution of the Catholic Canon

AD 60 to AD 200

> All scripture is given by inspiration of God, and is profitable
> for doctrine, for reproof, for correction,
> for instruction in righteousness:
> that the man of God may be perfect,
> thoroughly furnished unto all good works.
>
> —2 Timothy 3:16, 17

It is an accepted canon among New Testament scholars that there were no formal Christian Scriptures until Marcion. It was his challenge in the middle of the second century that forced the Great Church to assess the treasures they had been holding. Nothing could be further from the truth. The sectarians have always had their *litera scripta*, writings which they considered inspired and authoritative. Today, however, no one recognizes those writings for what they were, and they have been shelved in the museum of patristics as objects of curiosity.

The Bible of the first century proto-Catholics was nothing like any current Bible. When the pseudo-apostles left the fold, only a handful of New Testament books were in existence, and the few Pauline letters beginning to circulate were automatically rejected. The Gospel according to Matthew was the only genuine apostolic artifact they carried out with them. The *Didache* thus refers to Matthew as "the Gospel," "the Gospel of our Lord," and "His Gospel."[1] For half a century, it was the only written account they had of the life and teachings of Jesus Christ.

The false apostles manufactured their own New Testament. They penned a romantic version of the Acts of the Apostles which centered on Peter. They fabricated two epistles addressed to the apostle James. They wrote a volume of administrative procedures and devotional practices known as the *Didache*, something the apostles did not feel the need to codify. They later developed interpretational guidelines for the Old Law in the *Epistle of Barnabas*.

The Hebrew Scriptures made up the bulk of the Catholic canon until the end of the second century. The proto-Catholic teachers took over and used the Hebrew writings the same way as the first disciples. They were the "holy scriptures" Timothy had known from his youth.[2] The sectarians were very familiar with all the major books of the Old Testament, and quotations from the Law, the Prophets, and the Writings abound in the Church Fathers. It was thus entirely natural for the second century Hegesippus to refer to his canon as "the Law, the Prophets, and the Lord."[3]

Another class of books cited with the full weight of canonical authority was the Apocrypha. This is somewhat surprising as neither the Jewish rabbis nor the Christian apostles regarded them as Scripture. The Greek translation of the Old Testament, the Septuagint, contained these fifteen books and embellishments, and they were very popular in Palestine at the beginning of the Christian era. When the rabbinical authorities closed the Hebrew canon around AD 90, the Apocrypha was not included.[4] They limited the sacred writings to only twenty-four books; essentially the same as the Protestant Old Testament.[5] Bucking the consensus of both rabbinic and apostolic tradition, the false apostles brought these books into the church they founded.

When Jerome was commissioned by Pope Damascus I in AD 382 to produce a definitive Latin translation of the Bible, he started with the Greek Septuagint, which included the intertestamental books. By being included

---

1. *Didache* 8, 11, 15.

2. 2 Timothy 3:15. Also, the Bereans in Acts 17:11 who "searched the scriptures daily" were checking Paul's message against the Hebrew Bible.

3. *Eccl Hist* 4.22. We find the same Old Testament-laden canon in the *Didascalia Apostolorum* 2: "And if not, sit at home and read the Law, and the Book of Kings and the Prophets, and the Gospel the fulfilment of these."

4. m. *Sanhedrin* 10.1e; *Sanhedrin* 100b.

5. The Jews combine some of the books differently. The twelve minor prophets are all considered one book, for example. To further the confusion, sometimes the *Tanakh* (Hebrew Scriptures) were combined into twenty-two books—the number of letters in the Hebrew alphabet—and sometimes twenty-four.

in the translation, the Apocrypha was transmitted *en bloc* to the Vulgate, which became the standard Latin Bible of the Church. It has been enshrined in the Catholic canon ever since.[6]

> **Agrapha or Logion**—Agrapha, meaning "non-written," are sayings attributed to the Lord not found in the Bible. The *Clementine Homilies* contains 6 agrapha, the *Epistle of Barnabas* has 8, and *1* and *2 Clement* have 5 each. They disappear once the *Ekklesia Katholika* adopts the New Testament. There is even an agraphon in the New Testament: Acts 20:35.

The early Catholic presbyters were very partial to agrapha; sayings attributed to the Lord but not found in the canonical Gospels. They are also called logion. The *Epistle of Barnabas* contains eight of these pithy little proverbs, with the following being a typical specimen. "In like manner He points to the cross of Christ in another prophet who saith, 'And when shall these things be accomplished?' And the Lord saith, 'When a tree shall be bent down, and rise again, and when blood shall flow out of wood.'"[7] Genuine agrapha tend to have this same enigmatic, paradoxical quality about them.

The proto-Catholics had amassed a large body of agrapha and oral traditions by the middle of the second century. Papias, the presbyter of Hierapolis circa AD 130, collected those circulating among the churches of Asia Minor and set them down in a book called the *Expositions of the Sayings of the Lord*. The preface to this work underscores the great weight he put on the oral tradition.

> But I shall not be unwilling to put down, along with my interpretations, whatsoever instructions I received with care at any time from the presbyters, and stored up with care in my memory, assuring you at the same time of their truth. For I did not, like the multitude, take pleasure in those who spoke much, but in those who taught the truth; nor in those who related strange commandments, but in those who related the commandments given by the Lord to the faith, and which are derived from Truth itself. If ever anyone came who had been a follower of the presbyters, I inquired into the words of the presbyters, what Andrew or Peter or Philip or Thomas or James or John or Matthew or any other of the Lord's disciples had said, and what Aristion and

---

6. The Douay-Rheims Bible includes the following apocryphal books: 1 and 2 Maccabees, Tobit, Judith, the Wisdom of Solomon, Ecclesiasticus, Baruch (including the Letter of Jeremiah), the additions to the Book of Daniel (Prayer of Azariah, Susanna, Bel and the Dragon), and several additional chapters to the Book of Esther. Only three have been rejected by the Roman church: 1 and 2 Esdras, and the Prayer of Manasseh.

7. *Ep Barnabas* 12.

the presbyter John, the Lord's disciples, were saying. For I did not think that information from books would help me so much as the utterances of a living and surviving voice.
—*History of the Church* 3.39

Unfortunately, the text of the *Expositions* has not survived the ages. However, we have the testimony of Eusebius, who had read it, and he was not impressed. "He [Papias] seems to have been a man of very small intelligence, to judge from his book." The Hierapolitan elder is our first witness to the Gospel of Mark.[8]

The Pathway to Paul

The Scriptures employed in the *Epistle of Barnabas* are a fair representative of the Catholic canon in the first half of the second century. The eminent authority Adolf von Harnack dated this work to AD 131. Although it contains almost one hundred citations, the author does not display any knowledge of the New Testament beyond the Gospel of Matthew. He cites the Hebrew canon extensively, using the Septuagint version. This Greek translation includes the apocrypha, and pseudo-Barnabas invests the *Wisdom of Solomon*, *1* and *2 Enoch*, and *2 Baruch* with the full authority of Scripture. Finally, the *Epistle of Barnabas* is peppered throughout with agrapha.

The most noteworthy feature of *Barnabas* is what it lacks. There is not a single reference to Paul or his fourteen epistles. And, if you carefully read Papias' gallery of presbyters who came before him, there is no Paul. He left out the apostle who had brought the gospel to Asia in the first place. An astonishing "oversight," to say the least, one that Pauline Christians would never have made.

As we have learned, none of the Catholic presbyters before Marcion knew of Paul other than in his guise as Simon Magus. These men devoted plenty of space to such minor figures as Job, Jonah, and Zechariah, but not one of them ever acknowledged Paul, the apostle who wrote 50 percent of the New Testament by book count. The following list is not meant to be complete, but it does illustrate the astonishing number of first and early second century Catholic writings which are absent Paul.[9]

- *The Epistle of Peter to James*
- *The Epistle of Clement to James*

8. *Eccl Hist* 3.39.

9. *1 Clement* and the Ignatian letters should be dated AD 150 to AD 155, as discussed in chapter 14.

- *The Recognitions of Clement*
- *The Homilies of Clement*
- *The Didache*
- *Second Clement*
- *The Epistle of Barnabas*
- *The Apology of Aristides*
- *Peri Pascha* (*On the Passover*)
- *The fragments of Papias*
- *The writings of Hegisippus*
- *The Shepherd of Hermas*
- Justin Martyr's *First Apology*
- Justin Martyr's *Second Apology*
- *Dialogue with Trypho the Jew*

Only a couple of these writings can be dated with any degree of accuracy, but it is enough to establish a benchmark. The *Shepherd of Hermas* was, according to the *Muratorian Canon*, written when Pius was bishop of Rome, or between AD 140 to AD 154. The pre-Pauline Justin Martyr wrote extensively in the middle of the second century, both before and after AD 150. Therefore, with nothing but the literary evidence at hand, we could say that Paul was not accepted by the *Ekklesia Katholika* until after AD 150.

The letters of Paul had been in circulation for almost 90 years by this time. The New Testament Christians, who also began with just the Hebrew Scriptures, eagerly embraced the wisdom and solid teachings of Paul. They shared his epistles by passing them around, a practice Paul readily encouraged. "And when this epistle is read among you, cause that it be read also in the church of the Laodiceans, and that ye likewise read the letter from Laodicea."[10] The inspired quality of his handiwork was quickly recognized by the church, and Peter himself considered them Scripture. "Even as our beloved brother Paul, also according to the wisdom given unto him hath written unto you; as also in all his epistles, speaking in them of these things; in which are some things hard to be understood, which they that are unlearned and unstable wrest [twist], as they do also the *other* scriptures, unto their own destruction."[11]

---

10. Colossians 4:16.
11. 2 Peter 3:15–16, emphasis mine.

The Roman heresiologist Hippolytus (c. AD 215) is a rich gold mine of early Pauline texts. He takes us back to the early years of the second century. Hippolytus had personally read many of the Gnostic tracts, and preserved little snippets in his work *The Refutation of all Heresies*. We learn that one sect, the Naassenes, possessed the epistles to the Ephesians, Romans, and 1 and 2 Corinthians.[12] A lesser known Gnostic sect, the Peratae, considered 1 Corinthians to be "Scripture."[13] It is difficult to position these sectarians in either time or in space.[14]

> **Valentinus**—The most influential Gnostic of the second century left a huge mark on the *Ekklesia Katholika*. Valentinus grew up in cosmopolitan Alexandria before the Catholics had gained a foothold in Egypt. He was thus exposed to a wider range of Christian doctrine and apostolic writings than was available in Catholic circles. Valentinus moved to Rome in the late 140s, and was welcomed as a brother in Christ by the Catholic community. He even ran, unsuccessfully, for the office of the bishop. Valentinus introduced the Gospel of John to the Roman church and many exotic doctrines including a primitive Trinity, the Logos Christology, and the Real Presence in the Eucharist.

We are on firmer ground when it comes to the two great Egyptian theologians, Basilides and Valentinus. They were at the peak of their influence in the second quarter of the second century. Hippolytus cites several passages from the *Exegetics* of Basilides, including paraphrases from Ephesians, Romans, and 1 and 2 Corinthians.[15] It is clear that the epistles of Paul were *bona fide* Scripture to Basilides and his followers.

The other Alexandrian Gnostic, Valentinus, had his own claim of apostolic succession—not to Peter but to the apostle Paul. He boasted that his instructor, a man named Theudas, had been a disciple of Paul.[16] Valentinus was familiar with the same universe of Pauline texts as the Naassenes and Basilides, and he possessed Colossians as well.[17] Decades before anyone in the Catholic Church had ever heard of Paul, the Egyptian Gnostics were quietly discussing the finer points of his theology in their Sunday gatherings.

---

12. *Refutation* 5.1–3; They freely used the Gospel of John and the *Gospel of Thomas*.

13. *Refutation* 5.7.

14. Clement of Alexandria claimed the Peratae came from Peraea, the area east of the Jordan River (*Stromata* 7.17).

15. *Stromata* 5.13–15.

16. *Stromata* 7.

17. *Refutation* 6.29, 30; *Against Heresies* 1.3, 1.8.

The epistles of Paul cannot be traced back further than AD 120 in the patristic literature.[18] Save some startling new discovery, we will never know how the Pauline corpus was transmitted prior to Basilides and Marcion. The literary trail grows cold at that juncture and dies out.

The Canon is Modernized

The Catholic canon was in a continual state of flux throughout the third quarter of the second century. Never before or since has there been such a reshuffling of the deck. They sorted through the historic documents of the church; discarded the *Didache*, the *Preaching of Peter*, and the *Epistle of Barnabas*; brought in three new Gospels, most of the epistolary output of Paul and John; and gave their blessing to the Acts of the Apostles. Their efforts were documented in the first surviving canon of the church, the *Muratorian* fragment. Although damaged and incomplete, beginning in the middle of a sentence and ending just as abruptly, it gives us the tentative consensus of the Roman church around AD 180. We find they were using all of the current New Testament with the exception of 1 and 2 Peter, Hebrews, James, and 3 John.

> **Muratorian Canon**—This was the Catholic Church's first visible attempt to define a New Testament canon. It is the product of Rome, where reformers had been collecting the apostolic writings since Valentinus and Marcion had introduced them to Paul. The Greek-language fragment lists 22 of the 27 New Testament books. Pius, the Roman bishop until AD 154, had "recently sat on the *cathedra*," so a date around AD 180 cannot be far off the mark.

The omission of 1 and 2 Peter almost leaps off the page at us. How could the "home church" of Simon Peter not include his correspondence in their Bible? Under what scenario would that even be possible? It would make more sense if the Romans had *more* of his letters than anyone else; perhaps a personal note or two. It tends to blow the whole mythology about St. Peter and the Apostolic See right out of the water.

The compiler of the Muratorian Canon was not familiar enough with the new material to even get the chronology right. He maintained that John, who wrote to the seven churches of Asia, was the predecessor of Paul, who also wrote to seven apostolic churches. The truth, of course, is exactly the opposite. John received the vision on Patmos and passed the messages along

---

18. We are not considering forged documents (pseudo-Ignatius) or misdated documents (1 *Clement*).

to the Asian churches *after* Paul had gone on to his reward. The Canonist then asserts that Paul wrote his general epistles in the order given in the right column which, as can be seen, doesn't match the information derived from the book of Acts and the epistles themselves.

Approx. Date of Epistle	Muratorian Sequence
Thessalonians—Both in 52	Corinthians
Galatians—56	Ephesians
Corinthians—Both in 57	Philippians
Romans—57	Colossians
Philippians—60	Galatians
Colossians—61	Thessalonians
Ephesians—61	Romans

The author of the *Muratorian* fragment had to resort to a ruse to justify including the Gospel of John. The Fourth Gospel was still such a novelty at this time, its standing in the church so shaky, that he had to endow it with additional authority.

> When John's fellow disciples and bishops urged him to write, he said 'Fast with me from today for three days, and let us tell one another whatever will be revealed to each of us.' In the same night it was revealed to Andrew, one of his apostles, that John should write down everything in his own name, while all of them should review it.

We are asked to believe that John, who was counted among Jesus' inner circle, privileged to go up with him to the Mount of Transfiguration, and rested on his bosom at the Last Supper, had to have his work approved by a committee of his peers? Is that not laughable? John himself wrote of his unquestioned authority. "This is the disciple which testifieth of these things, and wrote these things: and we *know* that his testimony is true."[19]

The Gospel of John was not known to the proto-Catholics until the middle of the second century. The oldest Johannine codex in existence is the tiny fragment known as the Rylands papyrus—just a few precious verses of John 18—and it has been dated on paleographic grounds from AD 125 to AD 150. Found in the sands of Egypt, it is almost certainly Gnostic. The physical evidence meshes perfectly with the patristic record. In the *Refutation of all Heresies*, the Egyptian teacher Basilides quotes John 1:9 almost

---

19. John 21:24, emphasis mine.

verbatim and attributes it to "the Gospels."[20] His fellow countryman, Valentinus, moved to Rome "in the time of Hyginus" (c. AD 140) and attached himself to the Christian community. Shortly thereafter, Catholic authors in Rome begin to cite phrases and passages from the Fourth Gospel. The first crossover of John into Catholic literature occurs with Justin Martyr around AD 150. Justin's pupil Tatian compiled his harmony of the four Gospels, the *Diatessaron*, in the middle 160s, and Church Fathers subsequent to him quote freely from John.

The books of John raised more of a firestorm than the epistles of Paul. There were entire towns in the ancient heartland of Phrygia which flatly rejected the Gospel of John and the book of Revelation. Epiphanius christened this sect the *Alogi*, meaning "Deniers of the Word,"[21] but they were simply traditional Catholics who resisted the changes coming out of Rome. Irenaeus, a contemporary, tells us they "held themselves aloof from the communion of the brethren."[22] In truth, Catholics everywhere had reservations about the Johannine books. The Gospel of John had been used in Gnostic circles for decades, it had been brought to Rome by Valentinus, and for these reasons it was suspect. The *Alogi* took it a step further and claimed that the Fourth Gospel had been written by Gnostics.[23] The controversy smoldered for years, and even as late as the third century, Hippolytus felt compelled to write a tract, now lost, called *Defense of the Revelation and Gospel of John*.

There are real chronological disparities between the Gospel of John and the other three, further fueling doubt and suspicion. The synoptic evangelists depict the Last Supper as the evening Passover meal, with the crucifixion following the next morning. John seems to place the crucifixion in the afternoon before Passover, at the time when the paschal lambs were slaughtered.[24] The length of the Lord's public ministry also differed. There was a persistent belief in the early church that the ministry of Jesus only lasted one year, an impression left by the Gospel of Matthew.[25] The Fourth Gospel follows his travels over the course of three years, punctuated every Passover by the annual pilgrimage to Jerusalem.[26] Finally, the *Alogi* were appalled by the Christology presented in John's writings—the "Word made Flesh" doctrine. The first and second century Catholics understood Jesus to

20. *Refutation* 7.10.
21. *Panarion* 51.3.
22. *Against Heresies* 3.11.9.
23. *Panarion* 51.3.
24. John 18:28; 19:14, 31.
25. *Homilies* 19; *Stromata* 1.21.
26. John 2:23; 6:4; 11:55; 12.1.

be a prophet *extraordinaire* whom God had poured His Spirit into; not the divine Son of God.

The Gospel of John went on to become accepted throughout all Christendom. Not so with the book of Revelation. Ambivalence about Revelation remained until the fourth or fifth century in the western church,[27] and it was never given a place in the Syrian canon.

The *Diatessaron* was a mixed or composite Gospel. Tatian, a native of Adiabene, a border state east of the Euphrates River, had studied under Justin Martyr in Rome. He had witnessed first-hand the lively debate over the new Gospels and the epistles of Paul. He decided that the format of a single harmonizing Gospel was less confusing than the emerging consensus of four separate accounts.[28] Using the Johannine chronology as the basic framework, he wove details from the four Gospels together into a single seamless narrative. Tatian used over 95 percent of the Gospel of John, lesser percentages of the other three, and material from an unknown Judeo-Christian Gospel. He compiled the book in Rome and brought it to Syria in AD 172, where it became the standard Gospel text until the fifth century. We have to ask ourselves: Would the Syrian Christians have even considered using the mixed Gospel if they had been hearing the four canonical Gospels read from the pulpit every Sunday? The *Diatessaron* reached them just as the new Gospels and their place were being debated within the Catholic community.

The acceptance of Acts is closely intertwined with the acceptance of Paul. Our first glimpse of the genuine history of the New Testament comes, ironically, from the bogus proto-Catholic account of the period. The *Recognitions of Clement* has, at the end of book one, several recognizable incidents from the book of Acts, placed in a completely different setting. Would they have so blatantly plagiarized this material if it was well known? The present text of the *Recognitions* is pre-Pauline, but there are indications it had been substantially revised around AD 150. There is a single citation of Acts 1:9, without attribution, in what must be the last work of Justin Martyr,[29] and one of Acts 2:24 in *Polycarp's Epistle to the Philippians*.[30] They can both be dated very close to AD 155.

Acts was then put on the shelf and disappears from the patristic record for the next twenty years, the very time Paul marches triumphantly through

---

27. *Eccl Hist* 3.25.

28. The term *Diatessaron* comes from the music world, and it signifies a series of four harmonic notes.

29. *On the Resurrection* 9.

30. *Polycarp to Phil* 1.2.

the churches. It then reappears simultaneously in several writings at the end of the 170s: the *Epistle of the Apostles*, the *Muratorian Canon*, and the *Martyrdom of Vienne and Lyon*. The Acts of the Apostles then joins their canon and becomes their history.

The author of the *Muratorian Canon* makes the following observations about the book of Acts, revealing a paper-thin familiarity with the new material. "Moreover, the acts of all the apostles were written in one book. For 'Most excellent Theophilus' Luke compiled the individual events that took place in his presence, as he plainly shows by omitting the martyrdom of Peter as well as the departure of Paul from the city when he journeyed to Spain."

You would be hard-pressed to pack more misleading and factually challenged comments into just two sentences.

- The book does not exclusively cover the events that Luke experienced firsthand, as asserted. Luke does not begin to use the first-person pronouns until chapter 16.
- Paul did not go to Spain, as the Canonist claimed. After conveying this desire to the Roman church,[31] he was imprisoned and his plans thwarted.
- The Canonist clearly believed the legendary stories of Peter's death, and was surprised they were not confirmed by Luke.

Reading between the lines, we learn that the Acts of the Apostles neither verified their expectations of Paul's exploits in Spain, built up by thirty years of reading Romans, nor did it affirm the received tradition of Peter's martyrdom in Rome. The Canonist mollified his audience by saying that these things must have happened in Luke's absence.

Irenaeus is representative of the new canon coming out of Rome. He wrote the massive tome *Against Heresies* from Lyon, France around AD 185, immediately after the Roman reformation.[32] The five books that comprise this work explain and contest the intricate theology of the Gnostics. Irenaeus uses all of the New Testament except 1 Peter, 2 Peter, and 3 John. The fourfold Gospel was now solidly embraced by the western churches. "It is not possible that the Gospels can be either more or fewer in number than they are, since there are four directions of the world in which we live, and four principal winds."[33] Irenaeus treats the *Shepherd of Hermas* as Scripture,

---

31. Romans 15:15.

32. Irenaeus was an immigrant from Asia Minor and the second elder of Lugdunum, the Roman capital of Gaul.

33. *Against Heresies* 3.11.8.

and quotes uncritically from the apocryphal *Wisdom of Solomon*. Although well acquainted with the Acts of the Apostles, he still clung to the old Simon Magus mythology.

Alexandria was a backwater of the church until Origen took the helm in the third century. It retained the primitive Catholic canon far longer, as demonstrated by the *Stromata*[34] of Clement, written around AD 195. Clement of Alexandria recognizes the authority of the four Gospels, but he has no hesitation using the *Gospel of the Egyptians*, the *Gospel of the Hebrews*, and the *Traditions of Matthias*.[35] He cites the *Preaching of Peter* with every confidence it came from the hand of the apostle.[36] Agrapha are considered legitimate Scripture long after they disappear everywhere else.[37] And Clement considers the *Didache*, *1 Clement*, the *Epistle of Barnabas*, the *Shepherd of Hermas*, and the *Apocalypse of Peter* on par with the genuine writings of the apostles.

The eastern churches did not blindly follow the lead of the Roman reformers. This can be seen by comparing the unorthodox Scriptures employed by the Egyptian church with the modernity of Irenaeus' canon. The elasticity of the eastern canon is further illustrated by an incident that happened in a coastal village north of Antioch around AD 200. Bishop Serapion made a visit to Rhossus, learned they were reading the uncanonical *Gospel According to Peter*, and thought nothing of it. But later, after doing some research, he felt alarmed enough to warn them of the dangers.[38] According to the spurious *Doctrine of Addai*, the first New Testament of the Syriac-speaking church in the Euphrates Valley consisted of just the *Diatessaron*, the letters of Paul, and the Acts of the Apostles. The Cypriote churches known to Epiphanius were still reading *1 Clement* and *2 Clement* at the end of the fourth century.[39]

The designation of a "New Testament" did not enter the Catholic lexicon until late in the second century. Irenaeus, circa AD 185, was the first of the Fathers to recognize a two-fold division of Scripture. He refers to "both" testaments, the "new" testament, and even to the "two" testaments.[40] The nomenclature for an authoritative collection of apostolic writings appears to

---

34. Meaning "Patchwork."
35. *Stromata* 3.6, 9, 13; 5.14; 7.13, 17.
36. *Stromata* 1.29; 6.5–6, 15.
37. *Stromata* 1.27; 5.6; 3.7.
38. *Eccl Hist* 6.12.
39. "Clement himself convicts them of this in every way in his general epistles which are read in the holy church. . .." (*Panarion* 30.15.2).
40. *Against Heresies* 4.28, 32.

be brand new. Tertullian, just fifteen years later, protests Marcion dividing the deity into two gods, "one for each Instrument, or Testament, as it is more usual to call it."[41] This language suggests that the delineation of Scripture into two parts was well on its way to universal acceptance.

The Fathers of the Church had considerable trouble separating the divinely-inspired wheat of Scripture from the man-made chaff. Eusebius of Caesarea gives his assessment of the canon AD 325. He divides the sacred books into three categories: the accepted writings, the disputed writings, and the rejected or spurious writings.

> At this point it seems appropriate to summarize the writings of the New Testament. In the first place is the holy quartet of the Gospels, followed by the Acts of the Apostles. After this must be reckoned the epistles of Paul, then the epistle of John and that of Peter. After them should be placed, if it is really proper, the Revelation of John, concerning which we shall give the differing opinions at the proper time. These are the accepted writings. Those that are disputed, yet familiar to most, include the epistles known as James, Jude, and 2 Peter, and those called 2 and 3 John, either the work of the evangelist or of someone else with the same name. Among the rejected writings must be reckoned the *Acts of Paul*, and the *Shepherd*, as it is called, the *Epistle of Barnabas*, the *Teaching of the Apostles* [ie, *Didache*], and the Revelation of John, which some reject and others class with the accepted books.
> —*History of the Church* 3.25

It was not until AD 367 that the twenty-seven books of the modern New Testament, no more or no less, were all assembled in one place.[42]

The books that caused the most difficulty for churchmen were placed at the end of the New Testament: James, Jude, 2 Peter, 2 and 3 John, and Revelation. Allusions from the epistle of James can be detected as early as the *Shepherd of Hermas* and *1 Clement*, but the genuine letter was probably tossed out along with the *Epistle of Peter to James* and *Epistle of Clement to James*. The Church did not come across 2 Peter and 3 John until the third century, so it is not surprising their legitimacy would be suspect. Most of the Catholic Church went on to absorb the disputed books into their canon, but the Syrian, Maronite, and Nestorian rites, not convinced of their apostolicity, still do not recognize 2 Peter, 2 and 3 John, Jude, or Revelation.[43]

---

41. *Against Marcion* 4.1, also 4.6.
42. Athanasius, *39th Festal Letter*.
43. The Bible of the Syrian Orthodox and Maronite churches, the Peshitta, does not

10

The Meaning of the Eucharist

AD 100 to AD 160

> The cup of blessing which we bless,
> is it not the communion of the blood of Christ?
> The bread which we break,
> is it not the communion of the body of Christ?
>
> —1 Corinthians 10:16

We learned in chapter 7 that the Eucharist is the vestige of a first century church banquet. How did it get transformed from a minor mealtime ritual into the highly symbolic drama at the heart of the Mass? The steps leading to transubstantiation, the doctrine that the bread and wine are the literal body and blood of Christ, is the subject of this chapter.

The primitive eucharistic meal had none of the symbolism that has come to be associated with Holy Mass. The loaf was considered blessed bread, a notch up from common bread, but certainly nothing as mystical or metaphysical as the body of Christ. A fragment of Theodotus (c. AD 160), cited by Clement of Alexandria, expresses the idea. "The bread and the oil are sanctified by the power of the Name, and they are not the same as they appeared to be when they were received, but they have been transformed

---

contain these five books.

by power into spiritual power."[1] Invoking the name of God is a very Jewish concept, elevating what would otherwise be just ordinary food into something hallowed.

Matthew, the only Gospel known to the proto-Catholics for many years, articulates the new significance Jesus attached to the Passover *matzah* and cup of blessing.

> And as they were eating, Jesus took bread, and blessed it, and brake it, and gave it to the disciples, and said, Take, eat; *this is my body*. And he took the cup, and gave thanks, and gave it to them, saying, Drink ye all of it. *For this is my blood of the new testament*, which is shed for many for the remission of sins.
> —Matthew 26:26–28, emphasis mine

As long as they had the cultic meal, these words lay dormant on the page. This passage was not invested with any special or liturgical significance. And even for a few years after the separation into *agape* and sacrament, the Eucharist was still an empty symbol, a ritual in search of a meaning.

They found it in magic. For the first couple of centuries, the bread which had been blessed by prayer was believed to possess talismanic powers. It was, as pseudo-Ignatius told his imaginary friends circa AD 155: "the medicine of immortality and the antidote against death."[2] We would normally construe this kind of language to be mere hyperbole, but it was confirmed by Hippolytus a couple of generations later. "The faithful shall be careful to partake of the eucharist before eating anything else. For if they eat with faith, even though some deadly poison is given to them, after this it will not be able to harm them."[3]

A more powerful symbol fell into their lap when they acquired the Gospel of John. Valentinus, the freethinking Egyptian theologian who straddled the fence between Gnostics and Catholics, moved to Rome around AD 140. He brought his Bible with him, which included the Gospel of John. Valentinus was orthodox enough at the time to be a serious candidate for bishop and, as Tertullian tells the story, he barely lost. Tertullian credits him as "an able man, both in intelligence and eloquence."[4] It was the first time the Roman presbyters had seen the Fourth Gospel, and they were dumbstruck with the language of John 6.

---

1. Clement of Alexandria, *Excerpts of Theodotus* 82.
2. *Ig to Eph* 20.
3. *Ap Trad* 36.
4. Tertullian, *Against the Valentinians* 4.

> I am the living bread which came down from heaven: if any man eat of this bread, he shall live forever: and the bread that I will give is my flesh, which I will give for the life of the world. The Jews therefore strove among themselves, saying, How can this man give us his flesh to eat? Then Jesus said unto them, Verily, Verily, I say unto you, except ye eat the flesh of the Son of man, and drink his blood, ye have no life in you. Whoso eateth my flesh, and drinketh my blood, hath eternal life; and I will raise him up at the last day.
> —John 6:51–54

To their carnal minds, the bread to which he referred must be the bread of the Eucharist.

The Egyptian Gnostics had their own Eucharist. Like all Gnostics, Valentinus rejected the physical incarnation, insisting that Jesus only appeared to have a physical body. In a colorful turn of phrase, they taught that the Son of man had "passed through Mary like water flows through a tube."[5] The Jesus of the Gospels only *seemed* to get hungry, to thirst, to sweat, and to bleed. In Gnostic theology, matter was intrinsically evil, so the Lord's body could not possibly have been flesh and bone. Instead, his human form was thought to be ethereal and incorporeal, the curious doctrine known as docetism.

Irenaeus, the bishop of Lyon late in the second century, takes us inside the Gnostic Eucharist. "The bread over which thanks has been given is the body of their Lord, and the cup his blood."[6] What could a docetist possibly mean by the "body of the Lord" and "his blood" when they believed in neither? Irenaeus explains: Jesus had been "begotten by a [special] dispensation with a body endowed with an animal nature, yet constructed with unspeakable skill, so that it might be visible and tangible, and capable of enduring suffering. At the same time, they deny that He assumed anything material, since matter is incapable of salvation."[7] It was not that big of a stretch for them to believe that the spiritual body of Christ was infused into the bread by invocation and prayer.

The Gnostics believed in a bloodless Christ, yet the wine represented his blood. How exactly did that work? According to the Valentinian *Gospel of Philip*, the blood of the non-physical body of Christ was the Holy Spirit.[8]

---

5. *Against Heresies* 1.7.2.
6. *Against Heresies* 4.18.4.
7. *Against Heresies* 1.6.1.
8. "The cup of prayer contains wine and water, since it is appointed as the type of the blood for which thanks is given. And it is full of the Holy Spirit, and it belongs to the wholly perfect man. When we drink this, we shall receive for ourselves the perfect

> Flesh and blood shall not inherit the kingdom of God. What is it which will not inherit? This which is on us. But what is it which will inherit? It is that which belongs to Jesus and his blood. Because of this, he said, 'He who shall not eat my flesh and drink my blood has no life in him.' What is it? His flesh is the word, and his blood is the Holy Spirit.
> —*Gospel of Philip* 25

The wine was transformed by the word of prayer. "Pretending to consecrate cups mixed with wine, and protracting to great length the word of invocation, he [Marcus the Gnostic] contrives to give them a purple and reddish color, so that Charis, who is one of those who are superior to all things, should be thought to drop her own blood into that cup through means of his invocation, that those who are present should be led to rejoice to taste of that cup, in order that, by so doing, the Charis, who is set forth by this magician, may also flow into them."[9] So, after being consecrated by prayer (and trickery), the wine was presented as the blood of Charis, the feminine side of the Gnostic deity. The infused blood of Charis became, for the Catholics, the literal blood of Christ.

The doctrine of the Real Presence bursts very suddenly over the Catholic sky in the 140s. After being blessed by a priest, the bread and wine now becomes the literal body and blood of Christ. Justin Martyr, writing around AD 150, was one of its first spokesmen. "For not as common bread and common drink do we receive these; but in like manner as Christ Jesus our Savior, having been made flesh by the Word of God, had both flesh and blood for our salvation, so likewise have we been taught that the food which is blessed by the prayer of His word, and from which our blood and flesh by transmutation are nourished, is the flesh and blood of that Jesus who was made flesh."[10] Pseudo-Ignatius also delights in the new and mysterious doctrine. "I desire the bread of God, the heavenly bread, which is the flesh of Jesus Christ, the Son of God, who became afterwards of the seed of David and Abraham; and I desire the drink of God, namely his flesh. The Eucharist is the flesh of our Savior Jesus Christ, which flesh suffered for our sins and which God the Father raised."[11]

We are led in almost a straight line to a startling conclusion: The Catholic Church obtained its peculiar Eucharistic theology from Valentinus. Certainly the timing was right (early 140s), the place was right (Rome), the

---

man" (*Gospel of Philip*, 106).

9. *Against Heresies* 1.13.2.

10. *1 Apology* 66.

11. *Ig to Romans* 7.

means was there (Valentinus brought the Gospel of John), and the theology was half-right. The Catholics plagiarized the sacramental symbolism of the Gnostic mysteries, disassociated it from the docetism that made it plausible, and then justified it with passages from the new Johannine Gospel. The doctrine of the Real Presence, which made perfect sense within the contours of Gnostic theology, makes no sense whatsoever outside of it.

It was a profound misunderstanding of Christian spirituality. The abundant new life promised in the gospel flows from the words of Jesus, not from any ritual or ceremony. Jesus *was* the Word incarnate, and his teachings contain within themselves the germ of spiritual life when they are received with faith. As Peter defiantly told the temple priests, "God gives His Spirit to those who obey Him."[12]

Jesus made this point many times during his ministry. In the parable that explains all parables—the Sower and the Seed—the word is specifically identified as the seed of the heavenly Kingdom. "But he that receiveth seed into the good ground is he that heareth the word, and understandeth it; which also beareth fruit, and bringeth forth, some an hundredfold, some sixty, some thirty."[13] It is our response to his teachings which determines our spiritual fruitfulness and eternal destiny. At the beginning of his earthly ministry, the Lord summed up the Sermon on the Mount by saying they who heard his words and did them would be saved.[14] At the end of his ministry, he made this promise to his followers. "If a man love me, he will *keep my words*: and my Father will love him, and we will come unto him, and make our abode with him"[15]

The passage at the heart of transubstantiation is found in John 6. This chapter is entirely about bread, from the Miracle of the Loaves at the beginning to the revelation of Peter at the end. It was even set right before Passover, the feast of unleavened bread.[16]

After feeding the 5,000 with five barley loaves, the disciples rowed to the other side of the lake. The next day, Jesus chastises the people for seeking natural food instead of bread for their soul. They ask him how to do this, and Jesus tells them the work of God begins when they believe on His Son. They ask for a sign, pointing out that Moses had given them manna from heaven. Jesus declares that he is the true bread of life, and like the manna, he also came down from heaven. They murmur at this, knowing his natural

---

12. Acts 5:32.
13. Matthew 13:23.
14. Matthew 7:24, 25.
15. John 14:23, emphasis mine.
16. John 6:4.

parents, and he repeats that he is the bread of eternal life. "If any man eat of this bread, he shall live forever: and the bread that I will give is my flesh."[17]

The Jews wondered how they could eat his flesh. "Then said Jesus unto them, Verily, verily, I say unto you, except ye eat the flesh of the Son of Man, and drink his blood, ye have no life in you. Whoso eateth my flesh, and drinketh my blood, hath eternal life; and I will raise him up at the last day."[18] The Passover was nigh, and as they would soon be feasting on lamb, so they needed to feed on the Lamb of God.[19] He explains what he meant in verse 57. "As the living Father hath sent me, and I live by the Father: so he that eateth me, *even he shall live by me*." The disciples were still confused, so he clarified it further in verse 63. "It is the spirit that quickeneth; the flesh profiteth nothing: the *words* that I speak unto you, they are spirit, and they are life." Peter got the message loud and clear. "Then said Simon Peter unto him, Lord to whom shall we go? Thou hast the *words* of eternal life."[20] This discussion happened a full year before he instituted the bread and cup, and in a completely different context.

By the time Simon Peter wrote 1 Peter, he had been sharing the Gospel of the Kingdom for thirty-five years. He had explained the connection between the Word of God and the Spirit of God many times to many audiences. "Being born again, not of corruptible seed, but of incorruptible, *by the word of God*, which liveth and abideth forever. . . . . . The grass withereth, and the flower thereof falleth away: but the word of the Lord endureth forever. *And this is the word* which by the Gospel is preached unto you."[21]

---

17. John 6:51.
18. John 6:53–54.
19. John 1:29.
20. John 6:68, emphasis mine.
21. 1 Peter 1:23–25.

11

The Roman Reformation

AD 144 to AD 200

> All truth passes through three stages.
> First, it is ridiculed.
> Second, it is violently opposed.
> Third, it is accepted as self-evident.
>
> —Arthur Schopenhauer

For the Catholic intelligentsia living in the 140s and 150s, all roads led to Rome. They streamed in from every corner of the empire. Marcion came from Pontus, Valentinus from Egypt, Cerdo from Syria, Justin the Martyr from Samaria, Tatian from Assyria, and Hegesippus from Palestine. As the Roman Empire reached the pinnacle of its power, they were drawn to the city on the Tiber like iron filings to a magnet. All of their learning was not as revolutionary or transformative as the books they carried in their luggage.

The modern *Ekklesia Katholika* was forged at Rome. The remnants of the apostolic writings were brought together in one place for the first time, and the Catholic New Testament went from a single Gospel to twenty-plus books within two decades. The enlargement of their canon ushered in the most dynamic era of reform the Church has ever known. It was responsible for sweeping changes in their understanding of apostolic history, the nature of the Godhead, the person of Jesus Christ, and the Eucharistic formula.

The leadership of the Church passed from Asia Minor to Rome in the third quarter of the second century. For the first hundred years, the proto-Catholics were little more than a loosely-knit confederation of autonomous congregations. During that time, they had managed to spread far and wide across the Roman Empire. A concerted effort to consolidate and to centralize now appears, and the impulse springs entirely from Rome. There is nothing quite as unifying as a name, and they grandly began referring to themselves as the Universal Church, or *Ekklesia Katholika* in Greek.[1] Prior to this time, they were simply "Christians" who belonged to the "church of God."[2]

The Roman reformers laid the foundation for the top-down hierarchy that has characterized the Church through the ages. They saw with great clarity that the key to unity and uniformity of doctrine was a strong bishopric. Admonitions to obey the bishop are sprinkled throughout the documents of the period, both the genuine and the fictitious. *First Clement*, a letter from the Roman congregation to their fellow travelers at Corinth, touches on this theme at least half a dozen times. The bundle of forged letters attributed to Ignatius never misses an opportunity to exhort the laity to obedience. In every letter, there are admonitions to "love" (Ephesians), "reverence" (Magnesians), "do nothing apart from" (Trallians), "give heed to" (Philadelphians), or "to follow" (Smyrneans), their respective bishops.

The Acts of the Apostles

The reformers had to update their history library; not just once but twice. The *Preaching of Peter* was taken off the shelf, rewritten as the *Homilies/Recognitions of Clement*, and replaced twenty or twenty-five years later with the Acts of the Apostles. Justin Martyr, a highly regarded instructor in the Roman church, authored several long books on the cusp of the Pauline Revolution. It is crystal clear that, even at this late date (AD 150), his trusted source for church history was the *Preaching of Peter*, not the canonical Acts. He wrote about Simon Magus as an actual person who had hoodwinked the Roman authorities and whom the Romans themselves honored as a god.

> There was a Samaritan, Simon, a native of the village called Gitto, who in the reign of Claudius Caesar, and in your royal city of Rome, did mighty works of magic, by virtue of the devils operating in him. He was considered a god, and as a god was honored by you with a statue, which statue was erected on the

---

1. *Ig to Smyrn* 8.2; *Mar Polycarp* Prologue, 19.2; *Muratorian*.
2. *1 Clement* 1; *Polycarp to Phil* 1; *Shepherd* Sim. 9.18.

Tiber River, between the two bridges, and bore this inscription, in the language of Rome: To Simon the holy God...

... they again, as was said above, put forth other men, the Samaritans Simon and Menander, who did many mighty works by magic, and deceived many, and still keep them deceived. For even among yourselves, as we said before, Simon was in the royal city Rome in the reign of Claudius Caesar, and so greatly astonished the sacred senate and people of the Romans, that he was considered a god, and honored, like the others you honor, with a statue.
—*1 Apology* 26, 56

An obscure book written during this period tries to reconcile the *Preaching of Peter* with the Acts of the Apostles.[3] The Syriac *Teaching of the Apostles* starts out with the apostles on the day of Pentecost—obviously modeled on Acts 1—wondering how they were going to reach out to the Gentiles. They see tongues of fire, which alight on them, and each one hears in a different tongue. They perceive this is a sign telling them where they should preach, and they divide up the world accordingly. We are then treated to twenty-seven ecclesiastical canons, where we learn they prayed facing the east, kept the Sabbath on Friday evenings, and read the Law, the Prophets, the Gospel, and the Acts from the altar. The apostles then send Paul and Timothy to deliver these twenty-seven canons to the churches of Syria and Cilicia.[4] It concludes with a long list of countries where the apostles spent their days laboring for souls; all bogus, of course.

What are we to make of this? The author had a very limited familiarity with Paul and his exploits. He uses the early chapters of Acts as a framework on which to hang the old proto-Catholic legends. He pretends the apostles composed these "ordinances and laws" on the day of Pentecost and sent them to the churches instead of the letter of James. And in spite of all this, the Acts of the Apostles was read from the altar. It was an amateurish—and unsuccessful—attempt at reconciliation, and the book never gained any traction in the Church.

When the Acts of the Apostles was added to their New Testament, the Catholics had to revise their history of the apostolic age. The pioneering work of Paul was now acknowledged, but not in the strict Biblical sense.

---

3. It must have been composed after AD 170, because of the Pauline material and Acts, but not much later because the Church quickly embraced the Lucan version of events.

4. In the Acts of the Apostles, it was Paul and Barnabas who took the apostolic decision of Acts 15 to Syria and Anatolia, where they then met up with Timothy (Acts 15:22–27, 16:1–4).

Dionysius of Corinth, circa AD 175, shares the new consensus of the post-Acts church. "You have thus by such an admonition bound together the planting of Peter and Paul at Rome and Corinth. For both of them planted and taught us at Corinth. And they taught together in like manner in Italy, and suffered martyrdom at the same time."[5] Irenaeus (c. 185) promulgated the same odd belief about the foundation of the Roman church. "The blessed apostles [Peter and Paul], then, having founded and built up the church (of Rome), committed into the hands of Linus the office of the episcopate. Of this Linus, Paul makes mention in the epistles to Timothy."[6] We see in these statements the two streams of tradition, the old *Preaching of Peter* and the new Acts of the Apostles, mixing and merging together.

> **Christology**—The branch of theology which deals with the person and nature of Jesus Christ. How did his two natures, the human and the divine, interact? Was he really tempted in all points like us? Could he sin? How did he do the miracles?
>
> The false apostles embraced an adoptionist Christology. To them, Jesus was just another prophet—an exceptionally virtuous one—who was "adopted" by the Father at the River Jordan. By contrast, the apostles taught that Jesus was the pre-existent Son of God.

From Prophet to Deity

Their theology department also received a substantial upgrade in the third quarter of the second century. The pre-Pauline Catholics held very simplistic views of both the Godhead and the person of Jesus Christ. Their conception of the Supreme Deity was the uncompromising monotheism one would expect of a Jewish sect. Their Christology was the natural outgrowth of a long tradition of Hebrew prophets, ordinary men filled with the Holy Spirit who spoke as God gave them utterance.

The false apostles and their followers were adoptionists. They taught that Jesus was a mere mortal who, because of his purity and righteousness in keeping the Law, God chose (i.e., adopted) to be his Son. The celestial adoption occurred when the Holy Spirit descended upon him at the Jordan River. "And Jesus, when he was baptized, went up straightway out of the water: and lo, the heavens were opened unto him, and he saw the Spirit of God descending like a dove, and lighting upon him. And lo a voice from

---

5. *Eccl Hist* 2.25.
6. *Against Heresies* 3.3.3.

heaven saying, This is my beloved Son, in whom I am well pleased."[7] In adoptionist theology, there is a special relationship between the Holy Spirit and the Son of God. The Holy Spirit was the offspring of the Father and, after He was poured into Jesus bar Joseph at the River Jordan, Jesus became the Son of God.

Matthew, the sole Gospel of the sectarians for many years, does not breathe a word about the pre-existence of Christ. You would think the miracle of the virgin birth would spoil the theory, but according to Hippolytus, it did not.[8] The extant versions of the *Preaching of Peter*—the *Homilies* and *Recognitions of Clement*—speak repeatedly of Jesus as the "Prophet," the "true Prophet," or the "Prophet of truth."[9] To the proto-Catholics, Jesus was the prophet whom Moses had promised and foretold would come.[10] "I will raise them up a Prophet from among their brethren, like unto me, and will put my words in his mouth; and he shall speak unto them all that I shall command him."[11]

The Shepherd of Hermas was one of the last outposts of adoptionism in Catholic literature. It was written at Rome around AD 145, and quickly became one of the most popular books in the Christian world. It was so venerated that, for a few centuries, it was often bound together with the Holy Scriptures and read in the churches. The following passages from the *Shepherd* give us the flavor of the unfamiliar Christology.

> I wish to explain to you what the Holy Spirit that spake with you in the form of the Church showed you, for that Spirit is the Son of God.
> —Book 3, Similitude 9.1

---

7. Matthew 3:16–17.

8. *Refutation* 7.23.

9. "That unless a man be baptized in water, in the name of the threefold blessedness, as the true Prophet taught, he can neither receive remission of sins nor enter into the kingdom of heaven . . ." (*Recognitions* 1.69).

"If any one withdraw from God the Father and Creator of all, receiving another teacher besides Christ, who alone is the faithful and true Prophet, and who has sent us twelve apostles to preach the word . . ." (*Recognitions* 4.36).

"And, therefore, since amongst these *philosophers* are things uncertain, we must come to the true Prophet. Him God the Father wished to be loved by all, and accordingly He has been pleased wholly to extinguish those opinions which have originated with men, and in regard to which there is nothing like certainty. . . . " (*Recognitions* 8.62).

10. *Homilies* 3.53; *Recognitions* 1.41. This prophesy was also cited by the apostles in Acts 3:22 and 7:37.

11. Deuteronomy 18:18, see also 18:15.

> The Holy Spirit, who created all things, God made to dwell in flesh as He desired. This flesh [i.e., body] therefore, in which the Holy Spirit dwelt, was subject unto the Spirit, walking honorably in holiness and purity, without in any way defiling the Spirit. When it [i.e., Jesus] had lived honorably in chastity, and had labored with the Spirit, and had cooperated with it in everything, behaving itself boldly and bravely, He chose it as a partner with the Holy Spirit; for the career of this flesh pleased [the Lord], seeing that, as possessing the Holy Spirit, it was not defiled upon the earth.
> —Book 3, Similitude 5.6

As the twelve apostles walked the dusty roads of Galilee with Jesus, they perceived that he was more than just a prophet. One day, while trekking up to Caesarea Philippi, he asked his disciples, "Whom do men say that I, the Son of man, am? And they said, Some say that thou art John the Baptist; some, Elijah; and others, Jeremiah, or one of the prophets." Jesus then utters the words that have been the cause of so much contention between Catholics and Protestants.

> He said unto them, but whom say ye that I am? And Simon Peter answered and said, Thou art the Christ, the Son of the living God. And Jesus answered and said unto him, Blessed art thou, Simon Bar-jona: for flesh and blood hath not *revealed* it unto thee, but my Father which is in heaven. And I say also unto thee, That thou art Peter, and upon this rock I will build my church; and the gates of hell shall not prevail against it. And I will give unto thee the keys of the kingdom of heaven..."
> —Matthew 16:16–19, emphasis mine

Jesus was not just another prophet, like Elijah or Jeremiah, but he was the promised Messiah, the actual Son of God. This *revelation* is the great rock foundation of the Christian faith.

The doctrine of the pre-existent Son entered the *Ekklesia Katholika* by way of the Fourth Gospel. It is often called the Logos (or "Word") Christology because Jesus is equated with the Word of God. The Johannine Gospel begins with a glorious declaration of his divinity. "In the beginning was the Word, and the Word was with God, and the Word was God. The same was in the beginning with God. All things were made by him, and without him was not anything made that was made." In the eighth chapter, Jesus affirms his divine origin. "If God were your Father, ye would love me: for I proceeded forth and came from God; neither came I of myself, but he sent me."[12]

---

12. John 8:42.

Irenaeus of Lyon (c. 185), who had all of the Pauline and Johannine texts at his disposal, was one of the first proponents of the higher Christology. Irenaeus accurately reflects the liberal reforms that were coming out of Rome. A showdown between the old believers and the reformers occurred in the 190s, pitting the bishop of Rome, Victor, against Theodotus the Leathermaker. The adoptionists strenuously defended their turf, insisting, quite correctly, that their theology was the traditional teaching of the church.

> For they say that all the early teachers and the apostles received and taught what they now declare, and that the truth of the Gospel was preserved until the time of Victor, who was the thirteenth bishop of Rome from Peter, but that from his successor, Zephyrinus, the truth had been corrupted.
> —*History of the Church* 5.28

What a difference fifty years makes! Theodotus was put outside the camp and barred from communion. What was perfectly orthodox and almost canonized in the *Shepherd of Hermas* was now a dangerous heresy.

The adoptionists did not go down without a fight. The *Gospel of Barnabas* was a product of this period, and it is decidedly adoptionist; almost militantly so. This work was greatly expanded in the fourteenth century by anti-Trinitarian Muslims and exploited for their own purposes. The extant *Gospel of Barnabas* starts out by declaring that Jesus was a prophet, not the Son of God.

> Dearly Beloved, the great and wonderful God hath during these past days visited us by his prophet Jesus Christ in great mercy of teaching and miracles, by reason whereof many, being deceived of Satan, under the pretense of piety, are preaching the most impious doctrine, calling Jesus the son of God, repudiating the circumcision ordained of God forever, and permitting every unclean meat: among whom also Paul hath been deceived . . . . ."
> —*Gospel of Barnabas* Preamble

The Holy Trinity

The Jewish Christians grew up reciting the *Shema* ("Hear, O Israel") prayer twice daily, every morning and evening. This prayer is the most sacred creed of Judaism. It is the first prayer Jewish children learn from their parents and it is the last words on the lips of those facing martyrdom. The *Shema* begins with an affirmation of God's sovereignty and unity: "Hear, O Israel, the Lord is our God, the Lord is One."[13] The false apostles brought this same strict and uncompromising monotheism into the church they founded.

The Peter of the *Clementines* expresses a theology that would have sent the Nicaean Fathers spinning in their graves.

> Our Lord neither asserted that there were gods except the Creator of all, nor did He proclaim Himself to be God, but He with reason pronounced him blessed who called Him the Son of that God who has arranged the universe. And Simon [Magus] answered: "Does it not seem to you, then, that he who comes from God is God?" And Peter said: "Tell us how this is possible; for we cannot affirm this, because we did not hear it from Him. In addition to this, it is the peculiarity of the Father not to have been begotten, but of the Son to have been begotten; but what is begotten, cannot be compared with that which is unbegotten or self-begotten." And Simon said: "Is it not the same on account of its origin?" [Or, is not that which is begotten identical with that which begets it?] And Peter said: "He who is not the same in all respects as someone cannot have all the same appellations applied to him as that person." And Simon said: "This is to assert, not to prove." And Peter said: "Why, do you not see that if the one happens to be self-begotten or unbegotten, they cannot be called the same; nor can it be asserted of him who has been begotten that he is of the same substance as he who has begotten him?
>
> —Homilies of Clement 16.15–16

The doctrine of the Trinity was hammered out in the last quarter of the second century. As was common during this era, the Roman Catholics got the raw material from Valentinus. According to Marcellus of Ancyra, Valentinus was "the first to devise the notion of three subsistent entities in a work that he entitled *On the Three Natures*. For, he devised the notion of three subsistent entities and three persons—Father, Son, and Holy Spirit."[14] There is, within Gnosticism, no tradition of a triune Godhead, so Marcellus may not have it completely right, but they do speak of various aeons which emanate from the Unbegotten One. The *Apocryphon of John* (c. 160), also of Egyptian provenance, thus speaks of "the Father, the Mother, and the Child."[15]

---

13. Deuteronomy 6:4. This is followed by the familiar words of the next verse. "Thou shalt love the Lord thy God with all thine heart, and with all thy soul, and with all thy might."

14. Marcellus of Ancyra, *On the Holy Church* 9.

15. "Because of you the All came into being, and it is to you that the All will return. And I will praise and glorify you and Autogenes with the three Aeons: the Father, the Mother, the Child, the perfect power" (*Apocryphon of John* 9). The *Secret Book of John*

The first Catholic writer (c. AD 180) to reference the *Triados* was Theophilus of Antioch. The terminology he uses is right out of a Gnostic handbook.

> And as the sun remains ever full, never becoming less, so does God always abide perfect, being full of all power, and understanding and wisdom, and immortality, and all good. But the moon wanes monthly, and in a manner dies, being a type of man; then it is born again, and is a crescent, for a pattern of the future resurrection. In like manner, the three days which were before the luminaries are also types of the *Triados; of God, and His Word, and His Wisdom*. And the fourth is a type of man, who needs light, so that there may be God, the Word, Wisdom, and man.
> —*To Autolycus* 2.15, emphasis mine

You would be hard pressed to find a more anti-Trinitarian statement than this. The perfectly orthodox bishop of Antioch writes of "God" separate from "The Word" and "Wisdom." The Word, a minor member of the Gnostic Godhead, is identified with the Son elsewhere in this letter,[16] but the identity of Wisdom is left somewhat nebulous. There may be a good reason. In Valentinian cosmology, Wisdom was the emanation of the unknowable Father that gave birth to a formless substance and brought about the creation of the universe. Wisdom—Sophia in Greek—still occupies a central place in Eastern Orthodox mysticism. Indeed, the largest and most magnificent cathedral in the world for over a millennia was the Hagia Sophia ("Holy Wisdom") in Constantinople.

Bishop Theophilus lays out his understanding of the Godhead earlier in the letter. The God-Word-Wisdom Triad he presents is unfamiliar territory to Christians schooled in the classic Trinity.

> For if I say He [God] is Light, I name but His own work; if I call Him Word, I name but His sovereignty; if I call Him mind, I speak but of His wisdom; if I say He is Spirit, I speak of His breath; if I call Him Wisdom, I speak of His offspring.
>
> God, then, having His own internal within His bowels, begat Him, emitting Him along with His own wisdom before all things. He had this Word as a helper in the things that were created by Him, and by Him He made all things.
> —*To Autolycus* 1.3, 2.10

---

goes back to the middle years of the second century. Irenaeus (c. AD 185) seemed to know the work, see *Against Heresies* 1.29.

16. *To Autolycus* 2.22.

It is not the Nicene Creed, but you have to start somewhere.

Tertullian, a Carthaginian lawyer at the turn of the third century, was the first to define in precise language that which cannot be comprehended by the human mind. We learn that Catholic theologians had made tremendous strides in the two decades from AD 180 to AD 200. The Trinity has now become the familiar threesome of Father, Son and Holy Ghost.

> As if in this way also one were not All, in that All are of One, by unity (that is) of substance; while the mystery of the dispensation is still guarded, which distributes the Unity into a Trinity, placing in their order the three Persons—the Father, the Son, and the Holy Ghost: three, however, not in condition but in degree; not in substance but in form; not in power but in aspect; yet of one substance, and of one condition, and of one power, inasmuch as He is one God, from whom these degrees and forms and aspects are reckoned, under the name of the Father, and of the Son, and of the Holy Ghost.
> —*Against Praxeas* 2

The apostle John is our primary source on the Godhead. He depicts a closeness and a unity between the Father and Son that is beyond human understanding. "I and my Father are one"[17] and "Believest thou not that I am in the Father, and the Father is in me."[18] We are creatures of the dust, with limitations imposed upon us by a physical body. They are spirits, inhabiting a plane of existence we know little about. Perhaps the closest we can come in terms of human relationships are the two that become one-flesh in marriage.[19]

The Gospel seeks to bring us into the same intimate relationship with our Creator.

> Jesus answered and said unto him, If a man love me, he will keep my words: and my Father will love him, and we will come unto him, and make our abode with him.
>
> That they all may be one; as thou, Father, art in me, and I in thee, that they also may be one in us: that the world may believe that thou hast sent me. And the glory which thou gavest me I have given them; that they may be one, even as we are one: I in them, and thou in me, that they may be made perfect in one . . . .
> —John 14:23, 17:21-23

---

17. John 10:30.
18. John 14:10.
19. "For this cause shall a man leave father and mother, and shall cleave to his wife: and they twain shall be one flesh. Wherefore they are no more twain, but one flesh" (Matthew 19:5, 6).

At the heavenly marriage of the Lamb—the climax of all creation—we will be united with the bridegroom of our soul for all eternity.[20]

The Completion of the Eucharistic Prayer

The flood of new books, containing a wealth of new information, also changed the Eucharistic formula. The primitive Eucharistic prayer was a Christianized version of the *Birkat Hamazon*, with the same framework of three thanksgivings followed by a glorification of the Name. It was the universal prayer over the elements from apostolic times until the Pauline Revolution. The *Didache* is our earliest witness to the Table Grace, and it is nothing but the *berakah* rewritten in terms of the New Covenant. The patristic record is then blank until the time of Justin Martyr, who, as luck would have it, wrote just before the enlargement of the canon. He mentions the prayer of consecration in several passages and, although the language is vague, it abounds with thanksgivings.[21]

The primitive Thanksgiving prayer did not include the words of consecration. Now considered mandatory, these are the Lord's instructions at the Last Supper which dramatically changed the meaning of the ancient Passover. The bread and wine are no longer about bitter slavery and deliverance from oppression, but the Lord Jesus. Justin was the first of the Fathers to report on the institution narrative.

> For the apostles, in the memoirs composed by them, which are called Gospels, have thus delivered unto us what was enjoined upon them; that Jesus took bread, and when He had given thanks, said, 'This do ye in remembrance of Me, this is My body'; and that, after the same manner, having taken the cup and given thanks, He said, 'This is My blood;' and gave it to them alone.
> —*1 Apology* 66

Although these directives are mentioned in all three of the synoptic Gospels, the *anamnesis*, the command to "to this in remembrance of me," is only found in Luke and 1 Corinthians. Justin specifically tells us this instruction came from the "Gospels," which in this context can only mean the Gospel of Luke. The Third Gospel was thus beginning to broaden their understanding of the Eucharistic ritual, but they had not yet altered the accompanying liturgy.

That happened in the generation which followed. A second set of prayers was appended to the primitive nucleus of the Thanksgiving which

---

20. Revelation 19:7.
21. *1 Apology* 65.

links the taking of the bread and cup with the instruction to "do this in remembrance of me." We find a fully developed Eucharistic prayer incorporating the *anamnesis* in the *Apostolic Tradition*, written around AD 215. Sometime between the days of Justin Martyr and Hippolytus—both of them from Rome—the second half of the anaphora (Eucharistic prayer) took shape and was fused to the mealtime Grace.

We can narrow it down even further. The *Epistle of the Apostles* is a little-known Catholic work which, conveniently, dates itself to AD 180.[22] "And we said unto him: Lord, is it then needful that we should again take the cup and drink? [The Ethiopic version has: "Lord, didst not thou thyself fulfill the drinking of the Passover? Is it then needful that we should accomplish it again?"] He said unto us: Yea, it is needful, until the day when I come again with them that have been put to death for my sake."[23] The tenor of this exchange strongly suggests that the words of institution had not yet been added to the anaphora by AD 180.

Gregory Dix explored the liturgical boundaries of Irenaeus, a key figure of the period, and reaches the same conclusion. The bishop of Lyon believed in the Real Presence but, as late as AD 185, he did not take the bread and cup "in remembrance" of the Lord's death.

> Unmistakable, Irenaeus regards the eucharist as an 'oblation' offered to God, but it is as well to note the particular sense in which he emphasizes its sacrificial character. Primarily it is for him a sacrifice of 'first-fruits,' acknowledging the Creator's bounty in providing our earthly food, rather than as 'recalling' the sacrifice of Calvary in the Pauline fashion. It is true that Irenaeus has not the least hesitation in saying that 'The mingled cup and the manufactured bread receives the Word of God and becomes the eucharist of the Body and Blood of Christ,' and similar teaching is to be found in the passage above. . .but when all is said and done, he never quite puts these two ideas together or calls the eucharist outright the offering or the 'recalling' of Christ's sacrifice.
>
> —*Shape of the Liturgy* p. 114

---

22. "We said unto him, Lord: after how many years shall this come to pass? He said unto us: When the hundredth part and the twentieth part is fulfilled, between the Pentecost and the feast of unleavened bread, then shall the coming of my Father be" (*Ep Apostles* 17). The Coptic version reads: "When an hundred and fifty years are past. . ." The epistle was thus first written 120 years after the resurrection—or around AD 150—and then revised thirty years later.

23 *Ep Apostles* 15.

The oldest surviving Eucharistic prayer is that of Addai and Mari. Still in regular use by the Chaldean Syrian Church, the anaphora of Addai and Mari has *never* had an explicit institution narrative. It represents a living time capsule of the primitive church. In fact, many of the East Syrian liturgies do not even have a proper epiclesis, the petition directed toward the Holy Spirit to transform the offerings into the body and blood of Christ. They originated in Edessa, which was cut off from the main body of Byzantine Christianity when the Sassanian Persians swept across Syria in the AD 240s.

The new, enlarged Bible fueled an unprecedented period of growth for the Great Church. The rich spirituality of Peter, Paul, and John had far more appeal to the Graeco-Roman mind than the dry legalism of Torah and the *Clementina*. Eusebius marks their progress in his *History of the Church*: "About the same time, in the reign of Commodus (AD 180 to AD 192), our condition became more favorable, and through the grace of God the churches throughout the entire world enjoyed peace, and the word of salvation was leading every soul from every race of man to the devout worship of the God of the universe. So that now at Rome many who were highly distinguished for wealth and family turned with all their household and relatives unto their salvation."[24] The historian Cassius Dio tells us that Christianity even reached into the palace. "The tradition is that she [Marcia, the mistress of Commodus] very much favored Christians and did them many kindnesses, which she was able to do by possessing much influence with Commodus."[25]

---

24. *Eccl Hist* 5.21.
25. Cassius Dio, *Roman History* 73.4.

12

Easter: The Catholic Passover

> In the fourteenth day of the first month at
> even is the Lord's Passover.
> And on the fifteenth day of the same month
> is the feast of unleavened bread unto the Lord:
> seven days ye must eat unleavened bread.
>
> —Leviticus 23:5–6

If the Catholic Church descended from the false apostles, as we have asserted, there ought to be a remnant of the Hebrew holy days in their liturgical calendar. In fact, there is. Easter, the most hallowed season of historic Christendom, came straight out of Judaism. It is a vestige of the Passover (*Pesah* in Hebrew), which, along with the Feast of Unleavened Bread, formed the great national festival that defined Israel. The connection is seen in the Greek word *pascha*, which can mean either Passover or Easter, depending upon the context.

For Pauline Christians, the Old Testament Feast of Unleavened Bread was completely fulfilled in the New Testament breaking of bread.[1] The

---

1. "Therefore, let us keep the feast, not with old leaven, neither with the leaven of malice and wickedness; but with the unleavened bread of sincerity and truth" (1 Corinthians 5:8).

proto-Catholics also broke bread at the Sunday banquet, but they began to keep Christianized versions of the Jewish festivals as well. Our first glimpse of this comes from the Epistle to the Galatians, written just a year or two before the schism. Paul chided the faltering saints for observing "days, and months, and times, and years."[2] This would have definitely included *Pesah*, the most sacred and the most popular of the Jewish festivals. Four or five years later, he had to counsel the Christians in the upper Meander Valley not to let the neighboring Judaizers judge them "in meat, or in drink, or in respect of an holyday, or of the new moon, or of the Sabbath days."[3]

The false apostles completely revamped the Great Feast at the outset. Instead of a week-long *feast after* the 14th of Nisan, as Moses taught, they placed a week-long *fast before* the Passover. They were not allowed to fast on Sunday, as the old rabbinical rule against fasting on the Sabbath was transferred to Sunday,[4] and the resulting six days were considered a full week.[5] The instructional rubrics for this fast have been preserved in two passages, both ultimately going back to the same document. The *Didascalia Apostolorum* has a slightly more primitive cast, beginning the fast on the tenth day after the paschal new moon.

> Therefore shall you fast in the days of the Pascha from the tenth, which is the second day of the week; and you shall sustain yourselves with bread and salt and water only, at the ninth hour, until the fifth day of the week. But on the Friday and on the Sabbath fast wholly, and taste nothing.
> —*Didascalia Apostolorum* 21

From such humble beginnings were the extravaganza of Holy Week and Lent born.[6]

The proto-Catholics thus turned the Great Feast of the Jews on its head. Why did they do this? Epiphanius has preserved a passage from the *Apostolic Constitutions*, no longer in the extant version, which may explain their motivation. "And when the Jews are feasting, do you fast and wail over them, because on the day of their feast they crucified Christ; and while they are lamenting and eating unleavened bread in bitterness, do you feast."[7] The final drama of Jesus' life, played out against the backdrop of the Passover, was filled with sorrow and suffering. He went from the Last Supper

2. Galatians 4:11.
3. Colossians 2:16.
4. "Whoso afflicted his soul on the Lord's Day is under God's curse" (*Panarion* 6.70.11).
5. "Fast then . . . . six days, and it shall be reckoned to you as a week" (*Did Apost* 21).
6. See *Ap Const* 5.3.18 for the other version of this passage.
7. *Panarion* 6.70.11; see also *Ap Const* 5.3.15.

to Gethsemane, endured the betrayal in the garden, the midnight trial, the scourging and mocking, and finally, to a humiliating and painful death. The joyous atmosphere of the old feast no longer made sense.

The primitive *Pascha* of the proto-Catholics was an all-night affair. Like the Hebrew Passover, it started at eventide on the fourteenth of Nisan, the night of the full moon. The faithful gathered at the home of their presbyter, where they went for Sunday meeting, and brought baskets of food along. Although they had been fasting for several days at this point, tasting anything was considered a breach of the fast.[8] The vigil began with the ceremonial lighting of candles and recitation of a blessing. Over supper, the elder read Exodus 12, the story of Israel's miraculous deliverance from Egypt, followed by an exposition of its meaning. The long hours of the night were then spent reading the Scriptures, praying, and making intercession for Israel.

> From the even until cockcrowing keep awake, and assemble together in the church, watch and pray, and entreat God; reading, when you sit up all night, the Law, the Prophets, and the Psalms, until cockcrowing, and baptizing your catechumens, and reading the Gospel with fear and trembling, and speaking to the people such things as tend to their salvation: put an end to your sorrow, and beseech God that Israel may be converted, and that He will allow them a place of repentance...
> —*Apostolic Constitutions* 5.19

The Psalms mentioned in this extract were the Egyptian Hallel, Psalms 113–118. Psalms 113 and 114 are sung before the meal, and Psalms 115 to 118 are sung after the table grace and the third cup of wine.[9] Jesus and his apostles followed the *Pesah* protocol at the Last Supper. They passed around the cup of blessing—also known as redemption—and Jesus endowed it with a new meaning: "Likewise also the cup after supper, saying, This cup is the new testament in my blood, which is shed for you."[10] After declaring he would not drink the fourth cup—the cup of praise—they sang the concluding Hallel: "I will take the cup of salvation, and call upon the name of the Lord. I will pay my vows unto the Lord now in the presence of all his people. Precious in the sight of the Lord is the death of his saints."[11]

Psalms 118 and expressions of Alleluia carried over to the Christian Easter. The historian Sozomen reports that the Roman church was still

---

8. *Ap Trad* 29.
9. m. *Pesahim* 9.3d.
10. Luke 22:20.
11. Psalms 116:13-15.

singing Hallelujah on Easter in the fifth century.[12] Psalm 118 is now coupled with the reading of the Apostle in the Roman Easter Mass.

There was another dimension to the all-night vigil that was very real to the proto-Catholics. *They were watching and waiting for the Lord's return.* Jesus had warned his disciples many times during passion week to prepare for his second coming. "Watch ye therefore: for ye know not when the master of the house cometh, at evening, or at midnight, or at the cockcrowing, or in the morning: lest coming suddenly he find you sleeping."[13] The children of Israel have long expected the promised Messiah to appear at Passover season. Jewish households still set an extra goblet on the Passover table—known as Elijah's cup—and fill it with wine. It symbolizes the hope that Elijah, the herald and forerunner of the Anointed One, will come that very night and announce the redemption of the world.[14]

The Catholic Haggadah

The itinerary of the paschal vigil has survived in the work known as *Peri Pascha* (On the Passover). It has traditionally been attributed to Melito of Sardis, but no one really knows its origin.[15] The internal evidence all points to a date in the 140s. Pseudo-Melito cites Revelation but little else in the New Testament, the work is completely bereft of Paul, and there are far too many parallels and affinities with Justin Martyr not to be contemporaneous.

We learn that the primitive Easter service borrowed heavily from the Passover *Haggadah*. The *Haggadah* is a booklet or script which gives the order at the Seder table, designed to fulfill the command to "tell your sons" of their deliverance from bondage.[16] The head of each household was charged with telling (*Haggadah* in Hebrew) the story of the death angel and their hasty departure from Egypt. The false apostles took the traditional *Haggadah* and put a Christian spin on it.

They began the evening service by reading Exodus 12.[17] The Jewish head of house was prompted to explain its meaning by a question from the

---

12. "At Rome, hallelujah is sung once annually, namely on the first day of the festival of the Passover . . . ." (Sozomen, *History of the Church* 7.19).

13. Mark 13:35–36.

14. Malachi 4:5; Matthew 17:10–13.

15. Eusebius tells us that Melito of Sardis wrote two works on the Passover, see *Eccl Hist* 4.26.

16. Exodus 13:8.

17. "The scripture from the Hebrew Exodus having been read. . ." (*Peri Pascha* 1).

youngest child. "What mean ye by this service?"[18] This was changed in the post-Temple era to the more familiar query: "How is this night different from all other nights?" In *Peri Pascha*, the proto-Catholics were instructed to kick off the discourse by asking, "What is the Pascha?"[19] The Catholic homily then goes on to address the three topics Jewish fathers were obligated to cover. "The Passover—because the Omnipresent passed over the houses of our forefathers in Egypt. The Unleavened Bread—because our forefathers were redeemed in Egypt. The bitter herbs—because the Egyptians embittered the lives of our forefathers in Egypt."[20]

Their exegesis of "bitter herbs" is typical of the allegorical way the sectarians expounded Scripture:

> Bitter for you therefore is the feast of unleavened bread . . . bitter for you, Judas, whom you hired; bitter for you, Herod, whom you followed; bitter for you, Caiaphas, whom you trusted; bitter for you, the gall you prepared; bitter for you, the vinegar you produced; bitter for you, the thorns you culled. . .
> —*Peri Pascha* 93

There are even textual similarities between the Catholic homily and Passover passages in the Mishnah. Rabbi Gamaliel stated, "He brought us forth from slavery to freedom, anguish to joy, mourning to festival, darkness to great light, subjugation to redemption,"[21] and pseudo-Melito wrote, "It is he that delivered us from slavery to liberty, from darkness to light, from death to life, from tyranny to eternal royalty."[22]

The pre-Pauline *Pascha* was a commemoration of the Hebrew deliverance from Egypt, albeit from a Christian perspective. It was not a celebration of the resurrection of Jesus Christ. Indeed, only about twenty lines out of the eight hundred-plus sentences in *Peri Pascha* even allude to the resurrection. For pseudo-Melito and his contemporaries, the suffering of Israel in Egypt was fulfilled by the suffering of Christ. "What is the Pascha? It gets its name from its characteristic: from suffer (*pathein*) comes suffering (*paschein*). Learn therefore who is the suffering one, and who shares the suffering of the suffering one."[23] The Catholics did not link Easter with the resurrection until they added the New Testament to their canon in the middle of the second century.

18. Exodus 12:26.
19. *Peri Pascha* 46.
20. m. *Pesahim* 10.5.
21. m. *Pesahim* 10.
22. *Peri Pascha* 68.
23. *Peri Pascha* 46.

The Season of Baptism

The false apostles designed the entire cycle of Holy Week around the initiation rites of circumcision, immersion, and sacrifice. They were consciously following a long-established tradition that went back to the Lawgiver himself. Strangers and foreigners were circumcised before *Pesah* every year because it was a requirement to participate in the festival.[24]

Passover thus became the designated season for baptism. "Let him attend to frequent fastings, and approve himself in all things, that at the end of these three months he may be baptized on the day of the festival."[25] Several days before the 14th day of Nisan, the male initiates would be circumcised, and the multi-day fast which followed doubled as a time of healing. They would then spend the Passover vigil studying the Scriptures. "Spend the night in vigil, reading the Scriptures, and instructing them."[26] Just as Jewish proselytes were tutored in the finer points of the law before immersion, so Catholic catechumens were instructed as they awaited baptism.[27]

In the first centuries, the paschal fast would continue up until daybreak, when those assembled would form a procession and march to the waters of baptism. The catechumens were baptized at the crack of dawn.[28] After being immersed, they would eat bread sprinkled with salt as a substitute for their first offering.[29] In later years, if there were no candidates for baptism, they would end the fast at the third hour of the night by eating the Lord's Supper.[30] By the time the *Apostolic Tradition* was written in the third century, this meal had morphed into the reception of first communion.[31]

> **The Computus**—The formula used to compute the date of Easter is known as the *computus*. In the first century, the proto-Catholics observed Easter on the same day as the Jewish Passover, the 14th of Nisan. Easter Sunday was an innovation of the Roman church circa AD 115, and it gradually replaced the older observance. Easter is now celebrated on the first Sunday following the paschal full moon after March 21, the vernal equinox.

---

24. Exodus 12:43–48; Joshua 5:8–10.
25. *Recognitions* 3.67, see also 3.72.
26. *Ap Trad* 20.
27. The Two Ways section of the *Didache* was their first catechism. "And concerning baptism, baptize this way: Having first said all these things, baptize into the name of the Father . . .." (*Didache* 7).
28. *Ap Trad* 21.
29. *Homilies* 14.1.
30. *Did Apost* 21.19.
31. *Ap Trad* 23.

Quartodecimans and Easter Sunday

The New Covenant *Pascha* was tied to the same calendrical point as the Hebrew festival. The ancient patriarchs, following their flocks around the desert, measured time by the waxing and waning of the moon. The twelve tribes made their escape from Egypt on the fourteenth day after the new moon, the phase of the lunar cycle when there is a full moon in the sky. It was the ideal time for a large population to travel at night with their flocks and herds. The ecclesiastical year began in the spring and the first month, Nisan, was defined as the lunation in which the vernal equinox occurred. Moses commanded them to commemorate the passing over of the death angel on the fourteenth day of the month. The false apostles adopted this formula and it became the norm for centuries in Asia Minor, the cradle of Catholicism.

The intricacies of the Hebrew calendar were not familiar to their Greek converts. So how were they able to calculate the precise day? We assume that the false apostles—with their knowledge of paschal customs—made the critical determination in the first century. After these men died off, the Gentile churches were instructed to follow the lead of their brethren in Israel.[32] "Do not you yourselves compute [the date], but keep it when your brethren of the circumcision do: keep it together with them; and if they error in their computation, do not be concerned."[33] We do not know how the information was disseminated to the remote villages in Anatolia, but perhaps they sent special messengers from Israel, which was the custom of the Sanhedrin.

Rome was the birthplace of Easter Sunday. In the first or second decade of the second century, the Christians at Rome began to terminate the fast on the first Sunday after the paschal full moon. Irenaeus believed he could trace the convention back before the time of Xystus, the head of the Roman church from circa AD 115 to AD 125.[34]

---

32. "It behooves you, then, our brethren, in the days of the Pascha to make inquiry with diligence and to keep your fast with all care. And you shall make a beginning when your brethren who are of the People keep the Passover. For when our Lord and Teacher ate the Passover with us, He was betrayed by Judas after that hour; and immediately we began to be sorrowful, because he was taken from us. By the number of the moon, as we count according to the reckoning of the believing Hebrews, on the tenth of the moon, on the second day of the week... Whenever, then, the fourteenth of the Pascha falls, so keep it; for neither the month nor the day squares with the same season every year, but it is variable. When therefore that People keep the Passover, do you fast; and be careful to perform your vigil within their [feast of] unleavened bread" (*Did Apost* 21).

33. *Panarion* 6.70.10.

34. Sometimes spelled Sixtus.

Among these were the presbyters before Soter, who presided over the church which thou now rulest. We mean Anicetus, and Pius, and Hyginus, and Telephorus, and Xystus. They neither observed it [the 14th of Nisan] themselves, nor did they permit those after them to do so.
—*History of the Church* 5.24.14

Why did they make the change? We can only speculate, but transmitting information was slow and unreliable in the second century, and there were enormous distances between Palestine, western Turkey, and now Rome. The responsibility for making this vital calculation fell on the shoulders of the Roman elders, men who were not schooled in astronomy. Every year, in the springtime, they had to face the same bewildering and frustrating task. It was immeasurably easier just to use the first Sunday after the large and very visible Jewish community in Rome had eaten the lamb.

Rome, the mother church of the west, exported the simplified date to the children that sprang from her loins. Easter Sunday was not only planted in France, Greece, and Carthage, but also in Egypt, Judaea, Cappadocia, Edessa, and Mesopotamia. It was the only paschal observance these Catholics had ever known. The divergence in paschal customs between them and the Quartodecimans was papered over and ignored for several decades.

In AD 154, the growing rift was addressed in a formal way. Polycarp, the bishop of Smyrna, traveled to Rome that year to discuss the paschal differences with Anicetus, the Roman bishop. Each made a case for their tradition, citing the presbyters that came before them, but they were unable to find a compromise.[35] Despite this, a spirit of toleration and conciliation prevailed for the next several decades, until Victor was elected to the bishopric in AD 189. An overbearing, arrogant man, Victor enjoyed exercising the newly assumed authority of the Roman church. He proceeded to excommunicate the Quartodeciman observers.

Eusebius has preserved details of the Paschal controversy that erupted around AD 190 and the correspondence which sprang from it.

> A question of no small importance arose at that time. For the parishes of all Asia, *as from an older tradition*, held that the fourteenth day of the moon, on which day the Jews were commanded to sacrifice the lamb, should be observed as the feast of the Lord's Passover. It was therefore necessary to end their fast on that day, whatever day of the week it should happen to be. But it was not the custom of the churches in the rest of the world to end it at this time, as they observed the practice which,

---

35. *Eccl Hist* 5.24.

from apostolic tradition, has prevailed to the present time, of terminating the fast on no other day than on that of the resurrection of our Savior.
—*History of the Church* 5.23, emphasis mine

Polycrates, the bishop of Ephesus, wrote a passionate reply back to Victor on behalf of the Quartodeciman churches in Asia. He was quite adamant about the great antiquity and correctness of 14 Nisan.

> We observe the exact day; neither adding nor taking away. For in Asia also great lights have fallen asleep, which shall rise again on the day of the Lord's coming, when he shall come with glory from heaven, and shall seek out all the saints. Among these are Philip, one of the twelve apostles, who fell asleep in Hierapolis; and his two aged virgin daughters and another daughter, who lived in the Holy Spirit and now rests at Ephesus; and, moreover John, who was both a witness and a teacher, who reclined upon the bosom of the Lord, and, being a priest, wore the sacerdotal plate. He fell asleep at Ephesus. And Polycarp in Smyrna, who was a bishop and martyr; and Thraseas, bishop and martyr from Eumenia, who fell asleep in Smyrna. Why need I mention the bishop and martyr Sagaris who fell asleep in Laodicea, or the blessed Papirius, or Melito, the eunuch who lived altogether in the Holy Spirit, and who lies in Sardis, awaiting the episcopate from heaven, when he shall rise from the dead? All these observed the fourteenth day of the Passover according to the Gospel, deviating in no respect, but following the rule of faith. And I also, Polycrates, the least of you all, do according to the tradition of my relatives, some of whom I have closely followed. For seven of my relatives were bishops, and I am the eighth. And my relatives always observed the day when the people put away the leaven.
> —*History of the Church* 5.24

In the end, Victor was persuaded to back down, and the unity of the Church was restored.

The Quartodeciman churches enjoyed perfect communion with the rest of the Catholic world until the Council of Nicaea. When Constantine convened the first great council of the *Ekklesia Katholika* in AD 325, the principle item on his agenda was the standardization of Easter. The churches using the Roman rule had the votes and prevailed: "It is our duty not to have anything in common with the murderers of our Lord; and as the custom now followed by the churches of the west, of the south, of the north, and by some of those of the east, is the most acceptable, it has appeared good to all."[36] They settled on the first Sunday following the paschal full moon after the spring equinox. The church at Antioch went along with the majority and, at the Antiochene Synod of AD 341, cast out those who reckoned the festival "with the Jews."[37] The Quartodecimans now found themselves branded as heretics and put outside the camp.

The Nicene Council may have settled the Sunday Easter observance for all time, but they still could not agree on the correct *computus*, or formula for computing the date. The Roman church kept its 84-year paschal cycle while other churches retained their *computus*, so Christians around the world still found themselves celebrating the resurrection on different Sundays. The deviation between the paschal feasts of Rome and Alexandria reached an embarrassing four weeks in AD 387. After several centuries of experimentation, a variant of the 19-year cycle promoted by Alexandria, the astronomical center of the ancient world, became normative. The custom developed for the bishop of Alexandria to determine the proper day for the Church at large, and to transmit it by letter to the other bishops.

Despite all of these efforts, uniformity on Easter still eludes the daughters of Nicaea. After forcing an agreement on a Sunday observance and achieving consensus on the *computus*, the entire western calendar was recalibrated in the sixteenth century. The old Julian calendar had been getting further and further out of synch with the seasons each passing century. In AD 1582, Pope Gregory XIII commissioned a panel of experts, and they recommended that ten days be dropped from the calendar and altered the rules for adding leap years. The Roman Catholics adopted the papal reforms, but the Greek and Russian churches did not. Thus, in 2020, while the Latin and Protestant churches were joyously celebrating the feast on April 12th, their brethren in the Orthodox rites were still struggling to maintain the fast, which did not end for them until the following Sunday.

---

36. *Life* 3.
37. Canon 1.

13

Heresy and Dissent in the Great Church

---

*After the way which they call heresy,
so worship I the God of my fathers.....*

—Acts 24:14

Most of the Catholic world followed the lead of the Roman reformers, but there were pockets of old believers—most often in Asia and Phrygia—who put up resistance. As the Church changed course through the years, lurching from one novelty to another, conservative dissidents would spin off clutching the doctrine they had grown up with. Each change in direction would generate a new controversy and a new set of "heretics," Catholics who were guilty of nothing but keeping the faith of their fathers.[1]

Every epoch of the primitive Church was defined by its nonconformists. The 14th of Nisan Easter was not controversial until the Quartodecimans became a minority in the Church in the middle of the second century. They were finally cast out of communion at the Council of Nicaea AD 325. The Severians rejected Paul and the Acts of the Apostles, and split with the Roman reformers circa AD 175. The Montanists were early enthusiasts of

---

1. This is similar to the Samaritans in Israel. They were a spinoff sect of mixed Jews who kept to the Pentateuch, refusing to accept the historical and prophetic books of the Hebrew canon.

the apostle John, Quartodecimans who emphasized the charismatic gifts of the Spirit. The Adoptionists wanted to keep the traditional Christology of the sect, and fell afoul of the liberal reformers in the 190s. The *Alogi* refused to accept John and his writings, and were anathematized at the beginning of the third century.

We will look first at the Jewish wing of the Christian movement. The Church Fathers referred to the Jewish Christians who rejected Paul as Ebionites, and by the end of the second century they could distinguish them from the believing Jews, whom they called Nazarenes. In the Arab world, the followers of Jesus of Nazareth have always been known as *Nasrani*, or Nazarenes. The term goes back into New Testament days where Paul was called a Nazarene. "For we have found this man a pestilent fellow, and a mover of sedition among all the Jews throughout the world, and a ringleader of the sect of the Nazarenes"[2] Around AD 90, the rabbis added a malediction to the daily prayer of the Jews, the 18 Benedictions, which was directed toward "Nazarenes and other heretics."[3]

The later Church Fathers recognized that the Nazarenes held pretty standard Christian doctrines except, being Jews, they were circumcised and kept Torah. Our most complete source is the fourth century Cypriote bishop Epiphanius.

> They use not only the New Testament but the Old Testament as well, as the Jews do. For unlike the previous sectarians [Ebionites], they do not repudiate the legislation, the prophets, and the books Jews call "Writings." They have no different ideas, but confess everything exactly as the Law proclaims it and in the Jewish fashion—except for their belief in Christ, if you please! For they acknowledge both the resurrection of the dead and the divine creation of all things, and declare that God is one, and that his Son is Jesus Christ.
>
> They are trained to a nicety in Hebrew. For among them the entire Law, the Prophets, and the so-called Writings—I mean the poetic books, Kings, Chronicles, Esther and all the rest—are read in Hebrew, as they surely are by Jews. They are different from Jews, and different from Christians, only in the following. They disagree with Jews because they have come to faith in Christ; but since they are still fettered by the Law—circumcision, the Sabbath, and the rest—they are not in accord with Christians....

---

2. Acts 24:5.
3. b. Ber. 28b, 29a.

> Today this sect of the Nazoraeans is found in Beroea near Coelesyria, in the Decapolis near Pella, and in Bashanitis at the place called Cocabe-Khokhabe in Hebrew. For that was its place of origin, since all the disciples had settled in Pella after they left Jerusalem. Christ told them to abandon Jerusalem and withdraw from it because of its coming siege. And they settled in Peraea for this reason and, as I said, spent their lives there. That was where the Nazoraean sect began.
> —*Panarion* 29.7

The Ebionites

The few Jewish converts the false apostles made in Palestine remained frozen—arrested—in its primitive state. They did not develop and evolve along with the mainstream of the movement, and quickly lost contact with their Gentile brethren in far-off Phrygia. Justin Martyr, who was born in Samaria, wrote about them in the middle of the second century. He is long on philosophizing but short on detail.

> "But if some, through weak-mindedness, wish to observe such institutions as were given by Moses, from which they expect some virtue, but which we believe were appointed by reason of the hardness of the people's hearts, along with their hope in this Christ, and [wish to perform] the eternal and natural acts of righteousness and piety, yet choose to live with the Christians and the faithful, as I said before, not inducing them either to be circumcised like themselves, or to keep the Sabbath, or to observe any other such ceremonies, then I hold that we ought to join ourselves to such , and associate with them in all things as kinsmen and brethren. But if, Trypho, some of our race, who say they believe in this Christ, compel those Gentiles who believe in this Christ to live in all respects according to the law given by Moses, or choose not to associate so intimately with them, I in like manner do not approve of them. But I believe that even those, who have been persuaded by them to observe the legal dispensation along with their confession of God in Christ, shall probably be saved. And I hold, further, that such as have confessed and knows this man to be Christ, yet who have gone back from some cause to the legal dispensation, and have denied that this man is Christ, and have repented not before death, shall by no means be saved."
> —*Dialogue of Trypho* 47

HERESY AND DISSENT IN THE GREAT CHURCH

Irenaeus, circa AD 185, was the first of the Church Fathers to have any concrete information on them. We learn from the bishop of Lyon that they were now called Ebionites.

> "Those who are called Ebionites agree that the world was made by God; but their opinions with respect to the Lord are similar to those of Cerinthus and Carpocrates [ie, they were adoptionists]. They use the Gospel according to Matthew only, and repudiate the apostle Paul, maintaining that he was an apostate from the Law. As to the prophetical writings, they endeavor to expound them in a somewhat singular manner: they practice circumcision, persevere in the observance of those customs which are enjoined by the Law, and are so Judaic in their style of life that they even adore Jerusalem as if it were the house of God.
> —*Against Heresies* 1.26.2

Epiphanius tells us the Ebionites were governed by a patriarch and, below that, a class of ministers known as apostles."[4] This is reminiscent of the "apostles and prophets" of the *Didache*. The derivation of Ebion—Hebrew for poor—surely hearkens back to the false apostles. "Their boastful claim is that they sold their possessions in the time of the apostles and laid them at the apostle's feet, and have gone over to poverty and renunciation and thus, they say, they are called 'poor' by everyone.[5]

The Church Fathers could differentiate between the apostolic Nazarenes and the proto-Catholic Ebionites by their doctrine and Scriptures.

- The Ebionites did not believe in the virgin birth;[6] the Nazarenes did.[7]
- The Ebionites believed that Jesus was merely a man imbued with the Holy Spirit at baptism. The Nazarenes taught that Jesus was the pre-existent Son of God.[8]

---

4. *Panarion* 30.4.2.

5. *Panarion* 30.17.2.

6. "But the heresy of the Ebionites, as it is called, asserts that Christ was the son of Joseph and Mary, considering him a mere man . . ." (*Eccl Hist* 6.17).

7. "The adherents to this sect are commonly known as Nazarenes; they believe in Christ the Son of God, born of the Virgin Mary; and they say that He who suffered under Pontius Pilate and rose again, is the same as the one in whom we believe" (*Letter of Jerome to Augustine No. 75*).

8. "as I said before, he is a mere man who has come to be called the Son of God owing to the virtue of his life" (*Panarion* 30.18.6). "The Ebionites . . . say that Jesus was justified by fulfilling the law. And therefore it was that (he) was named (the) Christ of God and Jesus, since not one of the rest (of mankind) had observed completely the law. For if even any other had fulfilled the commandments in the law he would have been that Christ . . . for they assert that our Lord Himself was a man in like sense with all (the

- The proto-Catholic Ebionites rejected the apostle Paul;[9] the Nazarenes embraced Paul.[10]
- Of the Christian Scriptures, the Ebionites accepted only the Gospel of Matthew,[11] the Gospel of the first century proto-Catholics. The Nazarenes utilized the entire New Testament.[12]
- The Ebionites canonized the *Preaching of Peter*, which they called the *Travels of Peter*.[13] The Nazarenes used the Acts of the Apostles.
- The Ebionites immersed themselves daily for ritual purification.[14] The Peter of the *Homilies* and *Recognitions* also bathed daily.[15]
- The Ebionites observed the laws of family purity and uncleanness.[16]

The Severians

The Catholics who did not go along with the Paulinists in Rome were given the name of Severians, after their leader. We know nothing of this man. Irenaeus wrote about these old believers just thirty years after Paul's acceptance. He doesn't tell us much except that they had separated themselves from the "apostles," by which he means the Catholic mainstream.

---

rest of the human family)" (Hippolytus, *Against Heresies* 7.22). "For they acknowledge both the resurrection of the dead and the divine creation of all things, and declare that God is one, and that his son is Jesus the Messiah" (*Panarion* 29).

9. "Those who are called Ebionites . . . repudiate the Apostle Paul, maintaining that he was an apostate from the law" (*Against Heresies* 1.26.2).

10. "They use not only the New Testament but the Old Testament as well . . ." (*Panarion* 29.7.2).

11. "They use the Gospel according to Matthew only . . . ." (*Panarion* 30.3.7). "They too accept the Gospel according to Matthew. Like the Cerinthians and Merinthians, they also use it alone" (*Against Heresies* 1.26.2).

12. "They use not only the New Testament but the Old Testament as well, as the Jews do" (*Panarion* 29.7.2).

13. "But they use certain other books as well—supposedly the so-called *Travels of Peter* written by Clement, although they corrupt their contents while leaving a few genuine passages" (*Panarion* 30.15.1). It appears from this statement that the Ebionites used the original *Preaching of Peter* while Epiphanius knew the rewritten *Homilies of Clement*.

14. "In the *Travels* [ie, *Preaching of Peter*] they have changed everything to suit themselves and slandered Peter in many ways, saying that he was baptized daily for purification as they are" (*Panarion* 30.15.3).

15. *Recognitions* 6.11.

16. "The Ebionites added the rule about taking care not to touch a gentile; and that every day, if a man has been with a woman and has left her, he must immerse himself in water—any water he can find, the sea or any other" (*Panarion* 30.2.3, 4).

> But again, we allege the same against those who do not recognize Paul as an apostle: that they should either reject the other words of the Gospel which we have come to know through Luke alone, and not make use of them; or else, if they do receive all these, they must necessarily admit also that testimony concerning Paul, when he (Luke) tells us that the Lord spoke at first to him from heaven: 'Saul, Saul, why do you persecute Me? I am Jesus Christ, whom you persecute,' and then to Ananias, saying regarding him: 'Go your way; for he is a chosen vessel unto Me, to bear My name among the Gentiles, and kings, and the children of Israel. For I will show him, from this time, how great things he must suffer for My name's sake.' Those, therefore, who do not accept him, who was chosen by God for this purpose, that he might boldly bear His name, as being sent to the aforementioned nations, do despise the election of God, and separate themselves from the company of the apostles.
> —*Against Heresies* 3.15

Eusebius expanded on the Severians in the fourth century. We learn that they used more than one Gospel, but rejected both the Pauline texts and the Acts of the Apostles. This strongly implies they were still reading the *Preaching of Peter* in their congregations. The Severians may have been the last keepers of the old proto-Catholic flame.

> But a little later a certain man named Severus put new strength into the aforesaid heresy and thus brought it about that those who took their origin from it were called, after him, Severians. They, indeed, use the Law and Prophets and Gospels but interpret in their own way the utterances of the Sacred Scriptures. And they abuse Paul the apostle and reject his epistles, and do not accept even the Acts of the Apostles.
> —*History of the Church* 4.29

14

Chronology: Setting the Record Straight

What is history, but a fable agreed upon?

—Napoleon Bonaparte

It took one hundred years and three separate steps to complete the myth of apostolic succession. It began with the false apostles creating a connection with the twelve apostles which did not exist. They did this in their founding documents by misrepresenting Paul and portraying fictitious relationships with Peter and James. In stage two, Paul was invited into the church. This phase began in the middle of the second century with Marcion and ended with Polycarp's ringing endorsement. Finally, they had to close the chronological gap between step one and step two. There could not be an eighty or ninety-year hiatus—an unexplained break—in the historical record, so letters were manufactured to fill this void. These include the well-known letters written in the name of the bishop of Antioch, Theophorus Ignatius.

The Ignatian letters are the Piltdown Man of the patristic world. The most famous scientific hoax of the twentieth century was a human cranium fitted with the jawbone of an orangutan. The molars had been carefully filed, the jawbone broken at the critical spot where it joined the skull, and the bones chemically stained to impart the impression of great antiquity. To further the deception, the Piltdown quarry where they were found was

CHRONOLOGY: SETTING THE RECORD STRAIGHT

salted with the bones of extinct animals. Almost the entire British scientific community was taken in. French and American scientists, to their credit, were not as gullible and remained suspicious. Nevertheless, for nearly half a century, Piltdown Man was touted as the vital missing link that confirmed the theories of Charles Darwin. How were educated, presumably intelligent men so easily duped? Rather easily, as it turned out. It fit their preconceived ideas of what a missing link would look like, and advanced a theory they already believed in. They were blinded by their own biases.

We find the same blindness among scholars and churchmen regarding Ignatius. Not a single, solitary scrap of information is known about the man apart from what we are told in these letters. He is said to be the second or third Catholic bishop of Antioch, and there may be a kernel of truth in this. Peter is depicted in the pseudo-Clementine literature as bringing the Gospel to Antioch. Ignatius was thought for many years to have had the direct anointing of Peter, but by the third century, a man named Euodius had snuck in there.[1] This was done to push Ignatius' bishopric up to the turn of the first century, when we are told this group of letters was written.

What does the Bible tell us about the church at Antioch? According to Acts 11, the Syrian church was founded by Jewish Christians who, in their enthusiasm for the Gospel, had witnessed to local Greeks. It would not be untenable to suggest that the names of these men might be found among the "prophets and teachers" listed in Acts 13. "Now there were in the church that was at Antioch certain prophets and teachers; as Barnabas, Simeon that was called Niger, and Lucius of Cyrene, and Manaen, which had been brought up with Herod the tetrarch, and Saul." Barnabas was dispatched by the Judean leadership to sort things out, and no doubt he appointed the first elders and deacons. The Antioch mission was an unqualified success: "And much people was added to the Lord."[2] Paul and Barnabas taught the Antiochenes for a full year and often resorted there on their home visits.[3]

There is not a single point of intersection between the received Catholic tradition and the New Testament record. The Catholics claim a Petrine founding, followed by Euodius, and then Ignatius;[4] the Bible tells us that the Antiochene church sprang up spontaneously by unnamed disciples, who were then organized by Barnabas and taught by Paul. It would take a lot of ingenuity to reconcile these two accounts.

1. *Ap Const* 8.
2. Acts 11:24.
3. Acts 11:26.
4. The *Liber Pontificalis* gives Peter a seven year bishopric in Antioch, approximately AD 35 to AD 42. This was the very time when he was staying with Simon the tanner in Joppa and went up to meet Cornelius in Caesarea.

There are three separate collections of letters attributed to Ignatius, known as the short, middle, and long recensions. The seven epistles of the middle recension are considered genuine by most Roman Catholic and Orthodox theologians, and not a few Protestants as well. These letters are addressed to six different churches and one esteemed colleague:

- Ephesians
- Magnesians
- Trallians
- Romans
- Philadelphians
- Smyrnaeans
- The bishop of Smyrna, Polycarp

The short recension includes just three of these letters. Preserved only in Syriac, they are widely considered to be an abridgement of the middle edition epistles addressed to Polycarp, the Ephesians, and the Romans. On the other hand, the long recension is an expansion of the "accepted seven," and includes six additional letters whose authenticity no one will defend. This set of forgeries was a product of the fourth century, and it reflects the doctrinal controversies of that era. Indeed, the first attested citation comes from Stephanus Gobarus in the year AD 570.[5]

The story or scenario posited by the letters is as follows. The venerable bishop of Antioch has been arrested by Roman authorities and is en route to stand trial in Rome. Whenever the company makes a stop on the journey, Ignatius would dash off a pastoral letter to one of the above churches. Ignatius is traditionally assigned to the second half of Trajan's reign (AD 98 to AD 117), but the evidence for an early second century dating is extraordinarily weak.[6]

There is a mountain of evidence which indicates 1) the letters are fictitious, and 2) they belong to a later age. In the first place, Christians were tried and punished by local magistrates. They were simply not important enough to incur the cost of being transported to Rome for trial. There is not a single example from the Flavian age of a prisoner being brought to Rome for punishment who was not a citizen or a prisoner of war. If Ignatius had been a Roman citizen, he would have been beheaded, not fed to the lions. Finally,

---

5. Long Ignatius stands in a class of writings all its own: a forgery of a forgery.

6. Eusebius places his martyrdom within the reign of Trajan, without specifying the year (*Eccl Hist* 3.36).

CHRONOLOGY: SETTING THE RECORD STRAIGHT 159

an accused citizen who had appealed to Caesar could not be scourged or chained, as psuedo-Ignatius claimed in *Ignatius to the Romans* 5.[7]

Ignatius stands out as an anomalous outlier in the early years of the second century. Like an erratic boulder pushed down the mountain by glaciers and deposited in a grassy meadow, the Ignatian corpus is strikingly different from everything else written at that time. There are no agrapha, few allusions to the Old Testament, and only three direct citations from the Hebrew Scriptures. The prominent place accorded to bishops is at variance with every other Christian document of that period.

More serious are the anachronisms. It is not easy to compose something of this length without slipping up. One of the worst blunders is in the *Epistle to the Magnesians*. In the midst of a rambling sentence, he says of Christ: "who is his eternal Word, not proceeding forth from silence..."[8] This statement is meant to refute a signature tenet of Valentinus, who would not begin to teach for another thirty years. Another chronological lapse occurs in the *Epistle to the Philadelphians*. "If any confesses Christ Jesus the Lord, but denies the God of the law and of the prophets, saying that the Father of Christ is not the Maker of heaven and earth, he has not continued in the truth any more than his father the devil..."[9] This is an obvious jab at Marcion, who made the distinction between the God of the Law and Prophets, and the Father of Jesus Christ. Marcion would also not arrive on the scene for another thirty years. And pseudo-Ignatius refers to the *Katholika Ekklesia*, a designation which will not appear for another 50 years if the conventional chronology is adopted.

Moving ahead in the patristic record, what do we find? There is not a single witness to Ignatius between the time of his alleged martyrdom and the middle of the second century. He disappears for almost 50 years. The universally admired bishop of Antioch is, for some inexplicable reason, never mentioned by Papias, Hegesippus, pseudo-Barnabas, the *Shepherd of Hermas*, or Justin Martyr. The man who supposedly rocked the Christian world of his day did not merit a single acknowledgement by the generation that followed.

Our first sighting of Ignatius comes from the *Epistle of Polycarp to the Philippians*. This letter was most likely written in AD 155,[10] which provides us with a *terminus ad quem* for the fabrication of Ignatius. Even the *Epistle*

7. Lex de Iulia Publica
8. *Ig to Mag* 8.2.
9. *Ig to Phil* 6.

10. The death of Polycarp, documented in the *Martyrdom of Polycarp*, is placed in the reign of Marcus Aurelius (AD 161 to AD 180) by Eusebius, while a later addition to the *Martyrdom* puts it at AD 155 or AD 156.

of *Polycarp* is not without its problems. In chapter 9, we are told that Ignatius has not "ran in vain" and is "with the Lord." In chapter 13, he is very much alive and is writing letters.

The most parsimonious explanation for this contradiction is that chapter 13 is an interpolation. The *Epistle of Polycarp* reads seamlessly if chapter 12 is followed directly by chapter 14. The sole purpose of chapter 13 was to introduce the bishop of Antioch to the Church and to roll out the newly-minted Ignatian letters.

> The epistles of Ignatius, written by him to us, and all the rest (of his epistles) which we have by us, we have sent to you, as you requested. They are subjoined to this epistle, and by them ye may be greatly profited; for they speak of faith and patience, and all things that tend to edification in our Lord. Any more certain information you may have obtained respecting both Ignatius himself, and those that were with him, have the goodness to make known to us.
> —*Polycarp to the Philippians* 13

A production date of AD 150 is consistent with the internal evidence. The learned bishop who directed the affairs of the eastern Church was barely acquainted with Paul. Although claims are made for a broader familiarity, all we can say for certain is that pseudo-Ignatius had read 1 Corinthians.[11] He was ignorant of the Pauline missions, and it is unlikely he had ever seen the Acts of the Apostles. In the Ignatian letter to the Romans, for example, he writes as if Paul had never been a prisoner.[12]

We have weighed the authenticity of the Ignatian letters in the balance and found them wanting. We are not the first to question their authenticity. There has always been a cloud of doubt and skepticism hanging over the good bishop of Antioch. The introductory note to Ignatius in the Ante-Nicene Fathers series puts it like this: "The epistles ascribed to Ignatius have given rise to more controversy than any other documents connected with the primitive Church."[13] Their historicity has been endlessly debated by the

---

11. Even the passage Ignatius' supporters usually trot out for a broader awareness of Paul undermines their case. "Ye are initiated into the mysteries of the Gospel with Paul, the holy, the martyred, the deservedly most happy, at whose feet may I be found, when I shall attain to God; *who in every epistle makes mention of you in Christ Jesus*" (*Ig to Eph* 12:2, emphasis mine). Excluding the pastoral letters, the Ephesian Christians are mentioned in one and only one of Paul's epistles: 1 Corinthians.

12. "They were apostles, I am but a condemned man: they were free, while I am, even until now, a servant" (*Ig to Romans* 4). This is a patently false statement. Paul spent at least three years in Roman custody.

13. Roberts and Donaldson, *Ante-Nicene Fathers*, 46.

experts in the field because, like the Piltdown Man, the parts seem to fit but one cannot help feeling that something is not quite right.

First Epistle of Clement

There is a second way to close the ninety-plus year gap: Take genuine church documents and push their dating further back in time. It is commonly accepted that the letter known as *1 Clement* was written around AD 95, but this date rests on the flimsiest of foundations. The letter does not identify the author; only by a late tradition is it assigned to Clement, and then, taking another leap of faith, it is dated from an oblique mention of "sudden and successive" calamities. These calamities are arbitrarily identified with a persecution the Church Fathers cooked up under Domitian (AD 81 to AD 96).[14] It is—to say the least—not an airtight case.

We know from the twin testimonies of Dionysius of Corinth and Hegesippus that *I Clement* was circulating by AD 170.[15] That establishes a firm *terminus ad quem*. Polycarp of Smyrna (c. AD 155) *may* have known this letter—although I am not convinced—but other than him, there is not a single literary acknowledgement between AD 95 and AD 170.[16] It is the Ignatian Syndrome all over again. The Catholics assign very early dates to their writings with little or no hard evidence.

On the other hand, *1 Clement* could not have been published before AD 145 because of the Pauline connection. The author recommends *the* epistle Paul had sent to the saints at Corinth, indicating an acquaintance with 1 Corinthians but not 2 Corinthians.[17] He cites the Epistle to the Hebrews multiple times, and believes that Paul had journeyed to "the furthest bounds of the west," obviously picked up from Romans 15:24.[18] We conclude that *1 Clement* was written at the time when the Catholics were just beginning to flirt with Paul.

How did this letter come to be identified with Clement? There are a series of clues buried in the *Shepherd of Hermas* and the *Muratorian*

14. This persecution was a favorite place for Catholic Fathers to dump documents which are difficult to date. The modern consensus of opinion is that the Domitianic persecution never happened, see page 185.

15. *Eccl Hist* 4.21, 4.23.

16. Compare *Polycarp to Phil* 2.3 to *1 Clement* 13.1–2; *Polycarp to Phil.* 4.2–3 to *1 Clement* 1.3; *Polycarp to Phil* 4.2 to *1 Clement* 21.6; *Poly to Phil* 4.3 to *1 Clement* 21.3.

17. *1 Clement* 47.

18. It is equally obvious from this passage the author had never seen the Acts of the Apostles or he would have known that Paul's stated desire was interrupted by imprisonment.

Canon—both from Rome—which may help us uncover its origin. The first clue from the *Muratorian Canon* enables us to accurately date the *Shepherd of Hermas*. "But Hermas wrote the *Shepherd* very recently, in our times, in the city of Rome, while bishop Pius, his brother, was occupying the chair of the church of the city of Rome." Pius had the oversight of the Roman church for fourteen years, beginning in AD 140.

The second clue is from the *Shepherd of Hermas*. "You will therefore write two books, and you will send one to Clemens and the other to Grapte. And Clemens will send his to foreign countries, for permission has been granted to him to do so."[19] This Clemens may have been the Clement of the letter which now bears his name. He was apparently the secretary who corresponded with foreign churches on behalf of the Roman church. His name was probably appended to the original letter they sent to the Corinthians and then, as the letter was copied, it remained. This otherwise unknown scribe was quickly forgotten and his work attributed to the other, more famous, Clement.

At the time *1 Clement* was released, the Church was busy thumbing through and absorbing the letters of Paul. In his Epistle to the Philippians, Paul casually mentions an evangelist named Clement.[20] This breathed new life into the name of Clement—the legendary figure of their earliest mythology—and he now becomes synonymous with Paul's fellow-laborer. Thus, by AD 185, Clement of Philippi finds himself the author of *1 Clement* and third in line to the Roman succession.[21]

The Apostolic History of the proto-Catholics

The Syriac *Teaching of the Apostles* has preserved the most complete exposition of their apostolic mythology that we possess. Although the extant book was composed late in the second century—and amended later—it contains a significant amount of pre-Pauline material. This work gives us a list of the apostles and the countries they opened up to the gospel. Paul, who "labored more abundantly than they all," is conspicuously absent, and his legacy is parceled out among John, Simon Peter, Andrew, and Luke.

---

19. *Shepherd* Vision 2.4.

20. "And I intreat thee also, true yokefellow, help those women which labored with me in the gospel, *with Clement also*, and with other my fellowlaborers, whose names are in the book of life" (Philippians 4:3, emphasis mine).

21. Irenaeus, writing c. AD 185, believed that Clement was the third in succession to the Roman bishopric (*Against Heresies* 3.3.3). He consequently places *1 Clement* at the latter end of the first century.

CHRONOLOGY: SETTING THE RECORD STRAIGHT 163

The following citation retains the original numbering scheme.

1. Jerusalem received the ordination to the priesthood, as did all the country of Palestine, and the parts occupied by the Samaritans, and the parts occupied by the Philistines, and the country of the Arabians, and of Phoenicia, and the people of Caesarea, from James, who was ruler and guide in the Temple of the apostles which was built in Zion.

2. Alexandria the Great, and Thebais, and the whole of Inner Egypt, and all the country of Pelusium, and extending as far as the borders of the Indians, received the apostles' ordination to the priesthood from Mark the evangelist, who was ruler and guide there in the church which he had built, in which he also ministered.

3. India, and all the countries belonging to it and round about it, even to the farthest sea, received the apostles' ordination to the priesthood from Judas Thomas, who was guide and ruler in the church which he had built there, in which he also ministered there.

4. "Antioch, and Syria, and Cilicia, and Galatia, even to Pontus, received the apostles' ordination to the priesthood from Simon Cephas, who himself laid the foundation of the church there, and ministered there up to the time when he went up from thence to Rome on account of Simon the sorcerer, who was deluding the people of Rome with his sorceries."

5. "The city of Rome, and all Italy, and Spain, and Britain, and Gaul, together with all the rest of the countries round about them, received the apostles' ordination to the priesthood from Simon Cephas, who went up from Antioch, and he was ruler and guide there, in the church which he had built there, and in the places round about it."

6. "Ephesus, and Thessalonica, and all Asia, and all the country of the Corinthians, and all Achaia and the parts round about it, received the apostles' ordination to the priesthood from John the evangelist, who had leaned upon the bosom of our Lord; who himself built a church there, and ministered in his office of Guide which he held there."

7. "Nicaea, and Nicomedia, and all the country of Bithynia, and Inner Galatia, and the regions round about it, received the apostles' ordination to the priesthood from Andrew, the brother of Simon Cephas, who was himself Guide and Ruler in the church which he had built there, and was priest and ministered there."

8. "Byzantium, and all the country of Thrace, and the parts about it as far as the great river [the Danube], the boundary which separates from the barbarians, received the apostles' ordination to the priesthood from Luke the apostle, who himself built a church there, and ministered there in his office of Ruler and Guide which he held there."

9. "Edessa, and all the countries round about which were on all sides of it, and Zoba, and Arabia, and all the north, and the regions round about it, and the south, and all the regions on the borders of Mesopotamia, received the apostles' ordination to the priesthood from Addaeus the apostle, one of the seventy-two apostles, who himself made disciples there, and built a church there, and was priest and ministered there in his office of Guide which he held there."

—Syriac *Teaching of the Apostles*

"There must be a mistake," you say, "No one could possibly get it this wrong." However, earlier in the same book is another enumeration of the pioneering apostles and the place of their labors. "Also what James had written from Jerusalem, and Simon from the city of Rome, and John from Ephesus, and Mark from Alexandria the Great, and Andrew from Phrygia, and Luke from Macedonia, and Judas Thomas from India: that the epistles of an apostle might be received and read in the churches that were in every place." There really is no doubt. This is what the first century sectarians were taught and believed.

This is confirmed by several third century sources.[22] They were written after the Pauline Reformation, so Paul's contribution is now acknowledged. Origens' lost *Commentary on Genesis* is cited verbatim by Eusebius.

> Such was the condition of the Jews. Meanwhile the holy apostles and disciples of our Saviour were dispersed throughout the world. Parthia, according to tradition, was allotted to Thomas as his field of labor, Scythia to Andrew, and Asia to John, who, after he had lived some time there, died at Ephesus.
> —History of the Church 3.1

There are many such nuggets buried in this stratum of their history. Peter, who was the apostle to the Jews in the canonical Scriptures,[23] spent his life among the Greeks and Romans in the Clementine version of events. "The excellent and approved disciple, who, as being fittest of all, was commanded to enlighten the dark part of the world, namely the west, and was enabled to accomplish this.[24] Paul, of course, did more to "enlighten the west" than anyone. The *Apology of Aristides*, written in the 130s, also leaves out Paul's contribution. "He had twelve disciples who, after his ascension to heaven, went forth into the provinces of the world and declared His greatness. As for instance, one of them traversed the countries about us [Greece],

---

22. Acts of Thomas 1

23. "But contrariwise, when they saw that the gospel of the uncircumcision was committed unto me, as the gospel of the circumcision was unto Peter . . . ." (Galatians 2:7, 8).

24. *Clement to James* 1.

proclaiming the doctrine of the truth."[25] Paul, the first Christian missionary into Greece, was not one of the Twelve.[26] The third century *Didascalia Apostolorum* stockpiled many of their pre-Pauline legends, and proclaims that the Twelve evangelized the Gentiles. "But when we had divided the whole world into twelve parts, and were gone forth among the Gentiles into all the world to preach the word, then Satan set about and stirred up the People to send after us false apostles for the undoing of the word."[27] The Acts of the Apostles tells a different story.

Another source of these fanciful tales was a converted Jew named Hegisippus. He had traveled throughout much of the Christian world, from Palestine to Corinth to Rome, and by talking with elders in each place, he had soaked up their oral traditions and folklore. Snippets of his five-part book entitled *Memoirs* have been preserved by Eusebius. Hegisippus gives his understanding of heresy in the apostolic period in the following passage.

> In addition to these things the same man, while recounting the events of that period, records that the church up to that time had remained a pure and uncorrupted virgin since, if there were any that attempted to corrupt the sound teachings of salvation, they lay until then concealed in obscure darkness. But when the sacred college of apostles had suffered death in various forms, and the generation of those that had been deemed worthy to hear the inspired wisdom with their own ears had passed away, then the league of godless error took its rise as a result of the folly of heretical teachers who, because none of the apostles was still living, attempted henceforth with a bold face to proclaim, in opposition to the preaching of the truth, the 'knowledge which is falsely so-called.'
> —*History of the Church* 3.32

This would have been news to Peter, Paul, and John, who had plenty to say about the false prophets, false teachers, false apostles, deceivers, and antichrists in their midst. Peter, in his second epistle, addresses the false teachers who were bringing in "damnable heresies."[28] Jude devotes an entire letter to the ungodly men who had "denied" the Lord and turned the "grace

---

25. *Apology of Aristides* 2.

26. It is certain the author was referring to the apostle John. See paragraph 6 of the Syriac *Teaching* on p. 163.

27. *Did Apost* 23.

28. 2 Peter 2:1–2.

of God into lasciviousness."[29] No one familiar with the New Testament as it stands could possibly voice such an opinion.

The apostle John had the oversight of the Christian movement at the latter end of the sixties and possibly into the seventies. In his writings, he gives us first-hand information on the fracturing of the Truth during this critical period.

> Little children, it is the last time: and as ye have heard that antichrist shall come, even now there are many antichrists; whereby we know it is the last time. They went out from us, but they were not of us; for if they had been of us, they would no doubt have continued with us: but they went out, that they might be made manifest that they were not all of us.
> —1 John 2:18–19

You will notice that John wrote part of this passage in the past tense, indicating these things had already happened. John identifies the nature of the apostasy in his second letter. "For many deceivers are entered into the world, who confess not that Jesus is come in the flesh."[30] In his third epistle, John fingers one of the troublemakers by name: Diotrephes.[31]

Every time Hegesippus can be checked independently, he turns out to be wrong. We have his version of James' martyrdom in Eusebius.[32] Hegisippus would have us believe the brother of Jesus was known in all Israel—even among the priests—for his virtue and piety. He was invited to address the nation during Passover from the parapet of the temple. They asked that he restrain Israel from believing in Jesus, the very thing he was giving his life to advance. When James declares the divinity of Christ, he was thrown from the heights and clubbed to death. The historian Josephus gives a less rosy motivation. Instead of being honored for this righteousness, James was stoned to death as a lawbreaker during a chance interregnum of the Roman governor.[33] His account has far more credibility as he may have actually been living in Jerusalem at the time and personally knew many of the players involved.

29. Jude 4.
30. 2 John 7.
31. 3 John 9, 10.

32. *Eccl Hist* 2.23. The Hegesippan story was picked up and repeated by Clement of Alexandria, and it also forms the basis of the *Second Apocalypse of James*.

33. "Festus was now dead, and Albinus was but upon the road; so he assembled the Sanhedrin of the judges, and brought before them the brother of Jesus, who was called Christ, whose name was James, and some others [or some of his companions], and when he had formed an accusation against them as breakers of the law, he delivered them to be stoned..." (*Antiquities* 20.9).

> **The Paradox of Proximity**—It is a historical fact that the closer you get to the apostolic age, the less the Church Fathers knew about the characters and events of the New Testament. This is completely contrary to what you would expect if the *Ekklesia Katholika* actually did succeed the apostles. The first and second century literature reveals a church full of teachings and traditions remarkably untethered to the New Testament and quite often in contradiction.

The Missing Link

This brings us to a fascinating phenomenon associated with early Catholicism: *The closer you get to the apostolic period, the less they knew about the New Testament.* Hegesippus and his colleagues were completely oblivious to the false teachers and doctrinal disputes within the New Testament fellowship, believing the church had remained an "unsullied virgin," free of heresy, until the last apostle was gone. They did not know the fate of James, the leader of the Christian movement, even though it was known to Josephus, an outsider. They did not realize that Peter, whom they considered the emissary to the west, had spent most of his life ministering in and around Palestine. They did not acknowledge Paul, the one who had brought the gospel to the Gentiles, and they were ignorant of his exploits in Asia Minor and Greece. *As incredible as it sounds, the first and early second century Catholics knew almost nothing about the three main characters of the New Testament.*

How do you explain the abrupt break between the Christians who inhabit the New Testament and those we read about in the earliest Catholic writings? The *Ekklesia Katholika* only claims a couple of connecting links when there should be dozens, an unbroken chain of fellowship from Biblical times. The saints and young ministers of the New Testament should have become the grey-haired, old pillars of the faith. You would expect to see Christianity running into the second and third generations, as it had in Timothy's family. Paul could thus write to Timothy of "the unfeigned faith that is in thee, which dwelt first in thy grandmother Lois, and thy mother Eunice; and I am persuaded that in thee also."[34] We should find fourth and fifth generation Christians in the annals of the Church Fathers. We should know what became of Cephas and Apollos, perhaps something of the later exploits of Timothy and Titus, and we should possess the correspondence of a Silas. But no, a curtain suddenly falls with the last chapter of Revelation,

---

34. 2 Timothy 1:5.

and when the limelight of history begins to shine again, there is an entirely new cast of characters on the stage.

One of the key links in the Catholic chain of succession was Polycarp of Smyrna. Irenaeus claims that Polycarp had been "instructed by apostles," meaning—although he doesn't actually say it—the apostle John.[35] This is chronologically possible only if Polycarp and John had both lived to an extreme age. The famous bishop declared he had served Christ for eighty-six years when he was burned at the stake in AD 156,[36] and Irenaeus asserted that John "remained among them up to the times of Trajan," or AD 98.[37] How likely is it that both attained octogenarian status when very few men in the Roman Empire even made it to sixty? There is a simple explanation: They had to stretch John's life to an absurd length to make the chronology work.

We can check the Polycarp-John claim from another angle. Surely one who had been so close to John would have been intimately acquainted with his writings. Why then did Polycarp's successors refuse to accept two of John's letters—2 and 3 John—and why so much hesitation about the book of Revelation? Eusebius, some two hundred years later, classed the minor Johannine epistles among the "disputed" books, and neither letter has ever been given a place in the Syrian Bible. In his day (AD 325), the jury was still out on Revelation. Eusebius reported that the church was "evenly divided" on the Apocalypse, and the book did not find a settled place in the western canon until the Third Council of Carthage in AD 397.[38]

The writings under Peter's name are even more problematic. If the Roman bishops actually were the heirs to St. Peter's throne, would they not have had his genuine correspondence and would they not have known what was fake? Why, then, does the *Muratorian Fragment*, the canon of the Roman church AD 180, place confidence in the thoroughly fraudulent *Apocalypse of Peter*?[39] Why does the *Muratorian Canon* not include either of Peter's genuine letters, the epistles we now call 1 Peter and 2 Peter?[40]

---

35. *Against Heresies* 3.3.4.
36. *Martyr of Polycarp* 9.
37. *Against Heresies* 2.22.5.
38. *Eccl Hist* 3.25.

39. "We receive only the apocalypses of John and Peter, although some of us are not willing that the latter be read in church" (*Muratorian*).

40. Two other Roman works of the mid-second century, the *Shepherd of Hermas* and *I Clement*, also lack 1 and 2 Peter. Eusebius claimed that Papias was familiar with 1 Peter, but all we have is his word for it (*Eccl Hist* 3.39).

And the fact that Peter probably dispatched this letter *from Rome* does not help the case for Petrine succession.[41]

Peter's second epistle did not circulate in Catholic circles until the third century, and it seems to have been discovered in Egypt, not Rome. Although there are indications it may have been known to Clement of Alexandria, Origen, his successor, was the first to reference a second Petrine epistle. He expressed doubts about its authenticity.[42] As late as the fourth century, 2 Peter was classed by Eusebius among the disputed books, and it has never been given a place in the Aramaic-language Peshitta.

We began this book by exploring a movement founded upon fictitious books which were fabricated by false apostles. The church built on that foundation has been just as audacious in claiming the authority of the Twelve Apostles and writing under their name. The second century legends that spun off the founding documents—the myths of Peter at Rome—became as entrenched in their doctrine as the New Testament itself. The church orders of the third and fourth centuries continued the bold falsehood that they had been written by the apostles. In the fullness of time, however, the popes became powerful enough to drop this fiction, and they began to issue bulls and dogmas under their own "apostolic" authority.

The Church of Rome has been the source of terrible spiritual blindness and bondage, but at the same time we must acknowledge an incalculable debt. It was the institution which gathered up the precious literary remains of the apostolic age, preserved them in their purity, and transmitted them down the long road of history. Just as God used Pharaoh to accomplish his will in Egypt, so he used an adversary of the faith to transmit his written word to the world.[43]

The teachings of Jesus have been the light of the world for almost two thousand years. Originating in the heart of the Eternal, they are the only connection we have with our Maker and our only avenue to eternal life. His words will judge us all on the last day.

---

41. 1 Peter 5:13.
42. *Eccl Hist* 6.25.
43. Romans 9:17–24.

Supplemental Material

The Earliest Witnesses to the New Testament Books

Book	Approx. Date Written	Earliest Attestation	Approx. Date	Second Attestation	Approx. Date
Matthew	58	*Didache*	90	*Ep. Barnabas*	132
Mark	60	Papias	130	Justin Martyr	150
Luke	60 to 62	Basilides	130	Marcion	140
John	circa 65	Basilides	130	Justin Martyr	150
Acts	63	Polycarp to Philippians	155	Justin Martyr, *On the Resurrection*	155
Romans	57	Basilides	130	Marcion	140
1 Corinthians	57	Basilides	130	Marcion	140
2 Corinthians	57	Basilides	130	Marcion	140
Galatians	56	Marcion	140	Polycarp	155
Ephesians	61	Basilides	130	Marcion	140
Philippians	60	Marcion	140	Polycarp	155
Colossians	61	Marcion	140	Valentinus	140
1 Thessalonians	52	Marcion	140	Polycarp	155
2 Thessalonians	52	Marcion	140	Polycarp	155
1 Timothy	57	Polycarp	155	*To Autocylus*	170
2 Timothy	62	Polycarp	155	*Muratorian*	180
Titus	57	Tatian	160	Irenaeus	185

Philemon	61	Marcion	140	*Muratorian*	180
Hebrews	circa 62	*Shepherd*	145	*1 Clement*	150
James	47	*Shepherd*	145	*1 Clement* (?)	150
1 Peter	63	*2 Clement*	145	Polycarp	155
2 Peter	circa 64	Origen	220	Hippolytus	230
1 John	circa 65	Polycarp	155	*Muratorian*	180
2 John	65+	*Muratorian*	180	Irenaeus	185
3 John	65+	Origen	220	Dionysius of Alexandria	255
Jude	65+	*Muratorian*	180	Irenaeus	185
Revelation	69	Papias	130	Justin Martyr	150

The entire Ignatian corpus is fraudulent and, as discussed in chapter 14, the seven letters were forged very close to AD 150. *1 Clement* is considered genuine, but misdated. It has been placed in the middle of the second century instead of its traditional date at the end of the first century.

The New Testament in Historical Context

The Gospels, the Epistles, and the book of Revelation were all published before AD 70. The destruction of the Temple that year sent shock waves reverberating through the Jewish and Christian communities. When the daily sacrifice ceased forever on August 5th, it marked the end of provision for sin and uncleanness as they had known it. The effect upon institutional Judaism cannot be overstated. Yet, despite its importance, the New Testament is silent on the subject. True, Jesus had predicted it would happen, and his prognostications have proven accurate. But it was never exploited and capitalized upon by the apostles as they might had they been writing after the fact.

THE GOSPELS

The four Gospels were all produced within a ten-year period at the close of the apostolic age. The church was responding to the false teachings which were mounting at the time. Those who had walked with Jesus and knew the story most intimately felt the need to preserve the words and deeds of the Master. The Torah-observant teachers had confused many in the fifties, and the early sixties saw the emergence of the Gnostic movement. This highlighted the need for an authoritative text, and several of the apostles and their closest companions stepped in to meet this need.

Matthew was the first to set down his recollections and understanding of events. It would have been presumptuous for someone to write an account of the life and ministry of Jesus before one of the eye-witnesses. The

Gospel of Matthew was in circulation by AD 60—when the proto-Catholics broke fellowship—but not much earlier as Paul is never depicted carrying a written Gospel or preaching from one. The tradition that Matthew was written in the Hebrew language goes back to Papias, in the early years of the second century.[1] However, we note that the *Epistle of Barnabas*, a contemporary source, quotes from the Greek Gospel of Matthew. The Ebionites used Matthew exclusively, which the Catholic Fathers called "The Gospel of the Hebrews," so an early translation into Hebrew was indeed possible.

A remarkably early citation of Matthew is found in 1 Timothy 5:18. "For the scripture saith, thou shalt not muzzle the ox that treadeth out the corn. And, The laborer is worthy of his reward." The second half comes from Jesus' instructions to the Twelve in Matthew 10:10. This epistle is notoriously difficult to date, but in all likelihood it was written before Paul's imprisonment AD in 58. It is highly significant that Paul labels both Deuteronomy and the extract from Matthew's Gospel as "Scripture."

The Gospel of Mark—like Matthew—is anonymous. Marcus was the cousin of Barnabas, and both men were preachers of the gospel. His mother hosted the evening prayer meeting in Jerusalem where Peter went after being released from prison.[2] Thirty years later Peter refers to him as a "son" because of their long association in the gospel and respective ages.[3] Along with Matthew, the Gospel of Mark was probably one of the works alluded to in the introduction of Luke's Gospel: "Forasmuch as *many* have taken in hand to set forth in order a declaration of those things which are most surely believed among us, even as they delivered them unto us, which from the beginning were eyewitnesses and ministers of the word . . . ." We are getting ahead of ourselves here, but Mark was thus compiled AD 60 to AD 62.

Can we venture to guess where it was written? Mark is most closely identified with the missions in Asia, from the time he went with Paul and Barnabas until he finally joined Peter's greeting at the end of 1 Peter. He may have brought the manuscript to Rome when he joined Paul—finished or not—giving Luke immediate access to it.[4]

The Gospel of Luke was written after Matthew and Mark, but before the Acts of the Apostles. Luke begins the Acts in this way: "The *former treatise* have I made, O Theophilus, of all that Jesus began both to do and teach." The former treatise, of course, was the Gospel of Luke. The Acts of the Apostles terminates rather abruptly with events which can be dated to AD 62, giving

1. *Eccl Hist* 3.39.
2. Acts 12:12.
3. 1 Peter 5:13.
4. Philemon 23–24.

us a *terminus ad quem*. The "Beloved Physician" had accompanied Paul to Rome and possibly roomed with him during his house arrest.

At first, the Good News was proclaimed openly: "And many of the brethren in the Lord, waxing confident by my bonds, are much more bold to speak the word without fear."[5] As Nero's emotional conditioned worsened and the political situation deteriorated, open public meetings came to a halt. This left Paul and Luke with time to write. Paul set down for the ages some of his finest works, the five "prison epistles," as well as his theological masterpiece, Hebrews. Luke gathered in the recollections and stories of Paul, combined it with information from other sources, and wrote his Gospel. Luke was just one of several companions Paul had in the early part of the Roman imprisonment, but by the time Paul had an audience with Nero, he was the only one left. "For Demas hath forsaken me, having loved this present world, and is departed unto Thessalonica; Crescens to Galatia, Titus unto Dalmatia. Only Luke is with me."[6]

The first three Gospels are remarkably similar, both in order and in content, giving rise to what is known as the synoptic problem. Most scholars posit a priority of one—usually the Gospel of Mark—from which the others borrowed material, along with a lost common source "Q," from the German word *quelle* (source). But it is not necessarily to resort to plagiarism to explain the parallels. The gospel was strictly an oral message for the first thirty years and there was, by necessity, a lot of rote memorization. As the apostles went from town to town, they would tell the same parables and recount the same stories. Matthew, Mark, and Luke each set down what he knew of the common stock of apostolic teaching, what we now call "Q."

The Fourth Gospel offers up few clues about its date of composition, but the second half of the sixties is most probable. In John 5:2, we are given a description of the Pool of Bethesda *in the present tense*. This pool, with its five covered porticoes, was buried beneath rubble when the Romans leveled Jerusalem in the first century, and it was not unearthed until the nineteenth century. The author of the Johannine Gospel knew very specific architectural details that were hidden and undiscoverable after AD 70.

The Gospel of John is significantly different from the other three. After thirty-five years of preaching the Gospel, and decades of reflection, John had reached some conclusions about the person of Jesus Christ. To Jewish believers, he emphasized his divinity and sonship. "In the beginning was the Word, and the Word was with God, and the Word was God . . . And the Word was made flesh, and dwelt among us, (and we beheld his glory, the

---

5. Philippians 1:14.
6. 2 Timothy 4:10–11.

glory as of the only begotten of the Father), full of grace and truth."[7] To the emerging Gnostics, who were veering off in the direction of docetism—the odd doctrine that Jesus was a spiritual apparition without a physical body—he focused on his humanity. Jesus thus got tired, he hungered and thirsted, he wept, his body was pierced, and he bled like any other man.[8]

THE EPISTLE OF JAMES

James addressed his letter to the "twelve tribes scattered abroad," the believing Jews who had fled Israel after the persecution of Stephen c. AD 36.[9] They were living in the Levantine cities of Antioch, the island of Cyprus, Lebanon, Damascus, the other cities of the Greek Decapolis, and possibly Cyrene and Alexandria. These Jews were cut off from the larger Jewish community, facing some difficulties, and James felt they needed encouragement.

According to Suetonius, the reign of Claudius Caesar (AD 41 to AD 54) was marked with successive droughts and poor harvests.[10] One of those famines hit Palestine and the neighboring territories with special severity during the procuratorship of Tiberius Alexander, AD 46 to AD 48.[11] It was the "great dearth" mentioned in Acts 11, and the Antiochene Christians were moved to send aid to the mother church. "And there stood up one of them named Agabus, and signified by the Spirit that there should be great dearth throughout all the world which came to pass in the days of Claudius Caesar. Then the disciples, every man according to his ability, determined to send relief unto the brethren which dwelt in Judaea."[12] This drought may be alluded to toward the end of James' epistle. "Be patient therefore, brethren, unto the coming of the Lord. Behold, the husbandman waiteth for the precious fruit of the earth, and hath long patience for it, until he receive the early and latter rain.[13]

The economic distress this produced in an agrarian society exacerbated the normal tensions between landowners and laborers. "Behold, the hire of the laborers who have reaped down your fields, which is of you kept back by fraud, crieth."[14] Inflation, resulting from the scarcity of foodstuffs,

---

7. John 1:1, 1:14.
8. John 4:6, 7; 11:35; 19:1, 28, 34.
9. Acts 8:1; 11:19.
10. *Claudius* 18:2.
11. *Antiquities* 3, 20.
12. Acts 11:28–29.
13. James 5:7; 5:17–18.
14. James 5:4.

may be behind the words that "Your gold and silver is cankered [devalued], and the rust of them shall be a witness against you."[15] Finally, it may be significant that the letter contains no trace of the Gentile controversy that so dominated the council held at Jerusalem AD 49.

THE EPISTLES OF PAUL

The two letters to the Thessalonians are the oldest Pauline epistles extant. They hearken back to the first missions in Europe: Philippi, Thessalonica, Athens, and Corinth. While in Athens,[16] Paul decided to send Timothy to Thessalonica, and he and Sylvanus (Silas) headed for Corinth.[17] That is probably when Paul wrote to tell them Timothy was coming. During their time in Corinth, Paul was called before the proconsul Gallio, which ties this mission to the most secure dating landmark in the New Testament.[18] An inscription was uncovered in Delphi—barely 50 miles away—which declares that Gallio was the proconsul of Achaia "in the twelfth year of Claudius Caesar." That is AD 52 by our reckoning.

The epistles to the Galatians, the Romans, and the two to the Corinthian church should all be considered as a single unit. They address the false apostles who had followed Paul on his third journey. After passing through "Galatia and Phrygia," Paul spent two whole years at Ephesus.[19] He wrote to the Galatian churches not long after his arrival in AD 56. "I marvel that ye are *so soon* removed from him that called you into the grace of Christ unto another gospel . . . ."[20] After about a year in the Asian capital, he wrote to the Corinthians about such common pastoral concerns as unity, morality, faith, and charity.[21] Soon thereafter, the false apostles visited Corinth, and Paul left for Greece to head them off at the pass. While en route, he fired off his second epistle from Macedonia.[22] This time he vigorously defends his calling and apostleship, and refers to his detractors as "false apostles"

---

15. James 5:3.
16. 1 Thessalonians 3:1.
17. 1 Thessalonians 3:2.
18. Acts 18:11–17.
19. Acts 19:1–10.
20. Galatians 1:6.
21. 1 Corinthians 16:8, 19.
22. 2 Corinthians 7:5.

and "deceitful workers."[23] He wrote to the Roman church after arriving in Corinth circa AD 57, perhaps while staying with Gaius.[24]

First Timothy may also be the product of his three-month stay at Corinth.[25] We know from the opening lines that he had left Ephesus by way of Macedonia,[26] but we have no idea how much time has passed. This lengthy letter makes no mention of Paul's imprisonment, but it does mention Timothy's youth in passing.[27] Paul also commented on Timothy's age when he wrote to the Corinthians, and he uses virtually identical language about Titus when he wrote to him.[28] Paul took Timothy into the ministry in AD 51,[29] and he was still a young man when Paul wrote this letter. While not definitive, these observations point to an earlier rather than a later date. Paul had left Timothy behind in Ephesus—with all of its challenges—and he now passes along lots of practical advice. This letter is full of instructions on choosing elders, suggestions on how a young minister should treat an older presbyter, and counsel on dealing with the latest problem in the church, the circumcising teachers.[30]

Titus was contemporaneous with 1 Timothy. It is easy to get thrown off the trail by the language of Titus 1:5: "For this cause *left* I thee in Crete, that thou shouldest set in order the things that are wanting, and ordain elders in every city, as I had appointed thee." This seems to imply that Paul had been there with him. However, another rendering is that Titus had been *left* behind—and dispatched to Crete—instead of going with the other apostles to Jerusalem. Titus was probably expecting he would be among those who delivered the Gentile contribution to the poor saints at Jerusalem.[31]

A side-by-side comparison of selected passages from 1 Timothy and Titus leaves little doubt they were written in close temporal proximity.

---

23. 2 Corinthians 11:1–31.

24. Romans 16:1, 23.

25. Acts 20:1–3.

26. 1 Timothy 1:3.

27. "Let no man despise thy youth; but be thou an example of the believers, in word, in conversation, in charity, in spirit, in faith, in purity" (1 Timothy 4:12).

28. 1 Corinthians 16:11, "Let no man therefore despise him," and Titus 2:5, "Let no man despise thee."

29. Acts 16:3.

30. 1 Timothy 1:5–10.

31. "And there accompanied him into Asia Sopater of Berea; and of the Thessalonians, Aristarchus and Secundus; and Gaius of Derbe, and Timothy; and of Asia, Tychicus and Trophimus" (Acts 20:4).

1 Timothy	Epistle to Titus
1:2—Unto Timothy, my own son in the faith.	1:4—To Titus, mine own son after the common faith:
1:4—Neither give heed to fables....	1:14—Not giving heed to Jewish fables,
1:4—and endless genealogies, which minister questions,	3:9—But avoid foolish questions, and genealogy, and contentions,
1:6—From which some having swerved, have turned aside unto vain jangling.	1:14—That turn from the truth.........
3:2—A bishop then must be blameless, the husband of one wife, vigilant, sober, of good behavior, given to hospitality, etc.	1:6—If any be blameless, the husband of one wife, having faithful children not accused of riot or unruly.
4:12—Let no man despise thy youth;	2:15—Let no man despise thee.
4:12—But be thou an example of the believers,	2:7—In all things showing thyself a pattern of good works:

When Paul left Ephesus, the plan was to meet Titus in Troas, the chief port from Asia to Macedonia.[32] However, they ended up connecting on the Macedonian side.[33] It is highly likely that he dispatched Titus to Crete at that time. Titus was charged with setting things in order, ordaining elders, and above all, purging the churches of the Circumcisers.[34] Paul gives Titus the same list of qualifications for elders and deacons he had given to Timothy. Finally, we note that there is no hint in this epistle that Paul is— or has ever been—in prison.

Paul's correspondence to the Philippians, Colossians, Ephesians, Philemon, and 2 Timothy are known as the prison epistles. They were all written from Rome while Paul was waiting to appear before Nero, between AD 60 to AD 62. Three of the prison epistles were contemporaneous—Ephesians, Colossians, and Philemon. They were delivered by the same courier (Tychicus), and in the letters to the Colossians and Philemon, Paul is joined in salutations by the same five men: Epaphras, Marcus, Aristarchus, Demas, and Lucas.[35]

Philippians speaks of Caesar's court and Caesar's household.[36] It seems to have been written early in Paul's imprisonment when they still had the liberty to preach openly. "And many of the brethren in the Lord, waxing confident by my bonds, are much more bold to speak the word

---

32. 2 Corinthians 2:3.
33. 2 Corinthians 7:5–7.
34. Titus 1:10–15.
35. Colossians 4: 9–14, Philemon 23, 24.
36. Philippians 1:13, 4:22.

without fear."[37] Second Timothy also makes reference to Rome,[38] but it was probably written later in his imprisonment, after Nero's mental state had deteriorated and Paul's situation had taken a turn for the worse. Paul's letter carrier, Tychicus, had left for Ephesus,[39] and Demas, who had been in Rome when Colossians was written, had forsaken him and was headed for Thessalonica.[40]

A severe earthquake hit the lower Lycus Valley in the early sixties. The historian Tacitus lumps it in with events from the seventh year of Nero's reign (AD 54 to AD 68), or about AD 61.[41] He specifically mentioned just Laodicea, but the fifth century historian Orosius tells us that neighboring Colossae and Hierapolis had been damaged as well.[42] Paul's epistle to the Colossians makes no mention of the calamity, so either it had not yet happened or the news had not yet reached Rome. Laodicea was rebuilt, but Colossae slid into obscurity and remains an unexcavated mound to this day. In AD 69, when John received the vision on Patmos, Laodicea was counted among the seven churches of Asia but there was no church to mention at Colossae.

We should probably count Hebrews among the captivity epistles. Timothy had joined Paul in salutations at the beginning of the Philippian and Colossian letters, but we now learn that Timothy has been set at liberty and may be leaving.[43] If it is indeed this simple, then Paul wrote Hebrews after the Colossians/Ephesians/Philemon trio, but before 2 Timothy. Paul penned this letter anonymously because he was such a controversial figure in Israel. Nevertheless, he did not go out of his way to hide his identity, and it may be easily surmised. Hebrews 2:3 tells us the author was not an eye-witness; in 13:24, we learn that he was in Italy; in 10:34, he had been in prison; and in 13:23, he was a close associate of Timothy. Paul exalts Jesus Christ to his Jewish audience as the eternal High Priest of our faith, the fulfillment of the Law and Prophets.

---

37. Philippians 1:14.

38. 2 Timothy 1:16–17 "The Lord give mercy unto the house of Onesiphorus; for he hath often refreshed me, and was not ashamed of my chain: but, when he was in Rome, he sought me out diligently, and found me."

39. 2 Timothy 4:12.

40. Colossians 4:14; 2 Timothy 4:10.

41. Tacitus, *Annals* 14.27.

42. Orosius, *History Against the Pagans* 7.7.12.

43. Hebrews 13:23.

THE EPISTLES OF PETER, JOHN AND JUDE

In AD 62, the Sanhedrin took advantage of the death of Festus to get rid of the Lord's brother. After James was stoned to death, it was obvious that Israel was no longer safe for the Christian leadership. It appears that Peter fled to Rome that year to help out Paul, who was still under house arrest, and somewhat later John made his way to Ephesus and the Roman province of Asia.

First Peter was written at "Babylon," a common first century cipher for Rome.[44] Peter tells us that Mark was there at his side. By a happy coincidence, we learn from 2 Timothy 4:11 (one of Paul's prison epistles) that Timothy was going to bring Mark to Rome, and here, a year or so later, we find Mark is with Peter. The only question is whether 1 Peter was written before or after the Great Fire of Nero, which broke out on June 19, AD 64. The letter does not mention the burning of the saints or other atrocities, and so 1 Peter should be placed in AD 63 or the first half of AD 64.

Peter wrote this letter to assure the saints in Asia Minor—the product of Paul's ministry—of the surety of their faith. The situation was tense and, although open hostilities had not yet broken out, he repeatedly admonishes them to obey the civil authorities and not to make themselves a target.[45] Tacitus tells us that the Christians were considered "a class hated for their abominations," "a most mischievous superstition," and "evil."[46] It was easy for Nero to blame the fire in Rome on this despised minority, but these sentiments existed long before AD 64. No doubt they were shared by the Greek populace in Asia Minor and had been since Paul had the run-in with the Ephesian silversmiths.[47]

Jude, 1 John, and 2 Peter all address the proto-Gnostic menace which sprang up in the 60s. These teachers may have been emboldened by the leadership vacuum in Asia due to the imprisonment of Paul, the Neronian terror, and the war in the Holy Land. We get a fleeting glimpse of this teaching in 1 Timothy. "Turn away from godless chatter, and the opposing ideas of what is falsely called knowledge ("gnosis"), which some have professed and in so doing have departed from the faith."[48] Paul's letter to the Colossians, written about AD 61, almost reads like a Gnostic lexicon: principalities,

---

44. 1 Peter 5:13.
45. 1 Peter 2:12–15; 3:16–17; 4:14–16.
46. Tacitus, *Annals* 15.44.
47. Acts 19:23–41.
48. 1 Timothy 6:20, 21, NIV.

thrones, dominions, wisdom, mysteries, fullness, angels, and, above all, knowledge (or gnosis).

A few years later, Gnosticism had taken on a more definite shape. "Hereby know ye the Spirit of God: Every spirit that confesseth that Jesus Christ is come in the flesh is of God."[49] John, who could personally vouch that Jesus had come in the flesh and taken the nature of Abraham, was warning of the Christological error of docetism. Peter and Jude both speak of this doctrine as "denying the Lord."[50]

The author of Jude was probably the Lord's natural brother. He identifies himself in the opening line as "Jude, a servant of Jesus Christ, and brother of James." In Mark 6, we are provided with the names of Jesus' siblings, and one of them was Juda.[51] This gives us, along with Peter and John, another eyewitness to the resurrection who was still alive in the sixties of the first century.

The similarities between the epistle of Jude and 2 Peter are far too extensive not to be deliberate. We surmise that Jude was confronting the same issues as Peter, and when he read 2 Peter, he simply copied it under his own name. Today, we would do the same by forwarding an E-mail, but for some reason, Jude put the text into his own words and sent it on.

THE BOOK OF REVELATION

The Revelation of the apostle John, and the date it was written, is so intrinsically linked with speculation on the post-apostolic church that it is worth the time to examine the facts. The information which can be uncovered is devastating to Catholic tradition.

There is no substance to the tradition that John had been exiled to Patmos by the Roman authorities. You will search in vain for any reference in classical history to Patmos as a place of punishment. The arid, uninhabited island of Giaros (also Gyaros, Gioura), close to the Greek mainland, was the most common penal colony in antiquity. Because it is deficient in water, a sentence to this island was considered an extremely harsh punishment. The Roman poet Juvenal twice mentions Giaros in connection with exile, and in more recent times, Seventh Day Adventists and political prisoners have been banished there.[52]

49. 1 John 4:2.
50. 2 Peter 2:1; Jude 4.
51. "Is not this the carpenter, the son of Mary, the brother of James, and Joses, and of Juda, and Simon? And are not his sisters with us" (Mark 6:3)?
52. *Satires* 1.73, 10.170.

Tacitus wrote several volumes on Roman history from the late 90s until his death in AD 117. He was thus as contemporary with the alleged Johannine exile date of AD 95 as one could hope to find. He mentions three Greek islands where the Romans exiled dissidents and criminals. One was the aforementioned Giaros, and the other two were the remote Cyclades islands of Amorgos and Donoussa.[53] Curiously, both are fairly close to Patmos. It is safe to conclude that, outside of Catholic tradition, Patmos was not used as a Roman penal colony.

Then there is the date. Churchmen from the time of Irenaeus (c. AD 185) have placed John's stay on the isle of Patmos "toward the end of Domitian's reign" in a supposed pogrom of Christians.[54] That is the basis for the AD 95 date found in most Bible commentaries. However, there is a huge problem with the Second Great Persecution: it didn't happen. That there was a political reign of terror in the latter half of Domitian's reign is well documented. But outside the well-known execution of Flavius Clemens for "adopting Jewish customs," there is no evidence that religion played a role.

Suetonius, who was living in Rome during the latter part of Domitian's reign, never mentions Christians in connection with the period. He faithfully records Nero's treatment of those following this "malignant superstition," but the victims of Domitian's tyrannical cruelty does not include Christians.[55] Pliny, a member of the senate who also resided in the capital at this time, later wrote that he never had anything to do with the trial of Christians.[56] The Domitianic persecution does not appear in the Church Fathers until the end of the second century.

A more plausible date for John's vision is between the death of Nero in AD 68 and the fall of Jerusalem in AD 70. This squares nicely with the series of clues given in Revelation 17:9–10. "And here is the mind which hath wisdom. The seven heads are seven mountains on which the woman sitteth. And there are seven kings: five are fallen, and one is, and the other is not yet come; and when he cometh, he must continue a short space." The first part tells us in plain language what was meant by the "Mother of Harlots." Rome has long been known as the City on Seven Hills. Then, if we begin the count with Augustus, who was the first *imperator* (or "king") of the Roman Empire following the Republic, the fifth emperor, the last one "fallen," would be Nero. He fell by his own sword on June 9, AD 68. The king "now reigning" would therefore be Galba, and the one "not yet come" who would "continue

---

53. *Annals* 3.68, 4.30.
54. *Against Heresies* 5.30.
55. *Nero* 16.
56. *Pliny Letter No. 96.*

a short space" would be Otho, who sat on the throne from January to April of AD 69.

We also notice that the instructions from the angel to measure the temple were given in the *present* tense, which strongly suggests it was still standing.[57] Despite the best intentions of Titus to spare the Sanctuary, it was accidentally set afire in August of AD 70.

Revelation makes several references to those who worshipped the emperor and his statue, and some have been reluctant to place the beginning of the Imperial cult this early. But that is to miss the point. As the angel told John at the beginning and at the end of the book, he was revealing "things which must shortly come to pass" and "things which must shortly be done."[58] John had witnessed the early stages of emperor worship in Asia Minor, where it had been a feature of life since Augustan times, and he was warning the saints that the trial of their faith was going to intensify.[59] It was not long in coming. Vespasian, who acceded to the throne in November, AD 69, issued an edict condemning to death all who refused to worship his image.

By the use of highly symbolic imagery, the book of Revelation describes the horrific conditions for Christians in the second half of the 60s. Nero initiated a bloody pogrom in AD 64, blaming the torching of Rome in the early hours of June 19 on the much-maligned new sect. His meeting with Paul may have been fresh in his mind. The fire blazed for nine days; razing three entire districts of Rome to the ground, severely damaging another seven, and leaving only four unscathed. The Roman historian Tacitus describes the horror of that summer:[60]

> Therefore, to scotch the rumor (that he had started the fire), Nero substituted as culprits, and punished with the utmost refinements of cruelty, a class of men loathed for their vices, whom the crowd styled Christians. Christus, the founder of the name, had undergone the death penalty in the reign of Tiberius by sentence of the procurator Pontius Pilatus, and the pernicious superstition was checked for a moment, only to break out once more, not merely in Judaea, the home of the disease, but in the capital itself, where all things horrible or shameful in the world collect and find a vogue. First, then, the confessed members of the sect were arrested; next, on their disclosures, vast multitudes

---

57. Revelation 11:1–2.
58. Revelation 1:1; 22:6.
59. Revelation 13:15; 15:2; 16:2; 19:20; 20:4.
60. Suetonius also bore witness to the suffering of the saints under Nero. "Punishments were also inflicted on the Christians, a sect professing a new and malignant religious belief" (*Nero* 16).

were convicted, not so much on the count of arson as for hatred of the human race. And derision accompanied their end: they were covered with wild beasts' skins and torn to death by dogs; or they were fastened on crosses, and when daylight failed, were burned to serve as lamps by night. Nero offered his gardens for the spectacle, and gave an exhibition in his circus, mixing with the crowd in the habit of a charioteer, or mounted on his car. Hence, in spite of a guilt which had earned the most exemplary punishment, there arose a sentiment of pity due to the impression that they were being sacrificed not for the welfare of the state but to the ferocity of a single man.
—*Annals* 15.44

What had begun in the capital quickly spilled over into the provinces. Peter, writing to the saints in Asia Minor four or five years before, encouraged them to endure the "fiery ordeal" and the "trial of their faith" that had come upon them. It was just social harassment and verbal abuse—the actions of local magistrates—more than official policy. "Having a good conscience; that, whereas they speak evil of you, as of evildoers, they may be ashamed that falsely accuse your good conversation in Christ.... If ye be reproached for the name of Christ, happy are ye for the spirit of glory and of God resteth upon you."[61] However, difficulties for the Christians quickly escalated after Nero turned the public spotlight on them. A year or two later, Antipas was martyred at Pergamum, and the apostle John was forced into hiding on the remote island of Patmos."[62] Imperial Rome was indeed "drunken with the blood of the saints and with the martyrs of Jesus."[63]

At the eastern end of the Empire, the political turmoil in Palestine finally boiled over into outright rebellion. In AD 67, Nero's hand-picked general, Vespasian, attacked Judaea from the north. By AD 69, the country had been reduced to rubble, and the Roman army encircled the holy city. The end was eminent. The words of Revelation 6:6—"A measure of wheat for a penny, and three measures of barley for a penny; and see thou hurt not the oil and the wine."—are echoed almost exactly by Josephus when he described the final stages of the siege. "Many clandestinely bartered their possessions for a single measure of wheat, if they were rich, or barley, if they were poor;" and he later tells of the sacred wine and oil being distributed to the multitude and consumed.[64]

61. 1 Peter 3:16; 4:14.
62. Revelation 1:9.
63. Revelation 17:6.
64. *Wars* 5.10.2; 5.13.6.

The Year of the Four Emperors—AD 69—was one of the strangest episodes in Roman history. It was unending civil war and turmoil, and blood ran in the streets of Rome. Galba was murdered in January; Otho, his successor, committed suicide in April; Vitellus briefly took command and, in June, Vespasian was acclaimed Emperor by the army and left for Rome, where he was installed on the throne in November.

The Scarlett Woman, the Whore of Babylon, had made war on the people of God, and the life's work of the apostles was going up in flames. The saints in Rome had been burned alive, Israel lay in ruins, the Temple was in jeopardy, and Antipas had been martyred in Asia.[65] The Four Horsemen were galloping through the Empire, and it truly seemed the fulfillment of all things was at hand.

---

65. Revelation 2:13.

Epistle of Peter to James

Peter to James, the lord and bishop of the holy Church, under the Father of all, through Jesus Christ, wishes peace always:

1. Knowing, my brother, your eager desire after that which is for the advantage of us all, I beg and beseech you not to communicate to any one of the Gentiles the books of my preachings which I sent to you, nor to any one of our own tribe before trial; but if anyone has been proved and found worthy, then to commit them to him, after the manner in which Moses delivered *his books* to the Seventy who succeeded to his chair. Wherefore also the fruit of that caution appears even till now. For his countrymen keep the same rule of monarchy and polity everywhere, being unable in any way to think otherwise, or to be led out of the way of the much-indicating Scriptures. For, according to the rule delivered to them, they endeavor to correct the discordances of the Scriptures, if any one, haply not knowing the traditions, is confounded at the various utterances of the prophets. Wherefore they charge no one to teach, unless he has first learned how the Scriptures must be used. And thus they have amongst them one God, one law, one hope.

2. In order, therefore, that the like may also happen to those among us as to these Seventy, give the books of my preachings to our brethren, with the like mystery of initiation, that they may indoctrinate those who wish to take part in teaching; for if it be not so done, our word of truth will be rent into many opinions. And this I know, not as being a prophet, but as already seeing the beginning of this very evil. For some from among the Gentiles have rejected my legal preaching, attaching themselves to certain lawless and trifling preaching of the man

who is my enemy. And these things some have attempted while I am still alive, to transform my words by certain various interpretations, in order to the dissolution of the law; as though I also myself were of such a mind, but did not freely proclaim it, which God forbid! For such a thing were to act in opposition to the law of God which was spoken by Moses, and was borne witness to by our Lord in respect of its eternal continuance; for thus he spoke: "The heavens and the earth shall pass away, but one jot or one tittle shall in no wise pass from the law." And this He has said, that all things might come to pass. But these men, professing, I know not how, to know my mind, undertake to explain my words, which they have heard of me, more intelligently than I who spoke them, telling their catechumens that this is my meaning, which indeed I never thought of. But if, while I am still alive, they dare thus to misrepresent me, how much more will those who shall come after me dare to do so!

3. Therefore, that no such thing may happen, for this end I have prayed and besought you not to communicate the books of my preaching which I have sent you to any one, whether of our own nation or of another nation, before trial; but if any one, having been tested, has been found worthy, then to hand them over to him, according to the initiation of Moses, by which he delivered *his books* to the Seventy who succeeded to his chair; in order that thus they may keep the faith, and everywhere deliver the rule of truth, explaining all things after our tradition; lest being themselves dragged down by ignorance, being drawn into error by conjectures after their mind, they bring others into the like pit of destruction. Now the things that seemed good to me, I have fairly pointed out to you; and what seems good to you, do you, my lord, becomingly perform. Farewell.

THE RESPONSE

4. Therefore James, having read the epistle, sent for the elders; and having read it to them, said: "Our Peter has strictly and becomingly charged us concerning the establishing of the truth, that we should not communicate the books of his preachings, which have been sent to us, to any one at random, but to one who is good and religious, and who wishes to teach, and who is circumcised, and faithful. And these are not all to be committed to him at once; that, if he be found injudicious in the first, the others may not be entrusted to him. Wherefore let him

be proved not less than six years. And then according to the initiation of Moses, he *that is to deliver the books* should bring him to a river or a fountain, which is living water, where the regeneration of the righteous takes place, and should make him, not swear—for that is not lawful—but to stand by the water and adjure, as we ourselves, when we were regenerated, were made to do for the sake of not sinning.

5. "And let him say: 'I take to witness heaven, earth, water, in which all things are comprehended, and in addition to all these, that, air also which pervades all things, and without which I cannot breathe, that I shall always be obedient to him who gives me the books of the preachings; and those same books which he may give me, I shall not communicate to any one in any way, either by writing them, or giving them in writing, or giving them to a writer, either myself or by another, or through any other initiation, or trick, or method, or by keeping them carelessly, or placing them before *any one*, or granting him permission *to see them*, or in any way or manner whatsoever communicating them to another; unless I shall ascertain one to be worthy, as I myself have been judged, or even more so, and that after a probation of not less than six years; but to one who is religious and good, chosen to teach, as I have received them, so I will commit them, doing these things also according to the will of my bishop.

6. "'But otherwise, though he were my son or my brother, or my friend, or otherwise in any way pertaining to me by kindred, if he be unworthy, that I will not vouchsafe the favor to him, as is not meet; and I shall neither be terrified by plot nor mollified by gifts. But if even it should ever seem to me that the books of the preachings given to me are not true, I shall not so communicate them, but shall give them back. And when I go abroad, I shall carry them with me, whatever of them I happen to possess. But if I be not minded to carry them about with me, I shall not suffer them to be in my house, but shall deposit them with my bishop, having the same faith, and setting out from the same persons *as myself*. But if it befall me to be sick, and in expectation of death, and if I be childless, I shall act in the same manner. But if I die having a son who is not worthy, or not yet capable, I shall act in the same manner. For I shall deposit them with my bishop, in order that if my son, when he grows up, be worthy of the trust, he may give them to him as his father's bequest, according to the terms of this engagement.

7. "'And that I shall thus do, I again call to witness heaven, earth, water, in which all things are enveloped, and in addition to all these, the all-pervading air, without which I cannot breathe, that I shall always be

obedient to him who giveth me these books of the preachings, and shall observe in all things as I have engaged, or even something more. To me, therefore, keeping this covenant, there shall be a part with the holy ones; but to me doing anything contrary to what I have covenanted, may the universe be hostile to me, and the all-pervading ether, and the God who is over all, to whom none is superior, than whom none is greater. But if even I should come to the acknowledgment of another God, I now swear by him also, be he or be he not, that I shall not do otherwise. And in addition to all these things, if I shall lie, I shall be accursed living and dying, and shall be punished with everlasting punishment.' "And after this, let him partake of bread and salt with him who commits them to him."

8. James having thus spoken, the elders were in an agony of terror. Therefore James, perceiving that they were greatly afraid, said: "Hear me, brethren and fellow-servants. If we should give the books to all indiscriminately, and they should be corrupted by any daring men, or be perverted by interpretations, as you have heard that some have already done, it will remain even for those who really seek the truth, always to wander in error. Wherefore it is better that they should be with us, and that we should communicate them with all the fore-mentioned care to those who wish to live piously, and to save others. But if any one, after taking this adjuration, shall act otherwise, he shall with good reason incur eternal punishment. For why should not he who is the cause of the destruction of others not be destroyed himself?" The elders, therefore, being pleased with the sentiments of James exclaimed, "Blessed be He who, as foreseeing all things, has graciously appointed thee as our bishop;" and when they had said this, we all rose up, and prayed to the Father and God of all, to whom be glory forever. Amen.[1]

---

1. Alexander Roberts and James Donaldson, *The Ante-Nicene Fathers: Translations of the Writings of the Fathers to AD 325, Volume VIII*. Grand Rapids: Wm. B. Eerdmans, 1991. p. 215-217.

Epistle of Clement to James

Clement to James, the lord, and the bishop of bishops, who rules Jerusalem, the holy church of the Hebrews, and the churches everywhere excellently rounded by the providence of God, with the elders and deacons, and the rest of the brethren, peace be always.

1. Be it known to you, my lord, that Simon, who, for the sake of the true faith, and the most sure foundation of his doctrine, was set apart to be the foundation of the Church, and for this end was by Jesus Himself, with His truthful mouth, named Peter, the first-fruits of our Lord, the first of the apostles; to whom first the Father revealed the Son; whom the Christ, with good reason, blessed; the called, and elect, and associate at table and in the journeyings *of Christ;* the excellent and approved disciple, who, as being fittest of all, was commanded to enlighten the darker part of the world, namely the West, and was enabled to accomplish it—and to what extent do I lengthen my discourse, not wishing to indicate what is sad, which yet of necessity, though reluctantly, I must tell you—he himself, by reason of his immense love towards men, having come as far as Rome, clearly and publicly testifying, in opposition to the wicked one who withstood him, that there is to be a good King over all the world, while saving men by his God-inspired doctrine, himself, by violence, exchanged this present existence for life.

2. But about that time, when he was about to die, the brethren being assembled together, he suddenly seized my hand, and rose up, and said in presence of the church: "Hear me, brethren and fellow-servants. Since, as I have been taught by the Lord and Teacher Jesus Christ, whose apostle I am, the day of my death is approaching, I lay hands

upon this Clement as your bishop; and to him I entrust my chair of discourse, even to him who has journeyed with me from the beginning to the end, and thus has heard all my homilies—who, in a word, having had a share in all my trials, has been found steadfast in the faith; whom I have found, above all others, pious, philanthropic, pure, learned, chaste, good, upright, large-hearted, and striving generously to bear the ingratitude of some of the catechumens.

"Wherefore I communicate to him the power of binding and loosing, so that with respect to everything which he shall ordain in the earth, it shall be decreed in the heavens. For he shall bind what ought to be bound, and loose what ought to be loosed, as knowing the role of the Church. Therefore hear him, as knowing that he who grieves the president of the truth, sins against Christ, and offends the Father of all. Wherefore he shall not live; and therefore it becomes him who presides to hold the place of a physician, and not to cherish the rage of an irrational beast."

3. While he thus spoke, I knelt to him, and entreated him, declining the honor and the authority of the chair. But he answered: "Concerning this matter do not ask me; for it has seemed to me to be good that thus it be, and all the more if you decline it. For this chair has not need of a presumptuous man, ambitious of occupying it, but of one pious in conduct and deeply skilled in the word *of God*.

"But show me a better *than yourself*, who has travelled more with me, and has heard more of my discourses, and has learned better the regulations of the Church, and I shall not force you to do well against your will. But it will not be in your power to show me your superior; for you are the choice first-fruits of the multitudes saved through me. However, consider this further, that if you do not undertake the administration of the Church, through fear of the danger of sin, you may be sure that you sin more, when you have it in your power to help the godly, who are, as it were, at sea and in danger, and will not do so, providing only for your own interest, and not for the common advantage of all. But that it behooves you altogether to undertake the danger, while I do not cease to ask it of you for the help of all, you well understand. The sooner, therefore, you consent, so much the sooner will you relieve me from anxiety."

4. "But I myself also, O Clement, know the griefs and anxieties, and dangers and reproaches, that are appointed you from the uninstructed multitudes; and these you will be able to bear nobly, looking to the great reward of patience bestowed on you by God. But also consider

this fairly with me: When has Christ need of your aid? Now, when the wicked one has sworn war against His bride; or in the time to come, when He shall reign victorious, having no need of further help? Is it not evident to anyone who has even the least understanding, that it is now? "Therefore with all good-will hasten in the time of the present necessity to do battle on the side of this good King, whose character it is to give great rewards after victory. Therefore take the oversight gladly; and all the more in good time, because you have learned from me the administration of the Church, for the safety of the brethren who have taken refuge with us."

5. "However, I wish, in the presence of all, to remind you, for the sake of all, of the things belonging to the administration. It becomes you, living without reproach, with the greatest earnestness to shake off all the cares of life, being neither a surety, nor an advocate, nor involved in any other secular business. For Christ does not wish to appoint you either a judge or an arbitrator in business, or negotiator of the secular affairs of the present life, lest, being confined to the present cares of men, you should not have leisure by the word of truth to separate the good among men from the bad.

"But let the disciples perform these offices to one another, and not withdraw *you* from the discourses which are able to save. For as it is wicked for you to undertake secular cares, and to omit the doing of what you have been commanded to do, so it is sin for every layman, if they do not stand by one another even in secular necessities. And if all do not understand to take order that you be without care in respect of the things in which you ought to be, let them learn it from the deacons; that you may have the care of the Church always, in order both to your administering it well, and to your holding forth the words of truth."

6. "Now, if you were occupied with secular cares, you should deceive both yourself and your hearers. For not being able, on account of occupation, to point out the things that are advantageous, both you should be punished, as not having taught what was profitable, and they, not having learned, should perish by reason of ignorance. "Wherefore do you indeed preside over them without occupation, so as to send forth seasonably the words that are able to save them; and so let them listen to you, knowing that whatever the ambassador of the truth shall bind upon earth is bound also in heaven, and what he shall loose is loosed. But you shall bind what ought to be bound, and loose what ought to be loosed. And these, and such like, are the things that relate to you as president."

7. "And with respect to the presbyters, take these *instructions*. Above all things, let them join the young betimes in marriage, anticipating the entanglements of youthful lusts. But neither let them neglect the marriage of those who are already old; for lust is vigorous even in some old men.

"Lest, therefore, fornication find a place among you, and bring upon you a very pestilence, take precaution, and search, lest at any time the fire of adultery be secretly kindled among you. For adultery is a very terrible thing, even such that it holds the second place in respect of punishment, the first being assigned to those who are in error, even although they be chaste. "Wherefore do you, as elders of the Church, exercise the spouse of Christ to chastity (by the spouse I mean the body of the Church); for if she be apprehended to be chaste by her royal Bridegroom, she shall obtain the greatest honor; and you, as wedding guests, shall receive great commendation. But if she be caught having sinned, she herself indeed shall be cast out; and you shall suffer punishment, if at any time her sin has been through your negligence."

8. "Wherefore above all things be careful about chastity; for fornication has been marked out as a bitter thing in the estimation of God. But there are many forms of fornication, as also Clement himself will explain to you. "The first is adultery, that a man should not enjoy his own wife alone, or a woman not enjoy her own husband alone. If anyone be chaste, he is able also to be philanthropic, on account of which he shall obtain eternal mercy. For as adultery is a great evil, so philanthropy is the greatest good.

"Wherefore love all your brethren with grave and compassionate eyes, performing to orphans the part of parents, to widows that of husbands, affording them sustenance with all kindliness, arranging marriages for those who are in their prime, and for those who are without a profession, the means of necessary support through employment; giving work to the artificer, and alms to the incapable."

9. "But I know that ye will do these things if you fix love into your minds; and for its entrance there is one only fit means, viz., the common partaking of food. Wherefore see to it that ye be frequently one another's guests, as ye are able, that you may not fail of it. For it is the cause of well-doing, and well-doing of salvation. "Therefore all of you present your provisions in common to all your brethren in God, knowing that, giving temporal things, you shall receive eternal things. Much more feed the hungry, and give drink to the thirsty, and clothing to the

naked; visit the sick; showing yourselves to those who are in prison, help them as ye are able, and receive strangers into your houses with all alacrity. However, not to speak in detail, philanthropy will teach you to do everything that is good, as misanthropy suggests ill-doing to those who will not be saved."

10. "Let the brethren who have causes to be settled not be judged by the secular authorities; but let them by all means be reconciled by the elders of the church, yielding ready obedience to them. Moreover, also, flee avarice, inasmuch as it is able, under pretext of temporal gain, to deprive you of eternal blessings. "Carefully keep your balances, your measures, your weights, and the things belonging to your traffic, just. Be faithful with respect to your trusts. "Moreover, you will persevere in doing these things, and things similar to these, until the end, if you have in your hearts an ineradicable remembrance of the judgment that is from God. For who would sin, being persuaded that at the end of life there is a judgment appointed of the righteous God, who only now is long-suffering and good,3 that the good may in future enjoy forever unspeakable blessings; but the sinners being found as evil, shall obtain an eternity of unspeakable punishment. And, indeed, that these things are so, it would be reasonable to doubt, were it not that the Prophet of the truth has said and sworn that it shall be."

11. "Wherefore, being disciples of the true Prophet, laying aside double-mindedness, from which comes ill-doing, eagerly undertake well-doing. But if any of you doubt concerning the things which I have said are to be, let him confess it without shame, if he cares for his own soul, and he shall be satisfied by the president. But if he has believed rightly, let his conversation be with confidence, as fleeing from the great fire of condemnation, and entering into the eternal good kingdom of God."

12. "Moreover let the deacons of the church, going about with intelligence, be as eyes to the bishop, carefully inquiring into the doings of each member of the church, *ascertaining* who is about to sin, in order that, being arrested with admonition by the president, he may haply not accomplish the sin. "Let them check the disorderly, that they may not desist from assembling to hear the discourses, so that they may be able to counteract by the word of truth those anxieties that fall upon the heart from every side, by means of worldly casualties and evil communications; for if they long remain fallow, they become fuel for the fire.

"And let them learn who are suffering under bodily disease, and let them bring them to the notice of the multitude who do not know of them, that they may visit them, and supply their wants according to the judgment of the president. Yea, though they do this without his knowledge, they do nothing amiss. These things, then, and things like to these, let the deacons attend to."

13. "Let the catechists instruct, being first instructed; for it is a work relating to the souls of men. For the teacher of the word must accommodate himself to the various judgments of the learners. The catechists must therefore be learned, and unblameable, of much experience, and approved, as you will know that Clement is, who is to be your instructor after me. For it were too much for me now to go into details. However, if ye be of one mind, you shall be able to reach the haven of rest, where is the peaceful city of the great King."

14. "For the whole business of the Church is like unto a great ship, bearing through a violent storm men who are of many places, and who desire to inhabit the city of the good kingdom. Let, therefore, God be your shipmaster; and let the pilot be likened to Christ, the mate to the bishop, and the sailors to the deacons, the midshipmen to the catechists, the multitude of the brethren to the passengers, the world to the sea; the foul winds to temptations, persecutions, and dangers; and all manner of afflictions to the waves; the land winds and their squalls to the discourses of deceivers and false prophets; the promontories and rugged rocks to the judges in high places threatening terrible things; the meetings of two seas, and the wild places, to unreasonable men and those who doubt of the promises of truth. "Let hypocrites be regarded as like to pirates. Moreover, account the strong whirlpool, and the Tartarean Charybdis, and murderous wrecks, and deadly founderings, to be nought but sins. In order, therefore, that, sailing with a fair wind, you may safely reach the haven of the hoped-for city, pray so as to be heard. But prayers become audible by good deeds."

15. "Let therefore the passengers remain quiet, sitting in their own places, lest by disorder they occasion rolling or careening. Let the midshipmen give heed to the fare. Let the deacons neglect nothing with which they are entrusted; let the presbyters, like sailors, studiously arrange what is needful for each one. Let the bishop, as the mate, wakefully ponder the words of the pilot alone. Let Christ, even the Saviour, be loved as the pilot, and alone believed in the matters of which He speaks; and let all pray to God for a prosperous voyage. "Let those sailing expect every tribulation, as traveling over a great and troubled sea, the world: sometimes, indeed, disheartened, persecuted, dispersed, hungry, thirsty, naked, hemmed in; and, again, sometimes united, congregated, at rest;

but also sea-sick, giddy, vomiting, that is, confessing sins, like disease-producing bile—I mean the sins proceeding from bitterness, and the evils accumulated from disorderly lusts, by the confession of which, as by vomiting, you are relieved of your disease, attaining healthful safety by means of carefulness.

16. "But know all of you that the bishop labors more than you all; because each of you suffers his own affliction, but he his own and that of every one. Wherefore, O Clement, preside as a helper to every one according to your ability, being careful of the cares of all. Whence I know that in your undertaking the administration, I do not confer, but receive, a favor.

"But take courage and bear it generously, as knowing that God will recompense you when you enter the haven of rest, the greatest of blessings, a reward that cannot be taken from you, in proportion as you have undertaken more labor for the safety of all. So that, if many of the brethren should hate you on account of your lofty righteousness, their hatred shall nothing hurt you, but the love of the righteous God shall greatly benefit you. Therefore endeavor to shake off the praise that arises from injustice, and to attain the profitable praise that is from Christ on account of righteous administration."

17. Having said this, and more than this, he looked again upon the multitude, and said: "And you also, my beloved brethren and fellow-servants, be subject to the president of the truth in all things, knowing this, that he who grieves him has not received Christ, with whose chair he has been entrusted; and he who has not received Christ shall be regarded as having despised the Father; wherefore he shall be cast out of the good kingdom.

"On this account, endeavor to come to all the assemblies, lest as deserters you incur the charge of sin through the disheartening of your captain. Wherefore all of you think before all else of the things that relate to him, knowing this, that the wicked one, being the more hostile on account of every one of you, wars against him alone. Do you therefore strive to live in affection towards him, and in kindliness towards one another, and to obey him, in order that both he may be comforted and you may be saved."

18. "But some things also you ought of yourselves to consider, on account of his not being able to speak openly by reason of the plots. Such as: if he be hostile to any one, do not wait for his speaking; and do not take part with that man, but prudently follow the bishop's will, being enemies to those to whom he is an enemy, and not conversing with those

with whom he does not converse, in order that every one, desiring to have you all as his friends, may be reconciled to him and be saved, listening to his discourse.

"But if any one remain a friend of those to whom he is an enemy, and speak to those with whom he does not converse, he also himself is one of those who would waste the church. For, being with you in body, but not with you in judgment, he is against you; and is much worse than the open enemies from without, since with seeming friendship he disperses those who are within."

19. Having thus spoken, he laid his hands upon me in the presence of all, and compelled me to sit in his own chair. And when I was seated, he immediately said to me: "I entreat you, in the presence of all the brethren here, that whensoever I depart from this life, as depart I must, you send to James the brother of the Lord a brief account of your reasonings from your boyhood, and how from the beginning until now you have journeyed with me, hearing the discourses preached by me in every city, and *seeing* my deeds. And then at the end you will not fail to inform him of the manner of my death, as I said before. "For that event will not grieve him very much, when he knows that I piously went through what it behooved me to suffer. And he will get the greatest comfort when he learns, that not an unlearned man, or one ignorant of life-giving words, or not knowing the rule of the Church, shall be entrusted with the chair of the teacher after me. For the discourse of a deceiver destroys the souls of the multitudes who hear."

20. Whence I, my lord James, having promised as I was ordered, have not failed to write in books by chapters the greater part of his discourses in every city, which have been already written to you, and sent by himself, as for a token; and thus I dispatched them to you, inscribing them "*Clement's Epitome of the Popular Sermons of Peter*." However, I shall begin to set them forth, as I was ordered.[1]

---

1. Alexander Roberts and James Donaldson, *The Ante-Nicene Fathers: Translations of the Writings of the Fathers to AD 325, Volume VIII*. Grand Rapids: Wm. B. Eerdmans, 1991. p. 218-222.

The Didache

The Lord's Teaching Through the Twelve Apostles to the Nations

1. There are two ways, one of life and one of death, but a great difference between the two ways. The way of life, then, is this: First, you shall love God who made you; second, love your neighbor as yourself, and do not do to another what you would not want done to you. And of these sayings the teaching is this: Bless those who curse you, and pray for your enemies, and fast for those who persecute you. For what reward is there for loving those who love you? Do not the Gentiles do the same? But love those who hate you, and you shall not have an enemy. Abstain from fleshly and worldly lusts. If someone strikes your right cheek, turn to him the other also, and you shall be perfect. If someone impresses you for one mile, go with him two. If someone takes your cloak, give him also your coat. If someone takes from you what is yours, ask it not back, for indeed you are not able. Give to everyone who asks you, and ask it not back; for the Father wills that to all should be given of our own blessings (free gifts). Happy is he who gives according to the commandment, for he is guiltless. Woe to him who receives; for if one receives who has need, he is guiltless; but he who receives not having need shall pay the penalty, why he received and for what. And coming into confinement, he shall be examined concerning the things which he has done, and he shall not escape from there until he pays back the last penny. And also concerning this, it has been said, Let your alms sweat in your hands, until you know to whom you should give.

2. And the second commandment of the Teaching; You shall not commit murder, you shall not commit adultery, you shall not commit pederasty,

you shall not commit fornication, you shall not steal, you shall not practice magic, you shall not practice witchcraft, you shall not murder a child by abortion nor kill that which is born. You shall not covet the things of your neighbor, you shall not swear, you shall not bear false witness, you shall not speak evil, you shall bear no grudge. You shall not be double-minded nor double-tongued, for to be double-tongued is a snare of death. Your speech shall not be false, nor empty, but fulfilled by deed. You shall not be covetous, nor rapacious, nor a hypocrite, nor evil disposed, nor haughty. You shall not take evil counsel against your neighbor. You shall not hate any man; but some you shall reprove, and concerning some you shall pray, and some you shall love more than your own life.

3. My child, flee from every evil thing, and from every likeness of it. Be not prone to anger, for anger leads to murder. Be neither jealous, nor quarrelsome, nor of hot temper, for out of all these murders are engendered. My child, be not a lustful one. for lust leads to fornication. Be neither a filthy talker, nor of lofty eye, for out of all these adulteries are engendered. My child, be not an observer of omens, since it leads to idolatry. Be neither an enchanter, nor an astrologer, nor a purifier, nor be willing to look at these things, for out of all these idolatry is engendered. My child, be not a liar, since a lie leads to theft. Be neither money-loving, nor vainglorious, for out of all these thefts are engendered. My child, be not a murmurer, since it leads the way to blasphemy. Be neither self-willed nor evil-minded, for out of all these blasphemies are engendered. Rather, be meek, since the meek shall inherit the earth. Be long-suffering and pitiful and guileless and gentle and good and always trembling at the words which you have heard. You shall not exalt yourself, nor give over-confidence to your soul. Your soul shall not be joined with lofty ones, but with just and lowly ones shall it have its intercourse. Accept whatever happens to you as good, knowing that apart from God nothing comes to pass.

4. My child, remember night and day him who speaks the word of God to you, and honor him as you do the Lord. For wherever the lordly rule is uttered, there is the Lord. And seek out day by day the faces of the saints, in order that you may rest upon their words. Do not long for division, but rather bring those who contend to peace. Judge righteously, and do not respect persons in reproving for transgressions. You shall not be undecided whether or not it shall be. Be not a stretcher forth of the hands to receive and a drawer of them back to give. If you have anything, through your hands you shall give ransom for your sins. Do not hesitate to give, nor complain when you give; for you shall know

who is the good repayer of the hire. Do not turn away from him who is in want; rather, share all things with your brother, and do not say that they are your own. For if you are partakers in that which is immortal, how much more in things which are mortal? Do not remove your hand from your son or daughter; rather, teach them the fear of God from their youth. Do not enjoin anything in your bitterness upon your bondman or maidservant, who hope in the same God, lest ever they shall fear not God who is over both; for he comes not to call according to the outward appearance, but to them whom the Spirit has prepared. And you bondmen shall be subject to your masters as to a type of God, in modesty and fear. You shall hate all hypocrisy and everything which is not pleasing to the Lord. Do not in any way forsake the commandments of the Lord; but keep what you have received, neither adding thereto nor taking away therefrom. In the church you shall acknowledge your transgressions, and you shall not come near for your prayer with an evil conscience. This is the way of life.

5. And the way of death is this: First of all it is evil and accursed: murders, adultery, lust, fornication, thefts, idolatries, magic arts, witchcrafts, rape, false witness, hypocrisy, double-heartedness, deceit, haughtiness, depravity, self-will, greediness, filthy talking, jealousy, over-confidence, loftiness, boastfulness; persecutors of the good, hating truth, loving a lie, not knowing a reward for righteousness, not cleaving to good nor to righteous judgment, watching not for that which is good, but for that which is evil; from whom meekness and endurance are far, loving vanities, pursuing revenge, not pitying a poor man, not laboring for the afflicted, not knowing Him Who made them, murderers of children, destroyers of the handiwork of God, turning away from him who is in want, afflicting him who is distressed, advocates of the rich, lawless judges of the poor, utter sinners. Be delivered, children, from all these.

6. See that no one causes you to err from this way of the Teaching, since apart from God it teaches you. For if you are able to bear the entire yoke of the Lord, you will be perfect; but if you are not able to do this, do what you are able. And concerning food, bear what you are able; but against that which is sacrificed to idols be exceedingly careful; for it is the service of dead gods.

7. And concerning baptism, baptize this way: Having first said all these things, baptize into the name of the Father, and of the Son, and of the Holy Spirit, in living water. But if you have no living water, baptize into other water; and if you cannot do so in cold water, do so in warm. But if you have neither, pour out water three times upon the head into the

name of Father and Son and Holy Spirit. But before the baptism let the baptizer fast, and the baptized, and whoever else can; but you shall order the baptized to fast one or two days before.

8. But let not your fasts be with the hypocrites, for they fast on the second and fifth day of the week. Rather, fast on the fourth day and the Preparation [Friday]. Do not pray like the hypocrites, but rather as the Lord commanded in His Gospel, like this: Our Father who art in heaven, hallowed be Thy name. Thy kingdom come. Thy will be done on earth, as it is in heaven. Give us today our daily (needful) bread, and forgive us our debt as we also forgive our debtors. And bring us not into temptation, but deliver us from the evil one (or, evil); for Thine is the power and the glory forever. Pray this three times each day.

9. Now concerning the Eucharist, give thanks this way. First, concerning the cup: We thank thee, our Father, for the holy vine of David Thy servant, which You madest known to us through Jesus Thy Servant; to Thee be the glory forever. And concerning the broken bread: We thank Thee, our Father, for the life and knowledge which You madest known to us through Jesus Thy Servant; to Thee be the glory forever. Even as this broken bread was scattered over the hills, and was gathered together and became one, so let Thy Church be gathered together from the ends of the earth into Thy kingdom; for Thine is the glory and the power through Jesus Christ forever. But let no one eat or drink of your Eucharist, unless they have been baptized into the name of the Lord; for concerning this also the Lord has said, "Give not that which is holy to the dogs."

10. But after you are filled, give thanks this way: We thank Thee, holy Father, for Thy holy name which You didst cause to tabernacle in our hearts, and for the knowledge and faith and immortality, which You madest known to us through Jesus Thy Servant; to Thee be the glory forever. Thou, Master almighty, didst create all things for Thy name's sake; You gavest food and drink to men for enjoyment, that they might give thanks to Thee; but to us You didst freely give spiritual food and drink and life eternal through Thy Servant. Before all things we thank Thee that You are mighty; to Thee be the glory forever. Remember, Lord, Thy Church, to deliver it from all evil and to make it perfect in Thy love, and gather it from the four winds, sanctified for Thy kingdom which Thou have prepared for it; for Thine is the power and the glory forever. Let grace come, and let this world pass away. Hosanna to the God (Son) of David! If anyone is holy, let him come; if any one is not so, let him repent. Maranatha. Amen. But permit the prophets to make Thanksgiving as much as they desire.

11. Whosoever, therefore, comes and teaches you all these things that have been said before, receive him. But if the teacher himself turns and teaches another doctrine to the destruction of this, hear him not. But if he teaches so as to increase righteousness and the knowledge of the Lord, receive him as the Lord. But concerning the apostles and prophets, act according to the decree of the Gospel. Let every apostle who comes to you be received as the Lord. But he shall not remain more than one day; or two days, if there's a need. But if he remains three days, he is a false prophet. And when the apostle goes away, let him take nothing but bread until he lodges. If he asks for money, he is a false prophet. And every prophet who speaks in the Spirit you shall neither try nor judge; for every sin shall be forgiven, but this sin shall not be forgiven. But not everyone who speaks in the Spirit is a prophet; but only if he holds the ways of the Lord. Therefore from their ways shall the false prophet and the prophet be known. And every prophet who orders a meal in the Spirit does not eat it, unless he is indeed a false prophet. And every prophet who teaches the truth, but does not do what he teaches, is a false prophet. And every prophet, proved true, working unto the mystery of the Church in the world, yet not teaching others to do what he himself does, shall not be judged among you, for with God he has his judgment; for so did also the ancient prophets. But whoever says in the Spirit, Give me money, or something else, you shall not listen to him. But if he tells you to give for others' sake who are in need, let no one judge him.

12. But receive everyone who comes in the name of the Lord, and prove and know him afterward; for you shall have understanding right and left. If he who comes is a wayfarer, assist him as far as you are able; but he shall not remain with you more than two or three days, if need be. But if he wants to stay with you, and is an artisan, let him work and eat. But if he has no trade, according to your understanding, see to it that, as a Christian, he shall not live with you idle. But if he wills not to do, he is a Christ-monger. Watch that you keep away from such.

13. But every true prophet who wants to live among you is worthy of his support. So also a true teacher is himself worthy, as the workman, of his support. Every first-fruit, therefore, of the products of wine-press and threshing-floor, of oxen and of sheep, you shall take and give to the prophets, for they are your high priests. But if you have no prophet, give it to the poor. If you make a batch of dough, take the first-fruit and give according to the commandment. So also when you open a jar of wine or of oil, take the first-fruit and give it to the prophets; and of

money (silver) and clothing and every possession, take the first-fruit, as it may seem good to you, and give according to the commandment.

14. But every Lord's day gather yourselves together, and break bread, and give thanksgiving after having confessed your transgressions, that your sacrifice may be pure. But let no one who is at odds with his fellow come together with you, until they be reconciled, that your sacrifice may not be profaned. For this is that which was spoken by the Lord: "In every place and time offer to me a pure sacrifice; for I am a great King, says the Lord, and my name is wonderful among the nations."

15. Appoint, therefore, for yourselves, bishops and deacons worthy of the Lord, men meek, and not lovers of money, and truthful and proved; for they also render to you the service of prophets and teachers. Therefore do not despise them, for they are your honored ones, together with the prophets and teachers. And reprove one another, not in anger, but in peace, as you have it in the Gospel. But to anyone that acts amiss against another, let no one speak, nor let him hear anything from you until he repents. But your prayers and alms and all your deeds so do, as you have it in the Gospel of our Lord.

16. Watch for your life's sake. Let not your lamps be quenched, nor your loins unloosed; but be ready, for you know not the hour in which our Lord will come. But come together often, seeking the things which are befitting to your souls: for the whole time of your faith will not profit you, if you are not made perfect in the last time. For in the last days false prophets and corrupters shall be multiplied, and the sheep shall be turned into wolves, and love shall be turned into hate; for when lawlessness increases, they shall hate and persecute and betray one another, and then shall appear the world-deceiver as Son of God, and shall do signs and wonders, and the earth shall be delivered into his hands, and he shall do iniquitous things which have never yet come to pass since the beginning. Then shall the creation of men come into the fire of trial, and many shall be made to stumble and shall perish; but those who endure in their faith shall be saved from under the curse itself. And then shall appear the signs of the truth: first, the sign of an outspreading in heaven, then the sign of the sound of the trumpet. And third, the resurrection of the dead—yet not of all, but as it is said: "The Lord shall come and all His saints with Him." Then shall the world see the Lord coming upon the clouds of heaven.[1]

---

1. Roberts, Alexander and James Donaldson, *The Ante-Nicene Fathers: Translations of the Writings of the Fathers to AD 325. Volume VII.* Grand Rapids: Wm. B. Eerdmans, 1991. p. 377-382.

Bibliography

Amidon, Philip R. *The Panarion of St. Epiphanius, Bishop of Salamis*: Selected Passages. London: Oxford University Press, 1990.
Bauer, Walter. *Orthodoxy and Heresy in Earliest Christianity*. Philadelphia: Fortress, 1971.
Berding, Kenneth. "Polycarp's Use of 1 Clement: An Assumption Reconsidered." *Journal of Early Christian Studies* 19.1 (Spring 2011). http://muse.jhu.edu/article/424191.
Bradshaw, Paul F., Maxwell E. Johnson, and L. Edward Phillips. *The Apostolic Tradition*. Minneapolis: Fortress, 2002.
Connolly, R. Hugh. Translator. *Didascalia Apostolorum*. Oxford: Clarendon Press, 1929.
Daube, David. *The New Testament and Rabbinic Judaism*. Peabody, Massachusetts: Hendrickson, 1990.
Dix, Gregory. *The Shape of the Liturgy*. New York: Seabury, 1983.
———. *Apostolike Paradosis: The Treatise on the Apostolic Tradition of St. Hippolytus of Rome*, 2nd ed. London: SPCK, 1968; reprint Ridgefield, Conn.: Morehouse, 1992.
deSilva, David A. *Introducing the Apocrypha: Message, Context, and Significance*. Grand Rapids, Michigan: Baker, 2002.
Di Sante, Carmine. *Jewish Prayer: The Origins of the Christian Liturgy*, translated by Matthew J. O'Connell. New Jersey: Paulist, 1991.
Donin, Rabbi Hayim Halevy. *To Be a Jew*. New York: Basic, 1991.
———. *To Pray as a Jew*. New York: Basic, 2001.
Gavin, F. *The Jewish Antecedents of the Christian Sacraments*. Whitefish, Montana: Kessinger, 2007.
Grant, Robert M. *The Formation of the New Testament*. New York: Harper and Row, 1965.
Hahneman, Geoffrey Mark. *The Muratorian Fragment and the Development of the Canon*. New York: Oxford University Press: 1992.
Hall, Stuart George, ed. *Melito of Sardis—Peri Pascha*. Oxford: Clarendon Press, 1979.
Harris, Horton, *The Tubingen School*. Oxford: Clarendon Press, 1975.
Harnack, Adolf. *The Expansion and Mission of Christianity in the First Three Centuries, Volume II*, USA: Scholar Select Reprint, Published by Franklin Classics, 2018.
Harnack, Adolf. *Marcion: The Gospel of the Alien God*, translated by John E. Steely and Lyle D. Bierma. Eugene, Oregon: Wipf & Stock, 2007.

Hertling, Ludwig, S.J. and Engelbert Kirschbaum,, S.J. *The Roman Catacombs and their Martyrs*, translated by M. Joseph Costelloe and S. J. Darton. Milwaukee, Wis.: Bruce, 1975.

Hopkins, Clark. *The Discovery of Dura-Europos*. New Haven: Yale University Press, 1979.

Idelsohn, A. Z. *Jewish Liturgy and its Development*. New York: Dover Publications, 1995. Bibliography 198.

James, Montague Rhode. *The Apocryphal New Testament*. Oxford: Clarendon Press, 1924.

Jeremias, Joachim. *The Eucharistic Words of Jesus*. Philadelphia: Fortress, 1977.

Josephus, Flavius. *The Complete Works of Josephus*, translated by William Whiston. Grand Rapids: Kregel, 1991.

Klein, Isaac. *A Guide to Jewish Religious Practice*. New York: KTAV, 1992.

Metzger, Bruce M. *The Canon of the New Testament*. Oxford: Clarendon Press, 1987.

Neusner, Jacob. *The Mishnah: A New Translation*. New Haven: Yale University Press, 1988.

Neusner, Jacob. *The Tosefta: Translated from the Hebrew*, Volumes I & II. Peabody, Massachusetts: Hendrickson, 2002.

Niederwimmer, Kurt. *The Didache: A Commentary*, translated by Linda Maloney. Minneapolis: Fortress, 1998.

Oesterley, W.O.E. *The Jewish Background of the Christian Liturgy*. Oxford: Clarendon Press, 1925.

Osiek, Caroline. *Shepherd of Hermas: A Commentary*. Minneapolis: Fortress, 1999.

Petuchowski, Jakob J., ed. *Contributions to the Scientific Study of Jewish Liturgy*. New York: KTAV, 1970.

Ragg, Lonsdale and Laura Ragg, trans. *The Gospel of Barnabas*. Columbia, SC: Pantianos Classics, 2019.

Ramsay, William M. *The Cities and Bishoprics of Phrygia Volume 1, Part 2*. London: Oxford at the Clarendon Press, 1897.

Ramsay, William M. *The Letters to the Seven Churches: A History of the Early Church*. Whitefish, Montana: Kessinger Legacy Reprints, 2010.

Roberts, Alexander and James Donaldson. *The Ante-Nicene Fathers: Translations of the Writings of the Fathers down to AD 325*. Grand Rapids: Eerdmans, 1991.

Robinson, John A.T. *Redating the New Testament*. Philadelphia: Westminster, 1976.

van de Sandt, Huub and Flusser, David. *The Didache: Its Jewish Sources and its Place in Early Judaism and Christianity*. Fortress: Minneapolis, 2001.

Schaff, Philip. *The Nicene and Post-Nicene Fathers*. Grand Rapids: Eerdmans, 1989.

Schaff, Philip and Henry Wace. *The Nicene and Post-Nicene Fathers*. Grand Rapids: Eerdmans, 1991.

Schoedel, William R. *Ignatius of Antioch: A Commentary on the Letters of Ignatius of Antioch*. Philadelphia: Fortress, 1985.

Sheppard, A. R. R. R.E.C.A.M. "Notes and Studies No. 6: Jews, Christians and Heretics in Acmonia and Eumeneia." *Anatolian Studies* 29 (1979) 169–80. http://www.tor.org/stable/3642737.

Steinsaltz, Adin. *A Guide to Jewish Prayer*. New York: Schocken, 2000.

Suetonius Tranquillus, Gaius. *The Twelve Caesars*, translated by Robert Graves. Whitefriars: London, 1970.

Van Voorst, Robert E. *The Ascents of James*. Atlanta: Scholars, 1989.

Walker, Peter. *In the Steps of Saint Paul*. Oxford: Lion Books, 2013.

Williams, Frank. *The Panarion of Epiphanius of Salamis. Book 1 (Sects 1-46)*. Leiden, The Netherlands: SBL Press, 2009.

Wilson, Mark. *The 'Upper Regions' and the Route of Paul's Third Journey from Apamea to Ephesus*. Stellenbosch University. http://scriptura.journals.ac.za.

Index

Abercius, 102
Abgar, King, 58
Acts of Paul and Thecla, 101
Acts of Thomas, 38, 51, 164
Adoptionism, 53, 130, 131, 133, 151, 153
Agape, 90, 95, 122
Agrapha, 110, 111, 119, 159
Alogi, 116, 117, 151
Amidah, 67, 68, 69
Anacletus, Anicletus, 44, 45
Anicetus, 147
Antioch, Syrian, ix, xiii, 5–7, 10, 12, 13, 20, 26, 28, 37, 39, 41, 45, 81, 104, 119, 135, 149, 156–160, 163, 178, 208
Antioch of Pisidia, 5, 13, 19, 20
Antitheses, 100
Apocalypse of Peter, 119, 168
Apocrypha, 109, 110, 111, 207
Apocryphon of John, 134
Apology of Aristides, x, 112, 164, 165
Apostolic Constitutions, xi, 9, 10, 21, 29, 33, 35, 48, 63, 68, 69, 79, 141, 142
Apostolic Tradition, 33, 63, 65, 70, 73, 95, 138, 145, 207
Apostolikan, 99, 100, 102, 106
Athanasius, 120

Baptism, 23, 25, 29, 31, 51, 65, 67, 70–74, 78, 80, 145, 153, 203, 204
Baptismal vows, 74
Baur, Ferdinand, 27
Bardaisan, 58
Bar Kokhba Rebellion, 52, 56, 65
Barnabas (Clementine), 26, 28
Barnabas (New Testament), xiii, 5, 6, 13, 28, 38, 40, 58, 129, 157, 176
Barnabas, Epistle of, x, xi, xiv, 28, 33, 52, 99, 101, 109–112, 114, 119, 120, 176
Barnabas, Gospel of, XI, 28, 31, 133, 208
Beit Midrash, 66
Basilides, 78, 103, 113, 114, 115, 173
Berakah, 32, 86, 137
Birkat Hamazon, 32, 86, 87, 91, 92, 94, 137
Birkat Zimun, 87
Brit Milah, 50

Caesarea, ix, xiii, 4, 11, 12, 16, 22, 26, 28, 38, 41, 56–58, 120, 157, 163
Catacombs, 96, 208
Cathedra, ix, 42, 44, 114
Challah, 32
Chatzitzah, 72
Chronicle of Edessa, 58
Churching of Women, 74, 78

INDEX

Circumcision, xiii, 1, 5, 7, 8, 13, 15, 17, 18, 21, 25, 30, 31, 34, 38, 39, 41, 50–53, 56, 70, 71, 81, 93, 97, 102, 133, 145, 146, 151, 153, 164
Claudius Caesar, 37, 38, 45, 55, 128, 129, 178, 179
Clement (Catholic), x, 10, 11, 26, 28, 34, 35, 39, 42–45, 154, 161, 162, 193, 194, 196, 198, 199
Clement (New Testament), 28, 43, 44, 162
Clement of Alexandria, xii, 33, 113, 119, 121, 122, 166, 169
Clement, First Epistle of, 56, 64, 103, 111, 114, 119, 120, 128, 161, 162, 174, 207
Clement, Second Epistle of, ix, 103, 110, 112, 119, 174
Clement, Homilies of, ix, 11, 15, 23, 26, 27, 30, 39, 45, 47, 72, 77, 81, 87, 89, 112, 134, 154
Clement to James, Epistle of, viii, ix, xi, xiv, 23, 34, 35, 42, 112, 120, 193
Cletus, 43–45
Commodus, 139
Communion, 16, 67, 78, 87, 89, 91, 116, 121, 133, 145, 148, 150
Computus, 145, 149
Concordia (Peter's wife), 39
Constantine, xii, xiv, 20, 54, 148
Corinthians, First Epistle to, 13, 16, 34, 39, 64, 83, 99, 103–105, 113, 115, 121, 137, 140, 160, 161, 173, 179, 180
Corinthians, Second Epistle to, 10, 13–16, 51, 98, 99, 103, 104, 113, 115, 161, 173, 179–181
Cornelius, 4, 38, 157

Deacons, 32, 34, 41, 60, 62, 67, 86, 87, 88, 157, 181, 193, 197, 198, 206
Diatessaron, 58, 116, 117, 119
Didache, viii, ix, xi, xiv, 23, 29, 30–34, 51, 60–63, 65–67, 70, 86, 87, 89, 90–92, 94, 101, 108, 109, 112, 114, 119, 120, 137, 145, 153, 173, 201, 208

Didascalia Apostolorum, xi, xiv, 33, 34, 71, 88, 109, 141, 165, 207
Dio, Cassius, 37, 55, 139
Dionysius, 78, 130, 161, 174
Dix, Gregory, xii, 84, 85, 88, 90, 94, 138, 207
Doctrine of Addai, 191
Domitian, 49, 55, 103, 161, 185
Domitilla, 55

Easter, Passover, Pascha, *Pesah*, vii, x, 17, 18, 20, 34, 56, 70, 71, 74, 100, 106, 112, 116, 122, 125, 126, 137, 138, 140–150, 166, 207
Ebionites, 26, 27, 53, 151–54, 176
Edessa, 43, 57, 58, 139, 147, 164
Eighteen Benedictions, 32, 63, 64, 67, 74, 151
Ekklesia Katholika, x, xiv, 22, 28, 34, 62, 77, 85, 97, 107, 110, 112, 113, 127, 128, 132, 148, 167
Elchasai, 53, 54
Ephesians, Epistle to, 51, 73, 99, 103, 104, 106, 113, 115, 173, 181, 182
Ephesus, 13, 15, 16, 18, 20, 48, 100, 102, 148, 163, 164, 179, 180–183, 209
Epiphanius, xii, 116, 119, 141, 151, 153, 154, 207, 209
Epistle of the Apostles, xi, 103, 118, 138
Eucharist, vii, 32, 67, 83–85, 87–91, 94, 95, 113, 121–124, 138, 204
Eusebius, xi, xii, 17, 18, 56–58, 101, 111, 120, 139, 143, 147, 155, 158, 159, 164–166, 168, 169
Euodius, 157

False apostles, pseudo-apostles, x, xiv, 9–15, 17, 19, 22–25, 29, 30, 32–34, 36, 48, 49, 53, 60–62, 67, 76, 77, 85, 98, 102, 108, 109, 130, 134, 140, 141, 143, 145, 146, 152, 153, 156, 165, 169, 179
Fasting, 23, 29, 31, 74, 141, 142
Fiscus Judaicus, 49, 50

INDEX

Flavius Clemens, 55, 185
Fractio Panis, 196
Fraction, 85, 87, 89, 91

Galatians, Epistle to, xiii, 1, 6–8, 13–16, 18–20, 30, 38, 39, 41, 57, 81, 98, 99, 102, 115, 141, 164, 173, 179
Ger Tzedek, 5
Guides, 61
Gnostic, Gnostics, Gnosticism, 22, 103, 113, 115, 116, 118, 122–125, 135, 175, 178, 183, 184
Gobarus, Stephen, 105, 158
Gospel of Philip, 123, 124
Gospel of Thomas, 103, 113
Great Entrance, 88
Gregory Thaumaturgis, 20, 58

Hadrian, 52, 56, 103
Haggadah, 143
Hallel, Hallelujah, 142, 143
Hamotzi, 88
Hermas, Shepherd of, x, xii, 51, 99, 105, 112, 118–120, 131, 133, 159, 161, 162, 168, 208
Hegesippus, 17, 105, 109, 127, 159, 161, 166, 167
Hippolytus, xii, 44, 53, 103, 113, 116, 122, 131, 138, 154, 174, 207

Ignatius, 104, 114, 122, 124, 128, 156–160, 208
Ignatius to the Ephesians, xi, 104
Ignatius to the Romans, xii, 158–160
Irenaeus, xi, 18, 22, 43, 44, 53, 116, 118, 119, 123, 130, 133, 135, 138, 146, 153, 154, 162, 168, 173, 174, 185

James (Lord's brother), 6, 12–14, 17, 22–25, 35, 36, 38, 39, 41, 50, 81, 109, 110, 156, 163, 164, 166, 167, 178, 183, 184, 189, 190, 192, 193, 200
Jerome, 109, 153
John (the apostle), 14, 16, 22, 38, 41, 43, 47, 48, 53, 84, 106, 110, 114, 115, 136, 139, 148, 151, 162, 163–166, 168, 182–184, 186, 187
John (the elder), 111
John, Gospel of, 2, 3, 27, 45, 46, 75, 84, 99, 113, 115–117, 122, 123, 125, 126, 132, 136, 173, 177, 178
Josephus, xi, xii, 2, 5, 17, 166, 167, 187, 208
Justin Martyr, x, xi, 27, 56, 58, 66, 91, 99, 100, 105, 112, 116, 117, 124, 128, 137, 138, 143, 152, 159, 173, 174

Kedushat ha-Yom, 68

Lauds, 63
Liber Pontificalis, 44, 157
Linus, 43–45, 130
Logos, 53, 113, 132
Lord's Prayer, 31, 32, 65, 93
Lucian the Philosopher, 56
Luke, Gospel of, 2, 12, 17, 31, 39, 62, 65, 76, 81, 82, 84, 99, 100, 137, 142, 155, 173, 176, 177

Mani, 53, 54
Mark, Gospel of, 39, 62, 76, 80, 111, 143, 173, 176, 177, 184
Marcion, xi, xii, 97–104, 108, 111, 114, 120, 127, 156, 159, 173, 174, 207
Marcionite Prologues, 102
Martyrdom of Barsamya, xi, 43, 44, 61
Martyrdom at Vienne and Lyon, 57, 118
Martyrdom of Polycarp, xii, 103, 159
Matthew, Gospel of, 2, 8, 33, 39, 53, 57, 64, 66, 67, 76, 79, 84, 96, 99, 100, 105, 108–111, 116, 122, 125, 131, 132, 136, 143, 153, 154, 173, 175–177
Melito, 143, 144, 148, 207
Mikveh, 71, 77
Mishnah, xii, 30–32, 65, 72, 76, 77, 87, 89, 109, 142, 144, 208
Mitzvah, 50, 64, 75

INDEX

Mormons, 107
Muratorian Canon, xii, 112, 114, 115, 118, 128, 161, 162, 168, 173, 174, 207

Nazarenes, 67, 151, 153, 154
Nero Caesar, 40, 45, 47, 177, 181, 183, 185–187
Nicaea, Council of, xiv, 20, 57, 148–150, 163
Nicolaitans, 48
Niddah, 76–78

Offertory, 85, 87, 88, 91
Orante, 64
Origen, 20, 57, 119, 169, 174

Panarion, xii, 26, 53, 116, 119, 141, 146, 152–154, 207, 209
Pantaenus, 57
Papias, x, 18, 19, 99, 110–112, 159, 168, 173, 174, 176
Paul, vii, ix, xiii, 2, 2–16, 19, 20, 22–24, 26–28, 30, 33–45, 51–53, 56–58, 61–64, 68, 94, 97–107, 109, 111–120, 128–130, 133, 137, 139, 141, 143, 150, 151, 153–157, 160–162, 164, 165, 167, 176, 177, 179, 180–183, 186, 208, 209
Peri Pascha, x, 112, 143, 144, 207
Peshitta, 120, 169
Peter, ix, x, xiii, xiv, 3, 4, 6, 9–12, 14, 15, 22–30, 34–36, 38–46, 50, 53, 55, 58, 61, 62, 65, 71, 73, 79–81, 86, 87, 89, 95, 98, 109, 110, 112–114, 118, 120, 125, 126, 130, 132, 133, 134, 139, 154, 156, 157, 162, 164, 165, 167–169, 176, 183, 184, 187, 189, 190, 193
Peter, First Epistle, 41, 42, 73, 98, 118, 126, 168, 174, 176, 183, 187
Peter, Second Epistle, 36, 46, 95, 97, 112, 114, 120, 165, 168, 169, 174, 183, 184
Peter to James, Epistle of, viii, ix, xii, xiv, 9, 23, 24, 26, 111, 120, 189

Petronilla (Peter's daughter), 39
Pharisees, 3, 7, 8, 12, 31, 34, 74, 75, 79–81, 83, 86–88
Piltdown Man, 156, 157, 161
Pius, Bishop of Rome, 100, 104, 105, 112, 114, 147, 162
Pliny, 54, 90, 98, 185
Polycarp, xii, 22, 43, 103, 105–107, 117, 128, 147, 148, 158–161, 168, 173, 174
Polycarp to the Philippians, xii, 159, 160
Polycrates, 18, 19, 148
Preaching of Peter, 11, 22–26, 28, 29, 35, 43, 50, 114, 119, 128–131, 154, 155
Priscilla, Catacomb of, 96
Psalms, 32, 63, 65, 106, 142

Quadratus, 56
Quartodecimans, 18–20, 147, 148

Recognitions of Clement, ix, xii, 11, 13, 14, 23, 26, 28, 51, 60, 61, 72, 73, 81, 89, 112, 117, 128, 131
Real Presence, 113, 124, 125, 138
Revelation, book of, 15, 16, 19, 41, 42, 47, 48, 53, 66, 116, 117, 120, 137, 143, 167, 168, 174, 175, 184–188
Romans, Epistle to, 9, 16, 37, 38, 51, 99, 103, 104, 113, 115, 118, 161, 169, 173, 179, 180
Rome, vii, ix, x, xii, xiii, 16, 17, 23, 26, 28, 34, 36–45, 49, 55–58, 71, 77, 88, 91, 96, 100, 101, 104–106, 112–114, 116–118, 122, 124, 127–131, 133, 138, 139, 143, 146, 147, 149, 154, 158, 162–165, 169, 176, 177, 181–183, 185–188, 193, 207
Ruler, 61, 62, 163

Sadducees, 2, 3
Seal, 50, 51, 65, 66, 71, 101
Septuagint, 106, 109, 111
Serapion, Bishop, 119
Seven Benedictions, 67, 68

Severus, Severians, 150, 154, 155
Shape of the Liturgy, xii, 84, 138, 207
Shemoneh Esrei, 67
Simon Magus, x, 10, 23, 26–28, 111, 119, 128
Sophia (Wisdom), 135
Stephanus Gobarus, 105, 158
Suetonius, 37, 49, 50, 55, 178, 185, 187, 208
Syriac *Teaching of the Apostles*, xii, 45, 63, 129, 162, 164

Talmud, xi, xii, 4, 19, 70, 71, 75, 91
Tacitus, 38, 182, 183, 185, 186
Tatian, 58, 116, 117, 127, 173
Teaching of Simon Cephas, xii, 43–45
Teaching of Addaeus the Apostle, xi, 61, 164
Tefillin, 64
Tertullian, xi, xii, 32, 43, 44, 57, 58, 64–66, 72, 89, 95, 99–101, 120, 122, 136
Thanksgiving, 32, 69, 84–91, 94, 95, 137, 204, 206
Theodotus the Leathermaker, 133
Theophilus of Antioch, 135

Tiberias Caesar, 37, 100, 186
Titus Caesar, 186
Titus the Apostle, 15, 167, 177, 180, 181
Timothy the Apostle, 13, 15, 42, 44, 63, 109, 129, 130, 167, 179, 180, 182, 183
Tosephta, xii, 3, 68, 72, 80, 84
Trajan, 54, 58, 90, 158, 168
Triclinium, 84, 96
Trinity, 113, 133–136
Tubingen School, 27, 207
Two Ways, 30, 33, 145, 201

Valentinus, 22, 113, 114, 116, 122–125, 127, 134, 159, 173
Vespasian, 42, 49, 186–188
Victor, Bishop, 133, 147, 148
Vulgate, 102, 110

Xystus, Sixtus 43, 146, 147

Zacchaeus, 11, 12, 16, 22, 28, 61, 97
Zephyrinus, 113

www.ingramcontent.com/pod-product-compliance
Lightning Source LLC
Chambersburg PA
CBHW071436150426
43191CB00008B/1143